ANDREW ROSS

Fast Boat to China

Andrew Ross is Professor of Social and Cultural Analysis at New York University and is the author of seven books, including *No-Collar: The Humane Workplace and Its Hidden Costs*; *The Celebration Chronicles: Life, Liberty, and the Pursuit of Property Value in Disney's New Town*; and *Low Pay, High Profile: The Global Push for Fair Labor*. He has also edited six books, including *No Sweat: Fashion, Free Trade, and the Rights of Garment Workers* and, most recently, *Anti-Americanism*. He lives in New York City.

Fast Boat to China

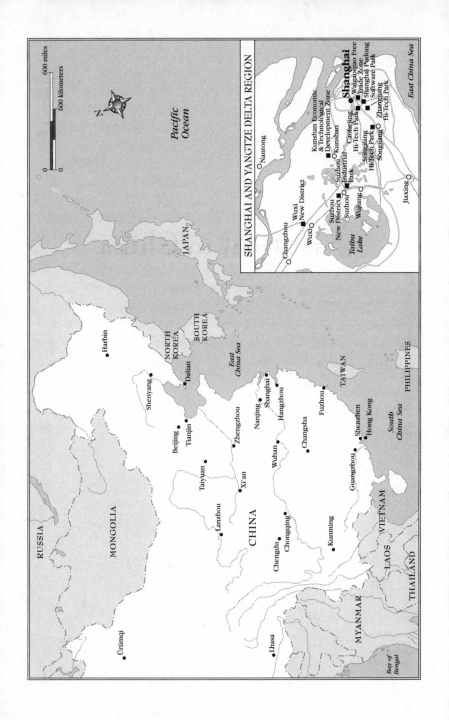

SHANGHAI AND YANGTZE DELTA REGION

Fast Boat to China

*High-Tech Outsourcing
and the Consequences of Free Trade—*

Lessons from Shanghai

ANDREW ROSS

Vintage Books
A Division of Random House, Inc.
New York

FIRST VINTAGE BOOKS EDITION, JUNE 2007

Copyright © 2006 by Andrew Ross

The Library of Congress has cataloged the Pantheon edition as follows:
Ross, Andrew, [date].
Fast boat to China : corporate flight and the consequences of free trade—
lessons from Shanghai / Andrew Ross.
p. cm.
Includes index.
1. Contracting out—China—Shanghai Region. 2. Foreign trade and employment—
China—Shanghai Region. 3. Wages—Effect of international trade on—China—
Shanghai Region. I. Title.
HD2365.R67 2006
331.7'92'095113—dc22   2005053487

Vintage ISBN: 978-1-4000-9554-4

Author photograph © Cynthia Del Conte
Book design by Virginia Tan

www.vintagebooks.com

Printed in the United States of America
10 9 8 7 6 5 4 3 2 1

Contents

Illustrations

(all photographs courtesy of the author)

Notes and Acknowledgments

In writing this book, I tried to meet my interviewees where they were, rather than presume that I knew how and why they got there. Though I have been a China-watcher for many years, I am not a China expert, and so my preconceptions were easy to ignore in any case. But I have not shrunk from interpreting the stories I gathered in a more analytic fashion than the actual informants would have done. China's transition is such a fascinating chapter in the history of economic civilization that to document any part of it is to imagine, for better or worse, that you have done much more.

All citations, when not otherwise indicated, are drawn from personal interviews with the author. Many of the names, and some of the identities, of my interviewees have been changed to protect their privacy. Chinese names are cited according to how that person prefers to be known—i.e., sometimes with an English name—and, for those living in Western countries, with the surname last.

Everyone knows that official statistics in China are far from accurate. Wherever they are cited in the book, readers should take this into account. In addition, many Chinese are paid with cash, or receive a cash supplement that does not show up in public accounting. Nor, as I was reminded by several businesspeople, is corporate accounting always truthful. Companies operating in China have many reasons for skewing accounts of their profits and revenues.

In writing this book, I was fortunate to have the help of many friends and colleagues. Wang Xiaoming and Wang Yuehua, at Shanghai University, were wonderful enablers and interlocutors. I can only hope to repay their generosity to me and my family during our residence on Fenyang Lu. Li Yihai, at the Shanghai Academy of Social Science, opened one crucial door for me; and Wang Fengzhen, at the Chinese Academy of Social Science, some others; and Kuan-Hsing Chen, at National Tsinghua University in Hsinchu, several more.

Zhou Laoshi, Fan Laoshi, and Li Laoshi, at my daughter's nursery school, and Mary Gallagher, Rob Cliver, Richard McGregor, and Kath Cummin were all part of the Shanghai mix. I would also like to thank staff and officers at Shanghai's American Chamber of Commerce.

I owe a great debt to my long-suffering language teachers, Xiao Xiao Jiao and Tian Tian in New York, and Zhang Laoshi in Shanghai.

A grant from the China Scholarship Council helped defray some of the cost of research. Alison Redick, Marcelo Penha, and Sybil Cooksey provided critical research assistance, and Alyssa Hepburn and Madala Hilaire, in the NYU American Studies Program, were a solid support team.

Among my colleagues at NYU, Xudong Zhang, Harry Harootunian, Angela Zito, and Doug Guthrie offered important help and advice.

The final drafting of the book benefited greatly from the insights of three brilliant regional experts—Ching Kwan Lee, Aihwa Ong, and Tani Barlow—who were kind enough to read the whole manuscript at a very busy time of year. Mitchell Duneier, ethnographer maestro, also gave a careful and generous reading of a draft.

The biggest credit goes to my partner Margaret Gray, who was often mystified by my comings and goings while we lived together in Shanghai, and finally had a chance to see what it was all about when she read the manuscript drafts. It turned out that she understood the book better than I did, and her rigorous editing is largely responsible for the final version.

For ushering the book into being, my gratitude to my editor, Vicky

Wilson, who figured out how to make me perform, and to my literary agent, Elyse Cheney, who already knew.

My mother, Jean, died in Scotland while I was doing my research in Shanghai. This book is dedicated to the memory of her own labors and her joie de vivre.

Fast Boat to China

Introduction

China's nonstop growth is now on everyone's lips, and the loose talk, once again, is about a threat from the East. For political hawks, the menace is a military one. For the environmentally minded, it is the high toll on global energy supplies and other natural resources. For national policymakers, the specter comes in the form of lopsided trade balances between China and more developed countries, or of the Chinese takeover of their national assets. And for those who work in industry and services vulnerable to offshoring, it is the loss of their livelihoods that has raised the alarm. Scaremongers have been exploiting Yellow Perilesque fears for well over a century, and the recent uptick proves that reserves of anti-Chinese sentiment are far from exhausted. Though they are often alarmist, the widespread concerns about China's economic development are not groundless. Prices on the retail shelves and at the gas pump, job security in the workplace, mortgage interest rates, and the career prospects of our children are only some of the things that are directly affected by the pell-mell transformation of China's economy and society.

But if this breakneck growth is a threat, it is not because Beijing harbors sinister ambitions for its industrial expansion. The real problem, as this book argues, is that China is playing host to the largest, and most corrosive, environment for offshore labor in the global free-trade economy. For more than a decade it served as a fast-track incubator for foreign investment in the low-wage export sector, cocooned from accountability to any principle not devoted to raw profit. In the last few years, as I describe in detail in these pages, investors have moved further up the value chain, in hopes of reaping the same offshore harvest from technology-driven manufacturing and white-collar services. Increasingly, these investors are global corporations, outsourcing skilled jobs and high-tech capital from developed countries with much firmer labor and environmental standards. Because of the temporary scarcity of skilled Chinese workers, companies are finding these new high-value sectors difficult to staff. Corporate managers cannot hold on to experienced engineers, project managers, and professional talent, and so wage inflation and job-hopping are endemic. But, while conditions are undeniably better than in the low-wage sweatshops of the export factories, the industrial relations are not appreciably different. Both skilled and unskilled workplaces share a climate rife with distrust and disloyalty on the part of employers and employees alike, chronic labor turnover and flightiness, extreme wage pressure from the threat to move to cheaper locations, and the shredding of economic and social security in the communities where investors have set up shop.

Free-trade zones in other developing countries have hosted much the same kind of cynical, runaway culture. So why is the China case so alarming? The answer lies not just in the jumbo scale of operations, but also in its all-encompassing spread. China is leapfrogging so fast up the technology curve it is attracting the highest-level investments—in product design and innovation, for example—from industry leaders. In the most telling development, the number of foreign-invested research and development (R&D) centers jumped from 200 to 600 in a space of only two years, from 2002 to 2004, when firms in a broad spectrum of industries followed the initiative of global first movers like GE, Microsoft, Honeywell, IBM, Ericsson, Bayer, and GM.[1]

No industrializing country has ever been able to compete for the top-end slots at the same time as it absorbs jobs lower down the production chain. Policymakers in advanced nations worry about the flight of jobs and capital at the higher end, but the problem is much greater than this. To command this spread—from the lowest assembly platform work to the upper reaches of industry and services—is to be in a position to set the global norm for employee standards as no country has before. Given the chronic disregard for job security and workplace rights in China's foreign-invested private sector, such a norm is a clear threat to the stability of livelihoods everywhere.

Again, let us acknowledge that this is not a threat hatched in Beijing. If China did not provide the most currently profitable mix of authoritarian governance, cheap, abundant labor, and investor-friendly policies, it would be sought out elsewhere. Though such conditions would not exist without government cooperation, the primary beneficiaries are global corporations. They stand to profit most from the normalization of an environment where jobs and capital can be transferred at a moment's notice and with complete impunity. If corporations cannot be held to consistent standards and responsibilities—and the working reality of offshore free trade does not demand any of these—then ordinary people in every corner of the globe will be at a loss to salvage any control over their futures and that of their communities.

We are only just beginning to understand how much our lives are touched by the rise of the Chinese and Indian economies. This sense of a mutually entwined destiny can rightfully be attributed to the impact of economic globalization as it has proceeded under the banner of free trade. But are we fully aware of who benefits and who loses? Should we assess neoliberal trade policy on its proven record—often catastrophic—in countries around the world, or wait to judge it in the long term, as its boosters insist? Many armchair critics have had their say on these questions. Research on the ground is less easy to come by, however, and least of all in China, the largest of the world's national economies to be jump-started by foreign investment and trade liberalization.

This book offers such research. It is based on field interviews with skilled Chinese employees and their managers in foreign-invested operations in Shanghai and the Yangtze Delta—the nation's fastest-growing regional economy—as well as in other parts of the mainland and Taiwan. The corporations that own the facilities I visited are the ones responsible for outsourcing jobs and skills from their home countries.

Their local employees, as I discovered, fear the fate doled out to their counterparts in East Asia, the European Union, and the United States, and most of them expect that their own time will come, when investors move on in search of a cheaper and more vulnerable workforce. They have no reason to trust their current employers, and few means to negotiate other than to emulate the footloose ways of the foreign bosses.

In factories and offices across the region, I found skilled employees with a savvy analysis of how the global production chain operates. They knew their place within it, though they were not always aware of how employers played them off against their counterparts in other regions. In any case, since they lacked effective channels of communication, never mind solidarity, with peers in those other locations, they were helpless to do much about it. These workplaces were still a novelty in China's private sector, and so it was tragic to come across the same intensity of work pressure and anxiety in Shanghai as in Taipei, Singapore, London, São Paulo, and San José. Everyone, everywhere, is working longer and harder.

The conclusions I reached in my inquiry differ from those of Thomas Friedman, probably the best-known journalist advocate of unfettered free trade. His recent book, *The World Is Flat,* also analyzes the contribution of offshore outsourcing to the economic rise of China and India, where he pays some visits. For Friedman, the deregulated conduct of global corporations is justified, and there is no alternative to the world of cutthroat competition between their workers in emerging economies and those in developed countries. As he puts it to his daughters: "My message to them is very simple: Girls, when I was growing up my parents used to say to me, 'Tom, finish your dinner. People in China and India are starving.' I say to my girls, 'Girls, finish your homework. People in China and India are starving for your jobs.' "[2] Friedman wants us to dwell on the contrast between his and his parents' comments. But what's more striking is how little has changed. In both cases, it's all about how affluent folks in the global North have to monopolize resources—food or knowledge—lest those less fortunate in the global South make off with them.

Friedman's flat world is governed by cutthroat competition. If workers in the developing countries win, then his daughters and their peers lose. The only option is to adapt to free trade rules that have been written explicitly to exploit distrust between people on different sides of the globe. The rules are seen as unalterable, and everyone is potentially expendable. Yet the price of accepting this thinly veiled social Darwinism is far too high. Job pressure offshore, as the Chinese testimony in this book shows, is no less severe than the anxiety experienced by those onshore. Almost everyone loses in the long run. We must not forget that there are global alternatives to the game of free trade. They come in the form of fair trade, sustainable development, and internationally recognized labor rights. But, so far, the Chinese workforce—barred by their government and employers from free association, independent organizing, and access to the global justice movement—have not been allowed to embrace them. If these alternatives are to succeed, then trust, cooperation, and solidarity will have to replace zero-sum competition as the guiding spirit of our engagement with China.

Open Doors

U.S.-China trade relations are a key part of the story told in this book. To give the reader some historical perspective on the topic, let me recount the contents of a volume—*A Guide to Nearly 400 Companies Interested in Developing Trade Between China and the U.S.A.*—that I came across while browsing through the private library of one of Shanghai's most prominent American residents. The firms featured in its pages ranged from renowned national corporations to obscure small-town enterprises, and there were more than sixty industries represented in its listings of almost 2,000 products and services. The goals of the publisher, the China-America Council of Commerce and Industry, were described as the removal of trade barriers, the encouragement of private enterprise, and "the transfer of American industrial techniques to China." American companies, the directory announced, were lining up to help reopen the door to U.S.-China trade, but they would not be coming at any price. Indeed, the council was calling for the following conditions in return for U.S. trade: nondiscriminatory tariffs and trade agreements; "adequate" commercial legislation along with trademark, copyright, and patent protection; "equitable and reasonable" taxation; the creation of "commercial arbitration machinery"; and the "development of China's exports as a basis for expanding her imports."[3]

Going on this information alone, the reader could hardly be faulted for assuming that this slick promotional guide was a recent publication. Yet the date on the cover was 1946, and the "closed door" of foreign trade mentioned in the guide's preface referred not to the communist state's command plan, but to a Japanese occupation that had endured for eight years. The Glemby Company of New York ("the largest importer of human hair and human hairnets") was one of the many listed firms to present itself dramatically as a steadfast Friend of China. Its supersized ad lamented that "China's ruthless enemy had halted her progress and her industries," and went on to promise that "we are returning to rebuild anew with a genuine hope that our growth will aid in the development of a Greater China." As an importer, Glemby was a distinct minority in these pages. The vast majority of firms were pitching their U.S.-manufactured products to the China market or angling for contracts for the reconstruction of China's cities and industrial plants. As it happened, the opportunity to bid on the contracts lasted only a few years. For foreign corporations, the open door would swing shut for the next thirty years with the onset of the Korean War.

The roll call of the 400 companies in the guide is a sober reminder of the sheer regional diversity of U.S. manufacturing as it existed at the dawn of the golden age of the American corporation. Sixty years later, many of the names are history. Today, Glemby hairnets are collector items in vintage flea markets. As a result of controversial free-trade policies, a goodly number of the better-known firms have shifted offshore and are exporting profitably to the United States from their affiliate factories in China. Many of the American towns and cities where they once provided stable, long-term employment are in pretty bad shape. So are their ex-employees, especially if the loss of a decently paid manufacturing job has resulted in a sizable wage reduction in some new service-sector job, as is the most common experience.[4] With the exception of a few fat years in the late 1990s, the real wage of the average American worker has been declining steadily since its postwar peak in 1973, around about the time that offshoring began. Among the other losers are the smaller domestic manufacturers who cannot afford to move offshore, and who are increasingly asked to match the "China price" of imports. In many cases the China price is below the cost of their materials.

In 1946, China's exports to the United States were limited to the commodities listed in the guide: spices, teas, bamboo, rattan, porcelain, silk, mohair, porcelain, and tung oil. Today there are very few goods of any kind that are not produced in China, and in the coming years, everything else will be. By contrast, aside from aerospace products, medical equipment, and plant machinery used to build factories, the leading U.S. exports to China are items like fertilizers, oil seeds, wood pulp, cotton, fats, waxes, grains, and raw animal hides. The two nations are well on their way to neatly swapping their trading profiles, and U.S. multinational firms are in no small measure responsible for this reversal. Indeed, the most relevant places to find their names listed today are in the ever-swelling directories of the American chambers of commerce of Shanghai, Beijing, or Guangzhou. Each fresh entry is a record of a new operation, facility, or office that has been transferred from a higher-cost country. The newer names reflect the march up the value chain that has characterized the most recent rounds of offshore investment in China; increasingly they represent the sectors of precision and high-tech manufacturing, biomedicine, information technology (IT), telecommunications, and financial and professional services.

Skilled employees everywhere have reason to be wary of this rapid advance into the high-value sectors. There are fewer and fewer kinds of jobs, in principle, that cannot be sent out on the fast boat to China. Job loss is not the only source of worry. The size and speed of China's buildup requires an imported supply of raw materials that is taking an unsustainable toll on the world's natural resources. Commodity and energy prices all skyrocketed in 2004, as China's growth sucked in more than 8 percent of the world's petroleum, 10 percent of its electricity, 19 percent of its aluminum, 20 percent of its copper, 31 percent of its coal, and 33 percent of its steel.[5] In China itself, almost every city suffers from rapidly deteriorating air quality, as well as chronic water and energy shortages. No less sustainable is the fragile dependence of the United States' own massively indebted economy on Beijing's hefty

An American IT company promotes its offshore services

annual purchase of dollar assets ($200 billion worth in 2004, and an estimated $300 billion in 2005) in the form of holdings like U.S. Treasury bonds.[6] In one of the most precarious trading arrangements in modern times, the world's "consumers of last resort" are relying on low-interest loans made available by Beijing's foreign-exchange earnings to go on buying goods exported from China. Not even the most ardent pro-free-trade economists believe this coincidence of interests (it is not a result of common interest) is a durable formula for stabilizing the global economy. Meanwhile, China's near monopolization of foreign investment flow has had a fundamentally depressing impact on the prospects of every other developing country.

Concerns like these have been relayed into acres of newsprint about the steepening curve of Chinese ascendancy, habitually depicted as a "threat." Some of this coverage fuels the same kind of virulent reactions that greeted the rise of Japan as an industrial superpower a quarter of a century earlier. Recent Chinese efforts to take over American companies have amplified the anxiety: Lenovo bought out IBM's PC division, Haier made a bid for Maytag, and, most sensitive of all, CNOOC tried to buy the Unocal oil corporation. Unlike Japan in the 1980s, China today is portrayed as a strategic rival by American hardliners, and so public fear about a new Asian Leviathan can all too easily be manipulated by those looking for a whipping boy. As a result, relations between Washington and Beijing are periodically fraught, and are tempered only by the growing commercial and financial interdependence of the two countries. But there is one other important difference between the resurgence of these two Asian nations. While Japan's rise was primarily home-grown, the hand of foreign corporate investors in China's recent growth is all too visible, and has provoked quite a sharp response in their countries of origin.

The Price of Nationalism

Consider the case of Lou Dobbs, CNN's top business analyst, who made a highly popular decision, in early 2003, to turn his nightly TV show entirely over to jaundiced reports about U.S. corporate outsourcing. For this "lifelong Republican," who had been staunchly loyal to the cause of free enterprise, the spectacle of unpatriotic American firms rushing to transfer jobs overseas prompted his conversion into a zealous critic of corporate greed. It also earned him the hostility of powerful sectors of the organized business community. Dobbs's CNN web page began to keep track of the 1,000 American companies that were "either sending American jobs overseas, or choosing to employ cheap overseas labor, instead of American workers." (No government agency had recorded or collected any such information.) *Exporting America*, the book that complemented this web hall of shame, was even more caustic. Blatantly nationalistic, it deplored the loss of the country's knowledge base, its technology, and its middle-class livelihoods, indicted "U.S. trade policies that haven't worked for three decades," and darkly warned against the "tight embrace" between "government and big business."[7]

Keeping company with Dobbs's 2004 election-year book was *Where the Right Went Wrong,* Pat Buchanan's most recent broadside at the "economic treason" of free-trade policymakers.[8] The most well-known right-wing convert to the cause of bashing global corporations, Buchanan's pitch for America First also included a helping of the anti-immigrant, anti-foreign sentiment that has often accompanied expressions of economic nationalism in U.S. history.[9] That record of chauvinism (and China-bashing has been its most persistent, and loathsome, form) is not, however, the sole preserve of conservative Christian fundamentalists like Buchanan. American labor unions, for example, have not been averse to exploiting anti-foreign sentiment in the effort to protect their members' jobs. China-bashing still has its uses within the AFL-CIO, just as it does for factions of the Democrat and Republican establishment. The result is unfortunate. What should be a clear-eyed focus on corporate responsibility for the grievous impact of capital flight and job transfers all too often gives way to a blame game in which scapegoating the Chinese serves some convenient political agenda or else assuages a generalized sense of personal hurt.

In a globally integrating economy, where barely anything is 100 percent nationally produced, and where hypermobility across borders has become a reality of economic life, there is little to be gained from any kind of crusade that promotes Us versus Them. Those guaranteed to lose the most are workers, whether unskilled or highly trained, who pit themselves against their overseas counterparts. For this is exactly the profit-happy game—economists call it "global labor arbitrage"—that multinational corporations have been playing for some decades now.

Despite growing public recognition of how domestic livelihoods have been damaged by free-trade fundamentalism, there is little awareness about the very similar challenges faced by overseas employees who are the presumed recipients of offshore job transfers. Lack of information makes it easier to blame the faceless foreigner who "took" the job, and that person, increasingly, is a stereotypical Chinese. The lives and attitudes of the Chinese employees in question are either taken for granted or entrusted to the least tolerant sector of the public imagination. While Americans have been fixated, for example, on domestic job loss, most are unaware that China has lost many more millions of jobs in the last decade, whether from the closure, restructuring, or sale of state-owned enterprises (with a further one-third of all state employees expected to be laid off in the next few years) or, more recently, from the pressure of World Trade Organization (WTO) requirements on farmers.[10] In fact, Chinese job loss is just as much the result of corporate globalization and neoliberal privatization as is U.S. job loss. In addition, the creation of a vast, floating pool of unemployed—as many as 150 million, mostly farmers—poses the same kind of threat to Chinese trying to hold on to their jobs as the threat of corporate offshoring does to U.S. employees. Because their prospects are now umbilically linked, the bread and butter of Americans is affected not just by workers' opportunities in China's well-developed coastal cities, but also by the job hunger of underemployed peasants in inland and western provinces, already earmarked as the next frontier for buccaneering foreign corporations.

One of the motives for writing this book was to put a human face on the job traffic that is usually summed up in U.S.-China trade statistics or in the latest employment figures. Little is known about the aspirations, fears, and beliefs of employees in China's transitional economy, not even those working for foreign firms who are the focus of this book. In the profiles drawn from my interviews with the latter, readers will encounter some emergent types—the "great Chinese engineer," the patriotic techie, the *xiaojie* (or "white-collar miss"), the self-directed professional, and the gray-collar worker, all of them working under expatriate managers from Taiwan, Singapore, India, Malaysia, Japan, the United States, and the European Union. As my research revealed, these mainland employees are all too often stereotyped by foreign managers who arrive with expectations of a compliant workforce and a fast profit. Consequently, managers tend to attribute most workplace conflict to cultural differences. In their mind, the Chinese have not yet become "modern individuals," and are still locked into a collective mind-set shaped by centuries of authoritarian discipline. In other words, their potential to become ideal corporate material is handicapped by local cultural traits.

There surely are such differences, yet I found that the conflict often has more to do with the unpredictability of a new industrial environ-ment where the rules of work are not yet fixed in place. What managers expect and what employees are willing to give is by no means a settled matter. Nor is the outcome a matter of purely local concern, relevant only to those with an interest in the regional labor market. China's key position in the global economy means that everyone has a stake in the result of this informal bargaining.

To gather evidence, I spent the best part of a year interviewing inside foreign-invested enterprises in Shanghai and the Yangtze Delta. Most were located in the industrial corridor that runs from Shanghai's shiny new urban center of Pudong on the east coast to the ancient upriver cities of Suzhou and Wuxi.[11] For technology-driven firms, where I did most of my interviewing, the supply chain in this corridor is almost complete. The Lower Yangtze is rapidly replacing the Pearl River Delta as the country's primary economic engine, and the lion's share of its foreign direct investment is flowing into the production of higher-value goods than are being made in the predominantly labor-intensive factories of the south. Indeed, the Yangtze Delta economy is increasingly the high-tech core of China's claim to be "the world's fac-tory." Shanghai's own booming service sector is spearheading China's less plausible aspiration to challenge India in also becoming the "world's office." Because all of this growth is based on comparative advantage in Asia as a whole, researching the book also took me to Tai-wan, the west of China, and India to see how companies played work-ers off against each other in regions with a lesser cost differential than with the United States.

Work and commerce in East Asia increasingly bears the footprint of corporate free trade, and it is especially visible in a resurgent city like Shanghai, which is being groomed to be the next financial capital of the Asia-Pacific region. In Shanghai, I sought contacts within the American business community that is a primary outpost for the free-trade traffic. Formal interviews and many hours of social chitchat with officers and members of the American Chamber of Commerce helped me document the psychology of the city's corporate expatriates during a turbulent period when outsourcing CEOs were being branded as

"Benedict Arnolds" by presidential contender John Kerry. Through my access to the Chamber of Commerce, I was able to track how this far-flung colony played a strategic role in influencing Washington's policy on the all-important China trade.

Running Out of Workers?

Shanghai's foreign investors are itching to transfer high-end manufacturing operations—such as product engineering, design, and R&D—into the Yangtze River Delta as fast as they can. The chief barrier to accomplishing these transfers is not the widely acknowledged concern about theft of intellectual property. The real obstacle, as I found out, has more to do with the difficulty of finding an adequate labor supply at the right price. From the moment I began to mingle with Shanghai's foreign businesspeople, I heard managers' complaints about the high cost of local wages and the scarcity or disloyalty of qualified employees. This flew in the face of the given wisdom that investors were flocking to China for its cheap, abundant labor supply. It seemed as if almost every scare-mongering newspaper story about outsourcing mentioned the 400,000 engineering graduates being turned out of China's universities annually. How could honest Americans compete, the stories implied, with this colossal industrial army of skilled workers? The answer, it appeared, was by no means straightforward.

Some of the reasons for the skilled-labor scarcity were technical, and could be applied to any local labor market governed by supply and demand. Others had to do with "Chinese characteristics": the declining birthrate in a one-child culture, for example, or the deviation from corporate norms produced by local customs, or the unfettered self-interest bred by novel exposure to economic pressure and opportunity alike. But increasingly the stories I was hearing about the dearth of employee loyalty suggested that something else was involved. Economic globalization, it appeared, was beginning to yield some unforeseen kinds of behavior on the part of workers.

Since it is now the world's largest recipient of foreign investment (having overtaken the United States in 2003, and netted more than

$60 billion in 2004), China is often seen as a primary beneficiary of corporate-led globalization. Yet the flightiness of multinational capital is no longer a secret, not even to the ordinary Chinese who watch the multimillion-dollar investments pour into their cities by the month. They have formed their own expectations from watching how corporations come and go in other countries. Many of the employees I interviewed saw little reason for loyalty toward managers who they believed were unlikely to be their bosses for very long. Soaring turnover in the private sector—I found rates of up to 40 percent in some high-skill precincts—is perhaps the most obvious indication of this attitude. In their ceaseless pursuit of the cheapest and most dispensable employees, multinational firms have made it clear they will not honor any kind of job security. Hooked on the habit of job-hopping, it looks as if workers in China's transitional economy might be returning the disrespect. In stark contrast to their weak ties to employers, loyalty to China itself, and the grander goal of growing the nation out of its technological dependence on foreign expertise, is a much more common cause of the allegiance of the skilled workers who appear in these pages.

At the low end of the labor market, among migrant workers who travel great distances from their inland homes to work on the coast, workplace bonds are especially thin. All over the developing world, low-wage export zones have seen high turnover rates, but in China any significant shifts in employment patterns are greatly magnified by the sheer scale of its workforce, and are more visible as a result. In 2004, after the annual week-long Spring Festival holiday, more than 2 million migrants (10 percent of Guangdong province's workforce) failed to return to the Pearl River Delta's export-processing factories in South China. Turnover is always up at this time of the year, but these numbers were unprecedented. Given their net impact, this was one of the most massive unorganized withdrawals of labor in recent times. It was quite different in character from the waves of workers' protests that had risen "like a violent wind" (in the description of the Ministry of Public Security) since mass layoffs in the state sector began in 1997.[12]

Domestic commentators rushed to explain the no-show, pointing to deep discontent with decade-long stagnant wage levels, the rising

Some of China's 150 million migrant workers,
outside the Suzhou railway station

cost of living on the coast, the absence of legal protection, and substandard workplace conditions that are notoriously hazardous to workers' health.[13] Some cadres took the occasion to praise the government's recently implemented tax relief for farmers, which had made the prospect of scratching out a living on the land preferable to staffing the sweatshops of Guangdong and Fujian.[14] The Ministry of Labor and Social Security interpreted the outcome as a collective act of resistance to the illegal factory conditions, and publicly called on South China's employers to heed the nation's labor laws. The region's export contractors, most of whom competed on razor-thin margins, were forced to recruit on the basis of the pathetic slogan "paying wages on time."[15] This was a response to China's biggest labor problem: the back wages owed to migrant workers.[16] Emboldened by seeing employers at a disadvantage, workers continued to walk out and wildcat strikes spread, and the aggrieved flocked to legal aid centers that were increasingly handling labor disputes as part of the country's rocky transition to a rule of law.[17] Despite government efforts to alleviate the shortage, and increases in the minimum wage of up to 30 percent, the shortfall in 2005 was similar if not worse, with many workers heading east toward the better conditions in Shanghai and its satellite cities.[18] As South China's multitude of small firms went into crisis mode, the international business press raised the alarm. *BusinessWeek* dutifully asked, "Is China Running Out of Workers?"[19]

How could this be in a country with such a bottomless supply of workers, and with so many unemployed and "floating" in search of work? While some demographers cite the declining birthrate as a possible explanation,[20] the most immediate reason is that foreign investors in the labor-intensive export sector only want to hire teenage girls (*dagongmei*), the cheapest, most pliable, and most expendable members of the workforce. So, too, in higher-skilled jobs, only those who are freshly graduated or who have some experience with international business and work practices need apply. The millions of workers who are skilled but who have worked for a state-owned enterprise are considered damaged goods, incapable of being retrained for the more punishing discipline of a capitalist work ethic. The labor shortage, then, is shaped by managerial requirements that are set by bias, and tailored to the maximum exploitation of the young and vulnerable. But even within the bounds of the labor pool considered acceptable, even among the ranks of workers who meet these selective standards, corporate managers are confronted with employee unreliability rather than the "flexibility" they would have preferred to see.

Readers of this book may find evidence, though not conclusive proof, that the easy international mobility enjoyed by capital-owners may be creating a workforce in its own mirror image: employees who simply will not commit. They are the flip side of the expendable workers whose jobs can be transferred or outsourced overnight, and they are nothing if not creatures of globalization. Indeed, the college-educated employees who feature in these pages have a carefully calculated sense of where their skills fit in the global industrial chain, relative to the high-wage West and to their counterparts in East Asian locations. As a result, they know exactly what they are worth to their employers of the moment. Many of them also know they are in the right place at the right time. Knowledge of this sort provides some leverage. In some cases—engineers with a few years of experience, for example—the result is an upward wage spiral that is plaguing their employers.

On the other side, local and central government cadres are pulling every power lever they have to ease the bottleneck and provide foreign investors with what they want: an abundance of skilled labor at a discount price. This is the latest in a long list of favors that officials in developing countries have had to offer as part of what is misnamed "free trade." Investors have come to expect a never-ending welcome parade of tax holidays and exemptions, acres of virtually free land, state-of-the-art infrastructure and telecommunications, discounts on utilities and other operating costs, and soft guarantees that labor laws and environmental regulations will never be seriously implemented. To stem corporate flight to China, officials in onshore locations have been forced to offer similar giveaways, further depleting the tax base of cities and counties in many countries in the OECD (Organization for Economic Co-operation and Development). Until recently, favors like these have pandered to companies looking to manufacture on the cheap. Now the model is being upgraded to suit the needs of those investing higher up the value chain.

If a surplus pool of talent materializes, and the current wage inflation is brought under control, then the way will be clear for corporations to transfer more and more high-skill operations and ever greater quantities of high-value investment capital into China. The much-lamented U.S. job loss and capital flight of the last few years may well be seen as a trickle in comparison with the mass migration to come. "There's nothing anyone or anything can do to stop it," the regional director of a U.S. multinational firm assured me, casually citing a Shanghai joke he had heard recently: "Pretty soon, lawyers will be the only people left with jobs in America." Given the rate at which the work of paralegals and junior associates is being sent offshore, even this may turn out to be a generous estimate.

Knowledge Transfer

Apart from reinforcing a sense of resignation about the outsourcing juggernaut, comments like the one above contribute to a climate of fear that can be debilitating for those worried about holding on to their jobs. Critics of outsourcing who believe they are delivering a wake-up call often generate the kind of panic that impels employees to accept pay cuts and other concessions just to keep their jobs above the red line. Time after time I listened to employees relate how the managers used this threat, even in mainland China, to extract longer hours or surplus enthusiasm on the job. This was especially evident in workplaces where employees had to compare their prospects with those of their counterparts in India, Taiwan, Singapore, Korea, or Malaysia, and vice versa.

The story laid out in this book is not intended to be alarmist, but it does encourage informed action. Corporate boosters of free trade have lavishly promoted the claim that the overall benefits of outsourcing far outweigh the costs. Without doubt there are short-term winners in this game, but there is absolutely no empirical basis to the free-trader belief that the communities losing the jobs and investment will see benefits in the long term. Moreover, it is not in the actual tally of jobs or dollars lost, but rather in downward wage pressure, and the establishment of a permanent climate of job insecurity, that we are likely to see the most sustained impact of offshore flight. Outsourcing is not a temporary economic trend. It is fast becoming a way of life, regarded more and more as a social as well as an economic norm, and inevitably it is altering our perception of what a job entails. In a postindustrial society, where uncertainty and risk have increasingly become burdens for individuals—rather than for employers or the state—to shoulder, work is less and less standardized, and a job no longer defines what a person is.[21] As the pace of outsourcing hastens on these changes, the definition of a job is mutating into something closer to its etymological origin— a discrete "lump" or "piece" of work that exists only for the duration of its fulfillment.

Free-trade ideologues have also insisted that advanced economies like the United States will automatically generate new higher-value jobs to replace those sent overseas. Yet all the past evidence suggests that in the sheer majority of cases, the outcome will be jobs of lesser quality, with lower pay and fewer benefits. In addition, East Asian economies are now all in the same game, hotly pursuing the skilled work that American, European, and Japanese employees have traditionally been assured is their birthright.[22]

The row over outsourcing is really only the most recent expression of popular revulsion at the faithless record of corporate conduct. Thirty years of capital flight have left communities battered and broken all around the world. Faced with the reality of runaway corporations, every town, city, and nation surely has a right to do whatever it takes to retain jobs and protect livelihoods, and elected officials have an obligation to respond. Piecemeal legislation of this sort has cropped up all over the United States, and popular opposition to free-trade policies played a prominent role in the 2005 national referendums in France and the Netherlands that rejected an EU constitution aimed at further liberalization of labor and capital markets.

But national legislation aimed at containing the damage has its limits. A new kind of social contract is needed if corporations are going to be made accountable to anyone other than their largest stockholder. While it should be locally binding, any such contract has to be international in scope. It will take its cue from the human rights and environmental standards that are habitually left out of free-trade agreements, whether brokered bilaterally or through the WTO. The push to recognize these standards has come from trade unions, non-governmental organizations (NGOs), and myriad activist groups that belong to the alternative globalization movement.[23] But the will to see them realized can only come from a deeper fraternity of workers and employees sharing knowledge, tactics, and goals across national borders. This will only happen if they are able to communicate with the same ease, trust, and conviction that their employers do.

It is not the intent of this book to offer practical prescriptions for establishing the global standards and the fraternity mentioned above. But my profile of the job traffic to China underscores the urgent need for such measures. One of my primary aims, for example, is to describe what lies behind "knowledge transfer," the corporate euphemism for white-collar outsourcing. Moving business assets from one place to another is no longer a matter of transplanting factories or offices.

Increasingly it means extracting thinking skills and processes from the heads of decently paid employees and moving these faculties to a human resource (to use another corporate euphemism) in a much cheaper part of the world. This is a more complex and fraught logistic than shipping out plant machinery on the next boat. It is also a much more insidious process, especially for employees who are expected to collude in the effort to upload the contents of their brain by actively training their likely replacements.

It is the chilling task of science fiction to imagine what kinds of future technologies will be developed to make this extraction all the more efficient. And yet the basic steps are already considered routine in most multinational companies, and the race is on to develop templates for the more advanced operations. Nor is knowledge transfer a recent innovation. The deprofessionalization that knowledge workers are currently experiencing is really only an update of the de-skilling undergone by the craft artisans of the nineteenth century, when industrialists used new factory technologies and other administrative measures to undermine artisans' control over their own work rhythms and schedules. Knowledge of their trade had to be extracted from them, too.

Today the human and economic scope of knowledge transfer encompasses a vast geographical playing field. Yet its outcome is not cast in stone. The long record of flawed Western forecasts about the destiny of China, in particular, should give us pause before predicting the upshot of its rulers' indulgence of market capitalism. History has not rewarded that species of confidence.[24] Since its liberation from foreign occupation in 1949, Beijing's path toward modernization has been resolutely unique, and the latest phase of the reform period is no exception. But if the prediction business is as dodgy as ever, the old spectator sport of China-watching has changed significantly. Westerners can no longer be passive beholders, transfixed by the latest epic unfolding in that far, ancient land. These days, our lives—and the ideas and things in them—are too connected to China for us to sit back and watch.

The Shanghai Squeeze

Corporations have been moving jobs and capital out of countries like the United States since the late 1960s. But in the public mind it is only recently that China has become the most likely destination. Almost overnight, it seems, the given wisdom is that if China's breakneck growth continues, its inexhaustible labor pool, its burgeoning high-tech skills, and its investment opportunities could effortlessly absorb the livelihoods of workers and professionals in every corner of the world. Worries are also mounting about how the world's resources are being drained to service this growth, but they do not yet compare to the widespread anxiety about the flight of industry and capital: in Mexico, whose NAFTA-based manufacturing sector has been hem-orrhaging jobs to Asia; in Japan, Taiwan, and Korea, where leading technology industries have come to depend on manufacturing on the mainland; in the United States and Western Europe, where offshore job transfer is sprinting up the value chain into the realm of profes-sional services; in the offshore sites of Eastern Europe and North Africa that are increasingly less profitable than Asian locations; and even in countries like Cambodia, Thailand, Vietnam, Burma, and India, whose low labor costs are now undercut by the comparative advantages of producing in the heartlands of the jumbo China market.

Workers everywhere tend to perceive the mercurial growth of China's economy as a threat. Most owners of mobile capital, by contrast, see only an investors' bonanza. This discrepancy is not surprising, but it is rare to come across a stark divide on such a scale and with so many far-flung consequences. One of the general aims of this book is to explain how these contrasting perceptions came about, whether they are justified, and what conditions are likely to change them. Is China's growth a timely outcome that will help to stabilize the world economy, or is it a textbook illustration of the lopsided benefits conferred by corporate globalization? How do offshore employees—among the presumed beneficiaries—fit into this equation, and how can their onshore counterparts—among the presumed losers—join with them to help remedy any imbalance? In the plunder-happy world of free trade, what are the responsibilities of governments, either in the West or in key cities like Beijing and Shanghai, to try to equalize the distribution of gains and offset the environmental damage?

My inquiry into these questions took me to the factories and offices of Shanghai's booming metropolis, neighboring cities in the Yangtze River Delta and other parts of China, and, ultimately, to Taiwan and India, but it begins here with a brief historical account of how the commercial traffic between the United States and China evolved.

How Outsourcing Became a Way of Life

Before the early 1990s, the bulk of job and capital flight to China was obscured by the maze of contracting chains that snaked all over East Asia. When export-processing zones were first established in the 1980s in South China, most of the suppliers to U.S. and European manufacturers and retailers were Taiwan-, Macao-, or Hong Kong–owned factories (registered in the Cayman or Virgin Islands) that operated with a low profile and with equally low operating capital. In most cases the only contact with the onshore firm was through a Hong Kong agent, and the identity of the parent manufacturer was generally not disclosed. Indeed, the system was designed to be nontransparent, making it difficult to trace the connections between the head and the tail of the chain. Because the U.S. apparel industry was the first to see the offshoring of labor-intensive operations, garment unions had the longest record of tracking the flight to Asia, dating back to the 1960s.[1] Labor advocates in the industry also had the longest experience of protesting substandard conditions in the factories—first in Japan, and then in Hong Kong and Taiwan—that supplied the apparel majors. Consequently, the concept of the Asian sweatshop producing for Western consumers was established early in the public imagination. The reality took on a more ominous profile when low-end assembly operations swept onto mainland China itself, all but concealing the factories and shops from international scrutiny.

The initial surge of job traffic to the export zones slowed after the 1989 crackdown in Tiananmen Square. International sanctions took their toll on most trade relations with China. Bill Clinton subsequently campaigned on a promise to take a firm stand against the "butchers of Beijing," and initially he tied the approval of China's Most Favored Nation (MFN) trading status to the improvement of Beijing's human rights record. But his fighting words soon dissolved in the face of pressure from the powerful U.S.-China trade lobby. His first administration approved Beijing's MFN status in 1994 over and above a barrage of complaints about appeasement.

Offshoring corporations developed a tight understanding with the governing class that each would press for the global liberalization of trade and investment. This entente among financial and political elites was part of the Washington Consensus, and its advocates promoted the doctrine that free-trade policies would bring wealth to all participants. Benefits flowed to those who profited from trade deregulation and privatization, but the more numerous "losers of globalization" were hard-pressed to see the silver lining. Rising inequality appeared in every poor country that lifted trade and investment barriers. Domestic protests surfaced wherever corporate-led free trade left its uneven footprint. Toward the end of the 1990s, a far-flung protest network—the global justice movement—was advocating a bottom-up vision of globalization, geared to human needs and sustainable development, rather than to short-term corporate profits.[2] With its scant domestic freedoms, and limited international exchange (though not for businesspeople), China emerged as the weakest link in the network, and the largest single obstacle to global cooperation on labor and environmental standards.

Partly as a result of this stepped-up global opposition to free-trade policies, a much fiercer fight over worker and human rights preceded congressional approval of China's Permanent Normal Trading Relations (PNTR) status in 2000.[3] The granting of PNTR, which was the prelude to China's accession to the WTO in 2001, opened the door wide for production shifts from the United States to the mainland. The exodus began in earnest. In the years that followed, the majority of China's ballooning exports were produced with foreign investment, and most of the goods were destined for the American market. Consequently the U.S. trade deficit with China soared (by 30 percent in 2004 alone, to top $162 billion), along with anxiety about the loss of livelihoods in the United States.

After PNTR was approved in 2000, Congress established a bipartisan commission (the U.S.-China Economic and Security Review Commission) to assess the economic and security implications of the worsening trade deficit with China. The first study to be commissioned on domestic employment impact reported a sharp escalation in production transfers out of the United States in the six months after the granting of PNTR. In this short period, more than eighty corporations announced plans to shift production to China. According to the survey, these were large, well-known, and highly profitable companies, and the majority of them were not producing for the China market. Moreover, the pattern of their investment in China showed a clear move away from low-skill light manufacturing toward more complex, value-adding industries like electronics, chemicals, machinery, metals, and financial services. The lost onshore jobs in these industries were more likely to have been unionized with higher wage and benefit packages than in labor-intensive sectors.

Each sizable plant closure, the commission's report continued, had a "ripple effect on the wages of every worker in that industry and that community, through lowering wage demands, restraining union organizing and bargaining power, reducing the tax base, and reducing or eliminating hundreds of jobs in the related contracting, transportation,

wholesale trade, professional and service sector employment in companies and business."[4]

The authors of the study estimated that in the eight years since
1992, 760,000 jobs had been lost due to U.S.-China trade, and predicted a rapid increase in the current rate (between 70,000 and
100,000 jobs each year) after China joined the WTO. There was also
evidence of a direct link between corporate investment in China in
selected industries and domestic job loss in those same industries at
home. The conclusion to the study was a sharp indictment of free-trade
policies pursued by Republican and Democratic administrations at the
behest of the business wings of their parties and U.S. multinational
investors in China: "Our research concludes that the U.S. and other
countries have moved ahead with trade policies and global economic
integration based on faulty arguments and incomplete information."[5]

A follow-up study, covering the period from January through
March 2004, did indeed show a sharp increase in the number of production shifts, as well as the number of industries involved, and
reported that corporations had established a pattern of simultaneous
transfers to multiple low-wage destinations, both near shore (i.e., Mexico) and offshore (China).[6] No government body had collected this
kind of data on the domestic impact of overseas trade policies, and the
studies flatly refuted what many economists had argued about the benefits brought to the United States by the "virtuous circle" of free trade.
A subsequent study, undertaken for the commission by the Economic
Policy Institute, found that the U.S.-China trade deficit was responsible for the loss of 1.5 million American jobs from 1989 to 2003. According to this survey, published in 2005, job displacement had doubled
since China joined the WTO, and the fastest growth was occurring in
highly skilled and technologically advanced areas, such as electronics,
computers, and telecommunications. Indeed, China now accounted
for the entire U.S. trade deficit ($32 billion) in "advanced technology
products."[7]

The commission's own field hearings, conducted in Columbia,
South Carolina (September 2003), San Diego, California (February
2004), Akron, Ohio (September 2004), and Seattle, Washington (Jan-

uary 2005), generated a wealth of testimony from politicians, economists, manufacturers, employees, and trade unionists about the debilitating impact on U.S. industries and communities of job and capital flight to China. The industrial sectors under investigation ranged from textiles, apparel, and furniture in South Carolina; to steel, auto, and machine tools in Ohio; high-tech in California; and aerospace and software in Washington. At each hearing the commission's findings were sharply critical of how policies that were introduced to promote free trade were, in practice, actively encouraging and, in some instances (involving the Export-Import Bank), funding the transfer overseas of manufacturing, services, and R&D. According to one commissioner, "We appear to be mortgaging a broad array of assets, pieces of our country's economic future, in a historic stampede for short-term gains in corporate profitability and consumer pricing."[8]

In the years following the onset of the recession, estimates of domestic job loss came thick and fast from many other quarters. By the end of 2003, the number most commonly cited was 3 million jobs lost since 2000, though all such estimates had to be balanced against how many jobs the economy would have been expected to create in a normal recovery. According to one such report, over the course of the actual recovery from the recession (from November 2001 to November 2003), 1.3 million jobs in manufacturing alone were lost, along with 272,000 jobs in information services and 93,000 jobs in professional/technical services. These were all in sectors that paid above-average wages. Job gains in this period were predominantly in lower-wage sectors.[9] By 2004, only 65.9 percent of employable adults—a sixteen-year low—had jobs or were looking for work. Though the bulk of the losses were in manufacturing, and were assumed to have migrated mostly to China, as many as 30 percent were estimated to be in white-collar, IT-enabled services, flowing abroad primarily to India. If those displaced found full-time employment, by far the majority were earning less than at their previous positions. On the whole, these earnings losses had been increasing since the mid-1990s.[10] Department of Labor figures that analyzed the job downturn showed a sustained impact on older, more experienced workers, a result that was consistent with patterns of outsourcing.[11]

Much of the headline-grabbing data about job loss, and projections of future flight, came from private consultancies like Forrester Research, the Gartner Group, TPI (Technology Partners International), the Boston Consulting Group, and the McKinsey Global Institute. Their research analysts played both sides of the issue. They advised their client firms to move offshore whatever assets they could, as soon as they could, while also issuing publicity-conscious reports that were guaranteed to scare the living daylights out of Americans who still had jobs in vulnerable sectors. The mainstream press followed the same schizophrenic path. Alarmist human-interest stories about jobs lost alternated with reassurances, often directly from the mouths of business economists, about the beneficial impact of outsourcing "in the long run."[12]

The analysts' most alarming reports offered estimates of unprecedented losses in white-collar services and skilled IT jobs. A much-cited Forrester Research report in November 2002 projected that by 2015 the United States would lose about 3.3 million such jobs. In July 2003, the Gartner Group estimated that by the end of 2004, one in ten technology jobs at American IT companies and one in twenty at non-IT companies would have moved offshore. In addition, only 40 percent of those who had lost jobs were likely to be retrained and redeployed by the firms surveyed.[13] Some estimates were even higher. Researchers at the Fisher Center for Real Estate and Urban Economics predicted that as many as 14 million white-collar service employees, or 11 percent of the nation's total jobs, were vulnerable to offshoring.[14]

Even after the U.S. economy began to add jobs in the winter of 2003–4, the estimates continued to rise. The market-research firm TPI reported that the second quarter of 2004 saw a 35 percent increase in the value of IT outsourcing contracts over the previous year, indicating that companies were increasingly committed to moving their entire IT operations out of house.[15] In March 2004, McKinsey reported that multinationals had moved $35 billion of investment offshore in 2002 alone, and forecast that the rate of offshoring would grow between 30 percent and 40 percent annually at least through 2008.[16] Outsourcing was no longer an option in services: it was considered a requirement of business-process jobs in call centers, loan processing, and back-office accounting; it was becoming an imperative in a whole range of engineering sectors and services like financial analysis; and it was marching steadily into the legal and medical professions. In July 2004, Boston Consulting Group adopted a more apocalyptic tone in warning firms that they faced extinction if they did not move offshore: "Companies that wait will be caught in a vicious cycle of uncompetitive costs, lost business, underutilized capacity, and the irreversible destruction of value."[17]

Most bluntly, the Boston Group's report undercut the free traders' argument that the export of low-end and middle-level jobs would free up corporations to create more high-value domestic jobs in areas like research and development. Surveying the companies that had already established large R&D operations in low-cost countries (LCCs), its authors reported that "one of the most intriguing advantages we have come across is faster (and lower cost) R&D. Because companies established in LCCs have eliminated a lot of automation and tooling requirements, they can be more responsive to R&D requests." The report concluded that firms could increase the amount of research they did by three to five times for the same budget they would devote onshore. A study from the University of California's Stimson Center reported that more than 200 foreign corporations—with names like GE, GM, Alcatel, Microsoft, IBM, Bayer, Ericsson, and DuPont—had already established R&D centers in China by 2002.[18] Over the next two years alone, that number would triple to 600. Every month a new R&D unit, with several hundred employees, opened in one of Shanghai's high-tech industrial parks. Firms could now operate on their own in China, free of the requirement to partner with local Chinese companies in joint ventures, and so security, in regard to intellectual property, was much tighter. The low cost and high quality of local engineers, combined with proximity to their expanding production centers, made it irresistible for companies of all sizes to move some of their most advanced operations offshore.

It was the same story in Silicon Valley, though with an extra twist in the tail. For the last three decades, the U.S. economy had relied on this region's high-tech industrial complex to seed innovative job creation.

Indeed, Silicon Valley hosted 13 percent of the new American jobs created between 1996 and 2000 alone. When the business of funding new technology start-ups resumed operations in 2003, it turned out that venture capitalists were primarily interested in backing "micro-multinationals," or companies that included offshoring in their business models. James Breyer, president of Accel, a leading venture capital firm, advised that, very soon, all Accel start-ups should have half of their workers based overseas. "If a company is not actively investing in China or India," he declared, "they need to provide a very compelling case to board members as to why they are not."[19]

The Balance Sheet

In the course of the last decade, "outsourcing" has become adopted in public currency as the default term, for better or worse, to refer to overseas job flight. Technically speaking, there are many varieties of outsourcing: offshore outsourcing, business process outsourcing, multi-sourcing, co-sourcing. In general, the term refers to the procurement of services or products from an outside supplier or manufacturer as a way of cutting costs and shedding benefit burdens. In principle, outsourcing is different, though not entirely distinct, from the practice of offshoring—when the company in question opens a plant overseas under its own name. Increasingly, however, public usage of the term "outsourcing" has been extended to all offshore transfers, and in this book I acknowledge the overlap, if not the exact equivalence, between the two terms.

However slippery this usage, it is simply the latest substitute for the original, more colorful name given to firms shifting jobs elsewhere to avoid regulation. In the 1950s, such companies were called "runaway shops," and they crossed state borders to escape labor and workplace sanitation laws, or to weaken the rights of their workers to tenure. The original runaways in the New York garment industry fled to New Jersey, while the New England textile mill owners moved to the Southern states after the Second World War to evade unionization. In fact, there is a direct line of descent from the so-called sweating system of the nineteenth-century garment industry to the outsourcing of today's global corporations. The garmento's practice of "putting out" ready-cut garments to be made up in journeymen's small shops or in workers' homes was the prototype for the wave of corporate subcontracting in the 1970s, which preceded offshore outsourcing as a strategy for offloading higher wages and benefits that had been hard won by decades of union organization.

Not much has changed, except for the scale and geographic scope of the operation. Migrating jobs offshore or to an outside contractor both creates and takes advantage of a transient work environment that feeds off workers' insecurity and immobility. While the jobs lost are frequently unionized, the new jobs created are almost always non-union, and therefore come at the expense of workers' rights. Indeed, employers often cite excessive union power as the reason for ordering the transfers, and so the threat of job and capital flight is used more generally to intimidate employees, in both onshore and offshore countries, who want to form unions. Well-placed officials in the less developed country may benefit in the short run from access to foreign exchange, not to mention kickbacks, but generally the recipient nation has no control over the vested capital or repatriated profits, and it has to negotiate hard, and often unethically, to ensure any benefits from technology transfer. So, too, the generous tax benefits customarily offered to foreign investors further deplete national revenues, and hasten the erosion of the public sector's capacity to provide a range of public goods, benefits, and secure employment. Workers' wages are by far the largest portion of the financial benefit to the host country.

As for the onshore country, it has to bear most of the costs of the corporate decision to outsource. Loss of jobs is a drain on the local tax base, and it raises the cost of unemployment benefits and government retraining programs. In addition, the social costs of job displacement are incalculable. If the transfer shuts down an operation that is central to a local economy, then the entire community can be decimated, along with trust in the shared bonds that ensure fairness in any society. The sense of betrayal is profound, whether the blame is directed at corporations (as is usually the case with blue-collar layoffs), at oneself (as is traditionally favored by white-collar employees), or at politicians in the thrall of free-trade ideologies. Jobs in industries threatened by cheaper imports, and manufacturing jobs in particular, have generally provided higher wages and benefits than jobs in export industries or in services. The majority of displaced workers experience a long-term decline in wages, security, and benefits, especially if the outsourcing is with a low-cost nation. Moreover, when outsourcing transfers move into the high-end range, some economists have argued that unless the onshore country competes vigorously, its entire economy will be hurt.[20] Finally, outsourcing undermines the sense of national sovereignty. Pride at the achievements of national industry, and confidence in its future, dissolve along with the capacity of the nation's managers to bring about an equitable adjustment of the economy.

By contrast, employers who ship out the jobs bear none of the costs of their decisions, and enjoy only the benefits. Among the latter are huge payroll savings, elimination of unions, and sharp reductions in social security, Medicare, and pension costs; looser environmental and workplace regulations; a raft of tax rewards, including immunity to taxation on foreign profits; higher corporate profits and stock prices; and the boosting of bonuses and returns for executives and investors. Access to new international markets on generally favorable terms inevitably erodes the sense of a firm's accountability to its society of origin. In the long run, however, the most valuable benefit to investors lies in the perpetuation of a climate of job insecurity in a global business environment where bigger gains can always be had by moving elsewhere. The threat to do so guarantees employee docility in the short term as long as the company lingers, and in the longer term if and when the move materializes.

This, at any rate, is an abstract way of assessing the balance sheet. Among the populace at large, there is a more powerful, emotional understanding of the impact of outsourcing. A typical poll (taken in May 2004 by the Employment Law Alliance) found that nearly 60 percent of U.S. survey participants believed that companies outsourcing work that could be done by Americans ought to be penalized by the U.S. government.[21] Contrary to Wall Street's undisguised enthusiasm for outsourcing, almost 66 percent of investors, according to an April 2004 Gallup poll, believed that it was "bad for the economy," and about a quarter expressed a sharp concern that they or someone in their households might lose their livelihood from offshoring.[22] Strong public sentiment like this fueled a political firestorm over the practice among lawmakers, opinion makers, lobbyists, and advocacy groups.

For those who felt their jobs were threatened, it wasn't just the statistics or warnings about job loss that generated concern. The underhanded manner in which company executives carried out the transfers provoked widespread disgust. Euphemisms were easy to spot. Eliminated jobs were most routinely described as "knowledge transfer," and there was a long list of related terms for which managers were officially advised to use neutral-sounding substitutes. Companies tried to disguise the transfers wherever they could, and rigid gag orders were imposed on employees who might be tempted to leak outsourcing plans to the press.

Because of IBM's status as a national industrial champion, leaks of its proposals to move several thousand high-level jobs overseas received particularly generous media attention. In July 2003, the *New York Times* outed the firm's secret plans to speed up its outsourcing of engineering and other white-collar positions.[23] For its story, the *Times* drew on a tape recording of an internal IBM meeting leaked by a nauseated employee to the Washington Alliance of Technology Workers (affiliated with the Communication Workers of America). Executives present at the event—a summit meeting for HR managers around the globe—warned that the job loss might create a "dignity issue" for displaced employees, and "that union organizing will become more aggressive over the coming months."[24]

The most highly publicized leak involved another set of internal IBM documents, obtained by the *Wall Street Journal* in January 2004, which detailed offshoring plans involving thousands more jobs, and actual projections of cost savings ($168 million annually). The memo included estimates from IBM's Shanghai office on the relative costs of labor and benefits for U.S. and Chinese programmers, project managers, and senior analysts (though the estimated 1:4 cost ratio was much lower than any wage structure I encountered in Shanghai). The memo included the draft of a "suggested script" for managers to use in breaking the news to employees affected. Terms like "resource action"—IBM language for layoffs—were to be avoided, as were "on-shore" and "off-shore." Empathetic talk was encouraged: "This action is a statement about the rate and pace of change in this demanding industry. It is in no way a comment on the excellent work you have done over the years."[25]

In some cases, leaks of impending plans prompted repressive action from company lawyers. In November 2003, the owner of American Champions, an anti-outsourcing website (www.american-champions.org), was ordered to remove a company document outlining plans for the overseas transfer of 70 percent of AT&T wireless jobs from Washington State. "It is disgusting to me that there is so little regard for those who have worked hard to make this company a success," declared one AT&T employee affected by the plan. "Some people are just livid. You come to work one day and you see people standing over your desk, discussing how to do your job. We spent many years of our lives learning how to do this, to become competent. We took pride in our jobs, stayed late without pay many times to make sure things worked. Now [the company] is saying to us, in effect, 'We don't really care.' "[26] In a practice that became quite common in many firms, employees whom AT&T slated to lay off were forced to assist directly in the knowledge transfer by training their overseas replacements or else lose their severance packages, and face possible legal action. The firm's managers had described this process, disingenuously, as a "pilot project," in which employees were invited to participate. "It kind of feels like you are talking to your hangman," reported one of the unlucky participants.[27] Stories like this became the stuff of workplace lore, and even prompted some politicians to try to outlaw the practice as inhumane.

All the New Economy talk in the 1990s about change and risk-averse behavior had not prepared its high-tech acolytes for the prospect of seeing careers migrate so rapidly. Moreover, the advanced technology that had played a starring role in the boom turned out to be the means by which their jobs could now be sent overseas with the flick of a router switch. Accustomed to enjoying humane workplaces with oodles of respect for their service on the job, they were shocked to be treated the same way as the blue-collar workers whose rust belt world of shuttered factories and welfare checks they had long regarded as the province of another species. Nor, like the manufacturing workers, did they have unions that could fight management for cutting and running. Instead, they did what techies do—they created websites to protest the wave of IT outsourcing. The list of sites, like the aforementioned American Champions, soared to well over a hundred (including the Rescue American Jobs Foundation, the Coalition for National Sovereignty and Economic Patriotism, the Information Technology Professionals Association of America, and the Organization for the Rights of American Workers), each publicizing an arsenal of resources for the aggrieved to adopt legal measures to save their jobs. Because of their professional status, mainstream journalists could more easily identify with their cause than with assembly-line workers, and so the movement and its protests got especially good press.

By 2003, the unemployment rate for computer scientists stood at 5.2 percent, and for electrical engineers at 6.2 percent. These were levels unthinkable during the previous two decades, when such professions were lionized as the leading edge of American job creation.[28] In the first quarter of 2004, the Bureau of Labor Statistics showed a 9.5 percent unemployment rate among computer programmers. Demand for skilled technology employees had fallen off precipitously, and the labor market slump was affecting some of the most highly valued occupations and industries in the American economy. Between 2001 and 2004, software-producing industries lost an even larger percentage of jobs (16 percent) than manufacturing (15 percent).[29]

In the face of such statistics, the most popular myth propagated at the height of the New Economy of the 1990s rapidly collapsed. Low-value manufacturing, it had been claimed, would keep on flowing to developing countries, but the high-value jobs, especially those in technology industries, would stay. Sustained growth in the service sectors would continue to offer opportunities for laid-off blue-collar workers who were willing to retrain away from the old "buggy whip" industries. By the beginning of the 2004 election year, it was no longer possible to push this line of argument among manufacturing workers. Nor could the same logic of moving up be applied to those laid off in high-tech or in producer services. To put it simply, there were fewer and fewer places at the higher end of the value chain—in finance, industrial R&D, high-tech, or professional services—where employees could move up in expectation of a stable career. Moreover, many of those high-value jobs were the same ones that every other technology-saturated country, especially those in East Asia, were hotly pursuing. By the time this fledgling international labor market fully matures, middle-class American parents might be hoping their children will grow up to be plumbers—precisely the kind of job that cannot be sent overseas.

While some business sectors were hard hit by the recession, the generous savings and handsome profits reaped from outsourcing more than compensated. Between 1990 and 2003, overall corporate profits rose 128 percent, CEO pay rose 313 percent, while average worker pay rose by only 49 percent.[30] In the three years following the recession's end, corporate profits showed the fastest growth rate since World War II, increasing at an annual rate of 14.5 percent after inflation.[31] By contrast, labor compensation recorded its lowest share of national growth for any recovery in the postwar period. As for the CEOs, who were rewarded for creating "shareholder value" by ordering the layoffs and transfers, they finally broke the barrier of the 300-to-1 ratio between their average pay and that of the average worker in 2003.[32] Average CEO compensation at the fifty firms outsourcing the most service jobs increased by 46 percent in 2003, compared with a 9 percent average increase for all CEOs.[33]

But it wasn't just in paychecks that domestic workers got the short end of the stick. Productivity rose by over 4 percent annually from 2002 through 2004, prompting business commentators to suggest that U.S. workers (who already worked much longer and harder than any other developed nation) could easily absorb the extra burden of job tasks inherited from their laid-off brethren.

Decades of public relations pounding from corporate America had sought public acceptance for the claim that companies had no choice but to ditch even their most valued and loyal employees if a cheaper and more competitive alternative became available. Growing capacity to pit workers against each other on a global scale fueled the "race to the bottom" (or "global labor arbitrage" as Stephen Roach, Morgan Stanley's senior economist, euphemistically termed it) that saw employers scouring the underdeveloped world for the lowest wage floor and best investment concessions. The same kind of PR was applied to the notion that employees had to fight to save their jobs from being "taken" by their counterparts in another region of the world. It was no wonder that some displaced workers found it easier to blame the faceless foreigner for taking their jobs than to hold companies accountable for paying Third World wages and asking First World prices.

Two City Views

If this was the climate at home, what was the mood offshore? How did the debate about outsourcing play overseas, among the corporate managers and executives whom John Kerry famously labeled as "Benedict Arnolds"? What did Chinese employees, who supposedly benefited from the transfers, have to say about their own prospects of job security? Shanghai was arguably the best place to find answers to these questions. It was the latest Asian boomtown to rebuild its fortunes on the strength of a massive influx of foreign investment, and it had lately attained a pivotal role in the global economy. To fully understand that role, we need to profile some of its history, as well as its quicksilver growth since the early 1990s.

First-time visitors to Shanghai can hardly avoid heading directly to the famous riverfront of the Bund. The Anglo-Indian name (for "embankment") recalls the port's contribution to the opium trade, and the neoclassical pomp of its buildings carries echoes of the foreign trading houses and banks that once controlled the economy, along with the social and cultural life, of colonial Shanghai. Needless to say, the symbolism of the 1.5-kilometer quay is highly contested. The Chinese street name Zhongshan Yilu (or Sun Yat-sen Road, Section One), honors the man whose own Western-inspired nationalism set in motion a long revolution that eventually drove the foreigners out of their most cherished Asian foothold after 1949. When the city was finally liberated, the Bund's grandest edifice, built for the Hong Kong and Shanghai Bank, which had been the most powerful financial institution in East Asia, was promptly converted into the city's Communist Party headquarters.

Fifty years later, one of the favorite sports of China-watchers was to record which foreign interests had been allowed back to lease space on the Bund. AIG, Citibank, and ABN AMRO were the first, followed by KFC, and then, in a shower of gloating publicity, the opening of Armani, Cartier, Gucci, Dior, Louis Vuitton, and Ermenegildo Zegna stores in 2004 sealed the Bund's reinvention as a trendy retail zone. But most bittersweet of all was the anticipated return of Jardine Matheson, the original monopolist of the hated opium trade, to take over management of that Jazz Era palace, the Peace Hotel. In a remarkable display of corporate deadpan, the local retail agent who brokered the deal commented to the Shanghai press: "As the Bund used to house Jardine's local office, the area has special meaning for the group."[34]

Since the late 1990s, the Bund has offered a different kind of window onto the reforms that have driven China's rapid makeover. The view across the Huangpu River now takes in the prospect of the new city of Pudong, boasting a zany collection of some of the tallest, boldest, and dottiest buildings in the world. Jumbo glass globes vie with lurid pink baubles in a skyline that generates wonder, mirth, and dread in equal measure. First envisaged by Sun Yat-sen himself in 1911 as the "Great Port of Pudong," but only approved for development by Beijing in 1990, the creation, as if overnight, of the Pudong cityscape is a national showcase for the belief that literally anything is possible in China's economy. This is exactly the kind of go-go verve that intoxicates the multinational firms that have set up shop in Pudong's financial district of Lujiazui. The same spirit is supposed to preside over its 220-square-mile sprawl—from the gaudy Oriental Pearl Tower and International Convention Center by the Huangpu's eastern bank to the gleaming new microchip factories on the broad acres of Zhangjiang

The skyline of the new city of Pudong, a view from the Bund

Hi-Tech Park, and even farther out, to the sci-fi Pudong International Airport by the East China Sea.

Pudong New Area, as it was officially termed, was granted more privileges by Beijing than any of China's export-oriented Special Economic Zones had previously enjoyed. The rapid development of its free-trade zones, top-end apartment complexes, golf courses, luxury malls and hotels, and stock exchange was aimed at restoring Shanghai's prewar status as the premier trading and finance center of the Asia-Pacific region. It was also planned as the ultimate global capitalist city, and in return for this hospitality, it was expected that foreign money would foot many of the bills. Japanese investors, in particular, were tapped to bankroll the corporate towers. Overseas Chinese, who had already led the way in funding South China's original export-processing zones, and whose blood ties to the motherland helped to sustain their position in the top ranks of foreign investors, were called upon again to develop much of the remaining real estate.[35] The Fortune 500 and their employees were expected to fill the downtown offices, technology parks, and upscale housing. Yet, in spite of the monumental scale of foreign direct investment (FDI), some commentators continued to see only the heavy hand of the state. After his visit, Milton Friedman, the high priest of privatization, dismissed the whole undertaking as "a statist monument for a dead pharaoh on the level of the pyramids."[36] The pharaoh in question was Deng Xiaoping, who had approved the project as a wide-open door to foreign trade.

Initial overbuilding of grade-A office space and luxury apartments produced the low occupancy rates that gave this new urban landscape a vacant, almost funereal air, but this is not what Friedman had in mind. However jaundiced (he was an inveterate anticommunist), his throwaway comment still spoke to the frank disarray of opinions held by economists about China's unique path of reform. What, after all, was the exact nature of the relationship between the state and the burgeoning private economy?[37] Was the ardent wooing of FDI just a means for China to subsidize its failing state sector, or did the recently revived health of many state-owned enterprises prove that gradual reforms and continued public ownership were a transitional bridge to a new kind of economy?[38]

Beijing had successfully evaded the disastrous shock therapy imposed upon the Warsaw Bloc economies by neoliberal institutions like the International Monetary Fund (IMF) and the World Bank.[39] China's slower, more evolutionary path to the market, directed by authoritarian rule at the center, appeared to have more in common with the "developmental states" of the East Asian tigers: Taiwan, South Korea, Singapore, and Hong Kong. Yet there were significant differences. Even at the dawn of the reform era in 1978, the daily sense of ownership and control in China was already quite decentralized. The vast campaigns of rural industrialization in the 1960s and 1970s, combined with the general undermining of Communist Party authority during the Cultural Revolution, had left local officials in townships and provincial cities with a considerable degree of practical power in their hands. They tried out new policies before any clear signals were received from Beijing. Indeed, some analysts argue that China's market-oriented reforms began in rural areas in the early 1970s and that they were only given official policy recognition by central government leaders like Deng toward the end of that decade.[40]

According to this revised timeline, the reforms took almost twenty years to reach Shanghai. When they fully arrived in the early 1990s, the city's comparative advantages, suppressed by Beijing for so long, generated runaway economic growth. Rents from the lease of land-use rights (massive profits at no costs) soon replaced extractions from state firms as the main source of government revenue.[41] Beginning in 1992, the city recorded double-digit GDP increases for twelve straight years (13.6 percent for 2004, with a GDP of $89 billion), far surpassing a national growth rate that was itself an object of marvel for the capitalist world. With only 1 percent of the population, the city accounted for 5 percent of China's GDP, 10 percent of its contracted FDI, 13 percent of the country's imports, and 11 percent of its exports. Not surprisingly, Shanghai was rated A+ by the World Bank for its investment conditions. More than half of the investment went into manufacturing, and a large portion of that was for export-processing for the developed countries.[42] But an increasingly substantial share was aimed at producing for the China market. By 2003, 46 percent of China's total imports were for "ordinary trade" in the domestic economy, and multinationals were developing mixed production strategies aimed at domestic sales as well as the export trade.[43] Business analysts had begun to talk about the "real," as opposed to the potential, China market. In Shanghai, at least, where one out of every ten employees worked in foreign-invested firms,[44] and where corporate management textbooks were hotter imports than Britney Spears, it was easy to see how the impact of foreign capital had left behind the isolated havens of the export zones and was encroaching on daily life.[45]

To better focus on this relationship between foreign money and domestic commerce, we would have to leave the sublime views of the Bund and Pudong, and move inside the city, through Nanjing Road's dense shopping precinct (with up to one million visitors a day) to its more upscale western section, where the Shanghai Center, stronghold of the city's foreign business community, sits opposite the golden-spired main hall of the Shanghai Exhibition Center. The architectural contrast between these two buildings is no less stark than the riverfront views, and the relationship between what they stand for is no less complex.

Shanghai's eclectic range of historic building styles is deservedly famous, and its most recent construction boom (which deployed, in one famous apocryphal estimate, the use of one-quarter of the world's cranes) had been like a fancy-dress ball invitation for the world's designer architects. As a result, the Exhibition Center, which stands as the city's unique period example of Soviet aesthetics, is no longer in the competition to dominate or dazzle the skyline. A lavish "gift from the Soviet people," the building began life as the Hall of Sino-Soviet Friendship, constructed in 1959 to mark the tenth anniversary of the founding of the People's Republic of China. It had been the city's highest tower until the 1980s, eclipsing the Park Hotel (1934), which had been the pinnacle building of Shanghai's International Settlement. To drive home the triumphalism, it was constructed on the former

Shanghai's Soviet-style exhibition hall—portal to the China market

twenty-five-acre estate site of the settlement's wealthiest resident, Silas Hardoon, one of the Baghdadi Jews who amassed a fortune from the city's periodic real estate booms. The building, with its palatial, somewhat campy, decor, now hosts weekly trade exhibits, showcasing industries of all types. Many are international fairs and expos, but the chief emphasis is still on the domestic market. The crisp People's Liberation Army guards at the gates and the immaculate upkeep of the grounds and interiors mark the site as a government enclave of high standing.

Symbolically speaking, the guards are protecting much more than the sanctity of the building. Aside from its inexhaustible reserves of cheap labor, the China market, that ever-elusive bounty, is the nation's most valuable asset, at least to Western eyes. Access to its untold riches is a perpetual draw for each new wave of foreign investors. Indeed, the prospect of selling to 1.3 billion consumers is the number-one fixation of many of the corporate suits that frequent the Shanghai Center across the road. For their part, government officials have learned how to bargain portions of market access for what China most needs: foreign exchange, advanced technology, and knowledge skills.

Boasting three stark towers, the Shanghai Center complex (known locally as the Portman Center, after its architect) was built in 1990 in the shape of the Chinese character for mountain (山). It has no guards, but is nonetheless shielded from the street by a bulbous concrete bunker that can be rented for arguably the ugliest form of advertising in the city. Inside, the cavernous compound is anchored by the Portman Ritz-Carlton hotel, and is studded with the familiar landmarks of global corporate culture: Starbucks and Häagen-Dazs; Salvatore Ferragamo, Paul & Shark, and Stefano Ricci; American Express and a string of international airlines, travel agencies, and consular offices. Office listings in the American International Center include Merrill Lynch, Morgan Stanley, the *New York Times* and the *Financial Times,* U.S. trade and commerce departments, the American Chamber of Commerce, and a batch of high-end legal and banking services. Nowhere else in Shanghai are all of the components of

Headquarters of the foreign business world—the Shanghai Center

business dealmaking so readily available, within a stone's throw of each other.

The center's City Supermarket is ground zero for the culinary needs of Shanghai's expatriate population. Even though they could be enjoying one of the world's great cuisines, expats who cannot not live without Duncan Hines brownie mix, Skippy Peanut Butter, or Old El Paso Nachos Kit can stock up there. None of the reading material I saw on display had a local flavor, with the exception of the very popular *Ayi Survival Guide,* a handbook for communicating effectively with servants (though readers would not find a chapter on how to persuade their *ayi* to cook with Betty Crocker Hamburger Helper). Among the freebies that shoppers could pick up was *China Brief,* a private consultancy's newsletter that advised the casual investor on the mechanics of setting up business in China. One of the articles detailed all of the costs involved in "A Practical Budget for Your South China Factory." Factor in up to 12 RMB ($1.50) a day for each employee's breakfast, lunch, and dinner, the reader was advised, and "please note this figure, as it will amount to quite a sum every month!" As for workers' accommodations, the author of the consultancy's guidebook, also on sale, noted: "While I have seen up to sixteen people crammed into a tiny cubicle, be fair to your working force, and you will gain in terms of lower turnover and a better attitude at work."[46] A lead article in the newsletter's September 2003 issue outlined how to purchase and convert a state-owned enterprise into a moneymaking instrument. This was not as risky as it used to be, but be warned: "existing workers' rights can be sticky." Since the country's first Labor Law was passed in 1994, regulations, on the page at least, had tightened considerably. Employees, the article went on to detail, could not be laid off without paying sizable severance packages. We were not in Kansas anymore, where you could shutter a plant and fire employees at will.

Localize or Die

The corporate expat community in Shanghai in 2005 numbered as many as 120,000 (out of a national total of 600,000),[47] and those who paid taxes accounted for 14 percent of the city's personal income tax revenue.[48] Like their pre-Liberation predecessors (labeled by historian Nicholas Clifford as the "spoilt children of empire"), their quality of life far surpassed what they could afford at home.[49] Likewise, for many of them, their days were numbered. This time around, it was their own companies, and not the Communist authorities, that wanted to send them packing. Over breakfast in the Tea Garden of the Ritz-Carlton, Tom Gougarty, executive director of the American Chamber of Commerce, explained why. First of all, he reported that FDI under $100 million no longer needed the approval of Beijing, which took away the need for costly representatives required to negotiate deals or massage government relations. Nor, since the bulk of FDI was now flowing into wholly owned foreign enterprises rather than into joint ventures, was there any need for managers to look after relations with the partnering state-owned enterprise. The era of China joint ventures in the 1980s and 1990s had been unprofitable for most foreign investors.[50] Gougarty conceded that many had lost their shirts, but the prospect of controlling their own operations, as they could now do, had brought them back in droves. However, they were more cognizant of operating costs on the ground, and were under pressure to localize as many employee positions as possible. Shanghai's cost of living for expats was now higher than Tokyo's and New York's. If a local could do the job competently at a fraction of the cost, it was no longer possible to justify the average expat package—which typically included prime-location villas at an average monthly rent of $9,400, similarly steep children's tuition rates, R&R trips, foreign service allowances, and even a special hardship premium, in some cases, for living in China.[51] Every expat was under pressure to train his or her own replacement. Moving Americans off the company payroll wasn't just an onshore-to-offshore process, it was happening here in Shanghai.

But with the city's thousands of foreign companies chasing a limited pool of qualified Chinese managers who were familiar with international business practices, localization was not a simple proposition. Sensing the vacuum, local engineers were seizing the opportunity to acquire cut-price MBAs and rush into managerial slots, leaving their own technical positions, critical to production, understaffed and subject to high turnover and wage inflation. As a result, Gougarty explained, it wasn't just Shanghai's expat salaries, but also the wages of skilled locals that had become too costly. "The education system," he observed, "isn't producing people fast enough," and so the labor supply was tight. Too tight, it appeared, for the comfort of many of his organization's members.

His was the first complaint I heard about high Chinese wages and lack of available skilled labor, but I soon found it echoed in almost every foreign-invested company office and factory I visited. Given that China's low wages were its main selling point, not to mention the bane of workers in developed countries, the payroll department was the last place I expected to hear such laments from foreign managers. Yet here in Shanghai, it was the complaint du jour. What were the implications of this tight labor market? Quite possibly, the livelihood of employees in a wide range of industries in the United States, Europe, and East Asia hung in the balance. If China could somehow produce a surplus of skilled employees at the right price (i.e., an employer's market), then multinationals could transfer their more advanced operations in the expectation of guaranteed savings. The impact on newly vulnerable onshore employees would be dramatic.

Gougarty was also the first of many businesspeople I met who absolved U.S. corporations of any responsibility for the politically sensitive trade imbalance between China and the United States. A breezy Midwesterner with a military demeanor, he had earned his stripes as a businessman in the 1980s, selling Japanese products to steel companies in what was fast becoming the rust belt. He recalled that he was "beat up" quite regularly for doing so, and so he had personal experience of American resentment about job loss to Asia. Noticing, for the first time apparently, that the waitstaff in the Portman Ritz-Carlton restaurant carried the initials P.R.C. on their name tags, he suppressed an impish smile, and explained that most U.S. corporations in China—75 percent, he estimated—had come to grab a share of the domestic market. The bulk of foreign investors in the export sector were East Asians, and so it was their exports to the United States that were largely responsible for the trade imbalance. Mainland Chinese, he added, had taken to setting up and registering their own companies in Hong Kong or in offshore tax havens like the British Virgin Islands, the Cayman Islands, Western Samoa, and Bermuda in order to enjoy the preferential treatment available to foreign investors. Naturally, the entrepôt goods that flowed out of Hong Kong, where most of the East Asian investors were registered, were included in the export figures.

Asian investors, in other words, and not U.S. corporations, were to blame for the United States' soaring trade deficit. This was a common argument inside the U.S.-China trade lobby, but it glossed over the reality of the supply chain that dictated the coastal export trade. In practice, most of the Asian investors were producing for U.S. and European corporations. The big brands relied on their Hong Kong agents or, increasingly, on mainland buyers to choose suppliers—Taiwanese, Korean, Macaoese, and Hong Kong middlemen—who could squeeze value out of the South China factories that assembled their products. The familiarity of those Asian investors with China's languages and cultures, and their capacity to operate under severe price pressure, with low margins, meant they were able to drive workers much harder and more brutally than Western managers could.[52] It was their no-name factories, producing for household retail names like Nike, the Gap, Disney, and Wal-Mart, which sprung to mind when Westerners thought of the modern Chinese sweatshop.

In pre-Liberation Shanghai, foreign capitalist taipans relied, in much the same way, on local compradores to extract ever more time and toil from their factory workforces. The term used to describe this was "squeeze," and its cruel art had resumed life, after a breathing space of over thirty years, when the export-processing zones of Guangdong and Fujian opened for business in the 1980s. As one Taiwanese shoe manufacturer put it, "China is like a sponge full of water, you just have to squeeze it hard until you get the last drop."[53] Factory owners like him operated on thin margins by buying imported materials, duty-free, and delivering the finished goods. The multinationals who placed the orders took the lion's share of the profits from the retail markups made possible by their marquee names. To conclude that the latter bore little responsibility for the flood of exports to the United States was disingenuous. The year before, in 2002, Wal-Mart alone accounted for $12 billion, or almost 10 percent, of the United States' imported goods from China, none of them produced in factories with WAL-MART painted on the side.[54]

Yet Gougarty's main point had been about producing for the China market. Corporations, he implied, were creating jobs that would probably not have existed otherwise, and least of all in the United States. Yet, again, it was difficult to prove this point. Corporate decisions to invest in emerging markets with anticipated higher returns usually rely on their ability to disinvest elsewhere. If a job in China produces more profit than one in Ohio, an employer will cut loose the domestic one in order to create more of the overseas ones. This doesn't mean that the actual job is transferred, though it may have the same impact. For a multinational corporation, layoffs in one country and recruitment in another are part of a global map of profit assessment that is constantly being adjusted and rearranged. Even when factories or operations are not being transferred directly from one location to another, this global balance sheet of investments still connects the winners and the losers together.

As for the China market itself, how long and for how many fevered minds had it cast its spell on the West? The fantasy of converting a vast population into faithful consumers of Western products had been around for several centuries.[55] For the would-be trader, the low point was the famous 1793 letter penned by Emperor Qian Long after King George III's ambassador, Lord Macartney, arrived in Beijing with a massive business delegation, requesting trading rights: "Our Celestial Empire possesses all things in abundance and lacks no products within its border. There is therefore no need to import the manufactures of outside barbarians in exchange for our own produce."[56] Even after foreign trade was imposed on China as a result of the Opium Wars and the humiliating treaty concessions, the domestic market remained almost entirely self-sufficient, and remarkably resistant to Western goods. Despite all of the favorable conditions it created for foreign trade, the Treaty of Nanking's first six years actually saw a decline in British exports to China.[57] Only kerosene and, later, cigarettes made any sizable impact on mass consumption.[58] Even the might of Manchester cotton, which made some initial headway, was vanquished when homegrown Chinese textile mills sprang up to undercut the prices. For half a century the folklore surrounding the fabled potential of the China trade was utilized by Shanghai's powerful British merchants to persuade the Foreign Office to exact even more concessions from Beijing. Trade lobbies, such as the powerful China Association, were organized to push for a British protectorate in the Yangtze region at the turn of the century. Suspicious of the overblown claims, sobered by the dismal trade figures, and wary of further imperial responsibilities, the British government repeatedly rebuffed the merchants, hewing to its policy of limited liability in China.[59] American exporters to China had their own problems. In 1905, when Washington refused to lift its Chinese Exclusion Act, U.S.-made goods were hit by a widespread boycott, which had a lingering legacy.

In the century of its commercial life as an entrepôt port, Shanghai saw a large volume of trade traffic, but very little that penetrated the provinces. The biggest domestic returns came from real estate—especially the business of building cheap housing for the hundreds of thousands of Chinese seeking haven from warlords, arbitrary taxation, and insurgencies in the countryside. Despite the deluxe appearance of the spoiling life enjoyed by its foreign business community, the commercial profits were never very great, and not even the real estate market recovered after the triple blow of the great communist strikes of 1925, the Nationalist takeover in 1927, and the Wall Street Crash of 1929.[60]

In *Four Hundred Million Customers*, his mordant 1937 memoir of a quarter-century spent watching Western manufacturers try in vain to pitch their wares, American advertising executive Carl Crow saw no reason to imagine that the Shanghai experience of his day would not be a permanent condition: "So long as people of one country make goods to sell to others, so long as ships cross the ocean and international trade exists, the golden illusion of the sales which may be made to China's industrious millions will always be an intriguing one. No matter what you may be selling, your business in China should be enormous, if the Chinese who should buy your goods would only do so."[61] Crow's book was a choice read for the foreigners who lived through the rocky era of joint ventures from the mid-1980s to the mid-1990s. It was expressly recommended to me by an ex-president of Shanghai's Chamber of Commerce. "I saw myself in every page," he reported, with a wan smile.

From the mid-1990s, foreign adventurers returned to Shanghai en masse, but outside of the export-processing trade, their investments were slow to show results, especially for a high-risk emerging market. By 1999, an American Chamber of Commerce survey found that only "12 percent of respondents said that their China operations generated returns above what the companies considered their cost of capital for China. Well over half had returns on investment below their cost of capital, and nearly a third significantly below."[62]

China's accession to the WTO in December 2001 gave the foreign investor another reason to believe. If authorities played by the rules set by the world's leading powers and their corporations, the entire domestic market would be integrated into the global capitalist economy. A new wave of FDI flowed in, far surpassing all previous tallies, and in 2003 the Beijing and Shanghai chambers of commerce reported that, finally, the majority of their member companies had turned profits, some of them substantial. Still, a significant majority (62 percent) of them had not achieved a margin greater than their global average.[63] The most profitable operations remained in the business of sourcing cheap goods for export, or in sectors like fast food, where McDonald's and KFC had no serious domestic rivals. Giants like Motorola and GM, who had made headway in new markets, saw their profits dwindle when domestic competition emerged.[64] The primary reason for lusting after the China market had not changed all that much; companies were there primarily to build their brand familiarity, or because "they could not afford not to be there" for fear of being left behind in that harvest of profits that lay just over the horizon, or at the end of the rainbow.

If the Western trading mentality had not changed its spots, Shanghai's economy itself had been transformed beyond measure. By 2004, it was the head of the dragon that formed the regional powerhouse of the

Showbiz sells soap—an American brand assails the China market

Yangtze Delta economy. In the first quarter of that year, the region finally overtook the Pearl River Delta as the center of China's economic gravity. After a 56 percent surge in exports, total foreign trade was worth $83 billion, while the Pearl River reported $69.3 billion.[65] More important, the region on the rise boasted an economy that was moving ever higher up the value chain. The industrial corridor of Greater Shanghai stretched over 120 kilometers from Pudong to the upriver cities of Suzhou and Wuxi. For its technology-driven companies, the supply chain in this corridor was almost complete, making it the first fully advanced production base in China.

Yet the history behind the city's role in the making of this regional economy was much less well known than the overtold tales about luxury, vice, and exploitation that continued to fuel the nostalgia binge for Old Shanghai.[66] What were the factors that had propelled Shanghai to its pivotal role in the world economy?

From Milk Cow to Gold Coast

By the time that General Chen Yi and the victorious peasant battalions of the PLA's Third Field Force entered Shanghai through the shaded boulevards of the French Concession in 1949, the city's reputation as the acme of foreign decadence and greed was long secure among the Chinese masses. Indeed, Chen's first mayoral administration seriously considered a proposal to dismantle and disperse Shanghai's factories, along with a population perceived as tainted by its complicity with the imperialists' ways.[67] The plan was put forward, in part, as a way of punishing the city for its parasitical past. Its proposed reallocation of industrial plant and skilled manpower would be aimed at developing neglected provinces in the interior. Whether because of the daunting magnitude of the task or the more pressing demands of the Korean War, the overall dispersal was never followed through. Nevertheless, in the two decades from 1956 to 1976, as many as 600 factories, colleges, and hospitals, and an estimated 2 million Shanghai residents— including up to 500,000 engineers and technicians—were transferred to underdeveloped provinces like Anhui, Sichuan, and Shaanxi.[68] The city's native capitalists fled to Hong Kong or Taiwan, and its existing industrial stock was converted into a superefficient production base that provided the primary source of revenue for national policymaking.

In Shanghai's factories in the early 1950s, a mere 1 percent of China's population was responsible for 20 percent of the nation's industrial output, but the task ahead required even more efficiency. Competing companies were combined into larger state enterprises in order to maximize production of the existing textile and basic consumer goods industries. In addition, petrochemicals, machinery, steel, and other heavy industries were introduced. Output soared, and for the next forty years Shanghai was the nation's milk cow, systematically drained of revenue to feed and develop the rest of the country. During the first Five-Year Plan, revenue from the city financed a full 64 percent of all basic state investment plans.[69] From 1953 to 1978, the growth rate for fiscal extraction averaged 17.5 percent annually.[70] At the same time as Shanghai money footed the nation's bills, the city was expected to show sustained industrial growth. Little revenue was coming back to Shanghai in the form of state investment, but the industrial infrastructure inherited from the 1920s and 1930s proved sound enough to foster this growth all through the Mao years.

By the 1980s, a combination of the brain drain, lack of new investment, and the deterioration of industrial stock finally took its toll. The neighboring provinces of Jiangsu and Zhejiang began to outpace the city, and the export-processing boom in Guangdong dominated the new coastal strategy of opening up to foreign trade. Output declined, and Shanghai brands lost their luster. In an effort to fill the gap left by students "sent down" to aid the countryside, hundreds of thousands of educated provincials were allowed to change their household registration and settle in the city.[71] These new entrants, combined with many more who moved illegally, helped to restore the initiative of a population that had been strictly controlled for fear that its city would rise as an alternative power base to Beijing. Shanghai was still held back, this time partly as punishment for the leading role its native Gang of Four had taken in directing the Cultural Revolution.

With the effective launching of the Pudong policy in 1992, Shanghai finally had its chance to sprint ahead. No longer the country's manufacturing mainstay, it would be playing a different role this time around, in the upgrading of the national economy. A designated finance hub, not only for China but for the Asia-Pacific region, its city officials elected to promote technology-driven and skill-intensive "pillar" industries, while also building strength in the tertiary service sector—in banking, hotels, advertising, culture, design, recreation, and real estate. The development of IT and high-tech enterprise got top-level support and funding, and a campaign to attract global R&D centers was kick-started. Central government, now in the hands of the Shanghai Clique of Jiang Zemin and Zhu Rongji, opened a free line of loan and credit for building the infrastructure to make it all happen rapidly.

Unlike the predominantly labor-intensive export economy of South China, Shanghai's new industries would all have a technology learning curve. Growth from these value-adding sectors was inclined to be higher, and the opportunities for absorbing technology and skills were considerably greater. As a result, government officials concentrated on luring American, Japanese, and European investors. Rather than relying on Asian middlemen suppliers as they had done in the south, multinational corporations wanted and, in general, needed to be able to exercise more direct control of the knowledge base of their higher-end operations. Yet the feat of transferring skilled technical and analytical knowledge to local employees would prove to be a much trickier process than teaching factory workers how to perform a stitching or glueing task on a sneaker.

By the end of 2003, more than 200 members of the Fortune 500 had set up in Shanghai, and their facilities were scattered all over the Yangtze industrial corridor. The Pudong policy's decade-long boom had seen its share of unhinged speculators and popped bubbles, but the rise in per capita income was real enough. The average 2003 disposable annual income increased by 12 percent over the previous year to 14,678 RMB per capita ($1,773), consistent with that of upper-middle-income nations, though, since most wages were paid in cash, these statistics (like most in China) were quite shaky. Nanjing Road and Huai Hai

Road were lined with top-brand stores, and city boosters made it appear as if Deng Xiaoping's vision of the "well-off society" was being realized on the banks of the Huangpu. The average Shanghainese income was seven times greater than that of the rural poor, in Anhui, while the World Bank's estimate of the nation's overall income disparity, as measured by Gini coefficient—the formula that measures the gap between a country's rich and its poor—soared from 0.15 in 1978, one of the lowest in the world, to 0.48 in 2003, putting China within reach of the most unequal nations.[72] Shanghainese lived in a global city, and changed their mobile phone models every six months, while peasants in the hinterland scratched together a meal.

Even so, the booster image of urbanites enjoying the high life was not all that accurate. Because of its history as the nation's industrial core, Shanghai was hit harder by state sector layoffs than any other region except for the northeast.[73] Nationwide, as many as 27 million workers were let go from shuttered or restructured state companies that had been considered "uncompetitive" in the transitional economy. Shanghai had a disproportionate share of those, and most of the workers laid off were *xia gang*, or "off-post," which meant that they were given a minimal stipend of a few hundred yuan per month from company and public welfare funds on the understanding that their jobs could be restored. As a result, they did not show up in the unemployment statistics. If they were middle-aged and low-skilled, they were all but unemployable, and the state's retraining programs were notoriously ineffective. Domestic and foreign firms in the private sector would not even hire the more skilled because of their "unproductive" work mentality. Nor did they have ready access to the low-wage service jobs that many of their Western counterparts in the rust belts had fallen back on. Shanghai's floating population of rural migrants (commonly estimated at between 3 and 4 million) were a preferred source of cheap labor for these positions, and, in addition, had provided the workforce that rebuilt and renovated the city during its construction boom.[74] Factoring in the meager but informal wages of these migrants, along with the *xia gang* stipends, would sharply reduce the city's otherwise optimistic per capita income figures.

For all the harsh and prejudicial treatment they suffered, migrants were doing better than they could in the countryside. By contrast, the *xia gang* laid-off had fallen much further, from the very pinnacle of job security all the way down into the shadowy crevices of the informal economy. In the heyday of Maoist welfare socialism, they had been the labor aristocracy, fully assured of their "iron rice bowl" privileges, which gave them access to housing, food, education, medical services, and state pensions.[75] Their labor had not been a commodity, and so they had not been vulnerable to shifts in its price or to competition from an alternative supply. In a non-market economy, work discipline had been light, and pressure from managers quite minimal. When the layoffs came, those who were lucky enough to find a job in a joint venture had to worry, for the first time in their working lives, about how their worth was being costed out. But the vast majority lingered in the *xia gang* limbo, despite the government's ambitious promise to solve the problem for good with a new unemployment benefits system.[76]

Seeing their jobs and state benefits decimated, and knowing that their managers and local officials profited royally from the corrupt sell-offs, was bad enough.[77] But many also lost their center-city locations when entire downtown neighborhoods of *longtang* alleys and lanes—considered community-rich by residents—were razed to make way for new hotels and luxury apartment complexes.[78] The evacuees were relocated to new high-rise housing estates at the edge of the city. In the space of ten years, Shanghai's urban working class had gone from being model citizens at the fêted center of the economy to unwanted castoffs at the physical margin of a city they could no longer afford.

Members of the younger generation who were able to find jobs in the new Shanghai economy felt a different, but no less acute, kind of pressure. The rules for conduct in a marketplace of waged labor were unfamiliar, housing prices soared to double the national average, and competition for opportunities was increasingly fierce. The official 2003 statistics showed Shanghai's unemployment rate at 4.9 percent, as against a national figure of 4.3 percent, but no one gave these numbers much credence. Both the World Bank and the Chinese Academy of Social Science offered estimates of around 12 percent, while some unof-

Longtang lane—Shanghai's fast-disappearing vernacular housing

ficial calculations put the figures as high as 23 percent.[79] While unemployment at these levels posed the threat of social instability to authorities, it should have made for a buyer's labor market, just as, in the nineteenth-century treaty port economy, the city's employers could rely on a steady influx of personnel to put pressure on wages. This applied at all levels, from the migrant workers at the low end all the way up to the college-educated returnees who flocked from abroad or from families in other provinces whose Shanghainese parents or grandparents had been sent down in previous decades.

Population pressure was a time-honored way of extracting "squeeze" in Shanghai, where density inside the inner ring was three times that of Tokyo, and where there was always a palpable awareness of encroachment. "That is why people have to fight their way in and out of the metro trains here," explained one of my first interviewees—a native twenty-five-year-old Shanghainese who did computer maintenance for a state bank. "We cannot afford to be polite because we know there is always someone else who will take our place. It not only affects how we walk in the street, but also how we see the future. China is a very crowded world and Shanghai is not a place you can ever relax. Even when I try to relax, I can feel the economy behind me, running up at my back." He had good reason to feel this way. As the city's GDP had soared, so had the unemployment figures for his peers—those between the ages of sixteen and thirty-five years. In 2004, youth were expected to account for up to half of those registered as unemployed.[80] Whatever the causes, this was a pattern that could not be attributed solely to state sector layoffs.

The economy of the Yangtze boomtown was in overdrive, fueled by record infusions of investment. But it looked as if there should still be more than enough slack in the general labor pool to fill the needs of most employers. So why were so many foreign managers complaining about rising wages and the shortage of talent? Were they exaggerating, or was there such a bad mismatch between supply and demand? In truth, they were expecting too much. Employees that foreign investors considered to be ideal had to meet very particular requirements. The managerial demand for specific skills and Western attitudes at China prices, as I would find out, was creating its own stubborn bottleneck in the labor market. With so much investment hanging in the balance, the result was being felt far beyond Shanghai's thrusting office towers and broad-acred industrial parks.

Raising the Bar

Arguing about free trade, offshore outsourcing, and high-tech flight on Capitol Hill or in a seminar room was one thing, but corporate expatriates in places like Shanghai were the people who had to implement the policies, and so they ought to know things the rest of us didn't. They had daily encounters with how the investments and transfers actually worked on the ground, and so their own views and insights about the balance sheet of free trade promised to be quite valuable. In my first two months in the city, I spent a good deal of my time getting to know their minds, their business networks, and their haunts, in an effort to understand the psychology of this key business community.

The 1990s real estate boom in Shanghai saw the construction of a throng of residential compounds, aimed at the market for expats and nouveau riche locals. Nowhere near as ostentatious as the colonial villa estates of Old Shanghai, many resembled a typical American gated community, except that the villas and town houses were smaller and more densely concentrated. Behind the gates, residents could, and often did, lead a lifestyle that had little to do with China. Not long after I arrived in Shanghai, I was invited to a private dinner party in one of these compounds, near the Hongqiao Airport. In fact, it turned out to be a barbecue, and I could not help but marvel at how meticulously every component of the feast, including the methods of preparation, were combined to replicate exactly the U.S. suburban prototype.

Gateway to an American-style villa compound

There was virtually no trace of anything local. It was an entirely imported event, and it reminded me of the publicity for a landscape-enhancement project at the Shanghai Center that was headlined "How You Live Is Where You Live"—the perfect slogan for the expat lifestyle.

Many of the guests, it turned out, were leading lights, including past and current presidents of Shanghai's American Chamber of Commerce (AmCham). For the most part, they were still basking in the glow from the post-SARS production boom. Assembly lines in the Shanghai auto factories of VW and GM were going full out, twenty-four hours a day, and all the important monthly figures—for exports, imports, and foreign investment—were on the upside. Yet the news from home was only bad, as many of the dinner guests acknowledged. In a jobless recovery from the 2001 recession, China-bashing had resurfaced at the center of the blame game being played by politicians and demagogues over the U.S. trade deficit with China. On Capitol Hill, members of the House and Senate on both sides of the aisle had introduced a raft of bills and initiatives all aimed at pressuring China to revalue its currency. Beijing, it was widely alleged, was undercutting American factories and workers by intentionally manipulating the yuan, and one of the results was the ballooning trade deficit ($124 billion in 2003, and 30 percent higher in 2004) with the United States.

According to the most widely cited version of this argument, China's currency was artificially undervalued by between 15 and 40 percent, ensuring that wages were kept down against the dollar, while goods exported to China were prohibitively priced. China-bashers called this "mercantilism," as opposed to the "free trade" that any presumably honest national policy should favor. Among those leading the charge were the latest pair of unlikely coalition partners, the National Association of Manufacturers (NAM) and the AFL-CIO. Though NAM's membership list and policy orientation had long been dominated by the multinationals who were doing business in China, the association was facing an open revolt from its smaller and more numerous domestically focused firms. These companies were losing business and profits to the China trade, since they lacked the capital and resources to move offshore themselves. While they were clearly being killed by free-trade fundamentalism, they were politically incapable of assailing the doctrine, so they took the low road of scapegoating Beijing. Joining them, for the time being at least, were their habitual antagonists, the house of labor, while the multinationals in China pushed discreetly but effectively to preserve NAM's traditional support for free-trade policies.[1]

As the run-up to the 2004 election season got under way, a goodly number of big Washington guns were being swung around to train on China. This time around, large U.S. corporations, ever more deeply entrenched in China, were positioned directly in the line of fire. Their returns on offshore investments, and their production shifts out of the United States, were being viewed with suspicion. As for the trade imbalance, even official Chinese estimates showed that almost 60 percent of the country's exports were from China-based affiliates of multinational corporations,[2] and assessments of the rate of return for U.S. corporate investment in the China export trade ranged from 14 percent to 21 percent.[3] This was hardly persuasive evidence of Beijing's "mercantilist" efforts to protect indigenous industries by hook or by crook, as some of the China-bashers alleged. On the contrary, the profile of the trade deficit showed clear evidence of the deliberate outsourcing strategies on the part of foreign corporations.

As the heat was turned up in Washington, Shanghai's expat executives began to run for cover. "We'll just try to keep our heads down," chuckled one of the guests at the dinner party, an AmCham board member and regional director of one of the largest multinationals in town. All things considered, it might have been sound advice, but it in no way reflected the policy that AmCham itself adopted. In the late summer of 2003, at the start of the election season, a columnist in the chamber's newsletter had warned members: "We have to come up with engaging ways of illustrating the positive role played by U.S.-China economic ties to counter the emotive but analytically weak appeals of the anti-China trade lobby. It will take some hard work to create effective sound bites in support of China trade. . . . It's up to those of us involved in business with China to make sure that it's not only the displaced workers that get all the air time."[4]

In a subsequent issue devoted to "Getting Heard Inside the Nation's Capital," Robert Kapp, president of the Washington-based U.S.-China Business Council, reinforced the warning: "You don't call Congress when you save money on a shirt, but you do when you lose your job."[5] The message was clear. Chamber members would have to enter the lobbying fray full tilt if they wanted to turn around the perception that U.S. businesses in China were actively draining the American workforce and its investment base. In the year that followed, the Shanghai and Beijing AmChams would be called on to take on a much more visible role than usual in the lobbying frenzy that churned around U.S.-China trade relations.

The global commitments of large American corporations made it increasingly difficult for their executives to reconcile their firms' interests with anything recognizable as "the national interest." If multinationals paid taxes at all to the IRS, the "creative accounting" of their fiscal officers ensured that they contributed as little as they could get away with. Their record of loyalty to U.S. employees and host communities was more and more threadbare. It fell to their regional managers abroad to execute policies that many workers and politicians at home saw as a betrayal of the national interest. Yet these managers, more than anyone on Capitol Hill or Wall Street, were in a position to gauge the pros and cons of the China trade investment from day to day, and if they were not too insulated, they also had some sense of the problems faced by local Chinese in finding a decent livelihood.

Expatriates are generally prickly about being called on their patriotism, and those in China were in an especially pivotal position to argue for the importance, to their country of origin, of the corporate presence there. On this topic, the membership of Shanghai's AmCham—more than 1,100 companies and 2,600 individuals (by the end of 2004)—offered a rich resource of opinion and conflicted sentiment. Though they represented firms that were likely to be in competition with each other, and hailed from industries with vastly disparate interests, they could be rallied by the chamber to a single voice with remarkable efficiency. Individually and privately, their anxieties, ambitions, beliefs, and prejudices were the grassroots that informed and reinforced the policy agendas of AmCham's friends and lobbyists in Beijing and Washington. But did they have anything like a group mentality, and could it be profiled?

As it happened, at least one writer had written such a profile—of the pre-Liberation British business community. In 1927, in a controversial article titled "The Shanghai Mind," the *Manchester Guardian* journalist Arthur Ransome wrote that "nothing could be further from the truth than to imagine that the Englishmen in Shanghai represent an English outpost or share the English point of view. The Shanghai-landers hold that loyalty begins at home and that their primary allegiance is to Shanghai. . . . Shanghailanders of English extraction belong, if they belong to England at all, to an England that no longer exists." Ransome had little difficulty in capturing the fierce insularity of this pampered business colony—"they seem to have lived in a comfortable but hermetically sealed and isolated glass case since 1901." But he went on to warn that the demands they had recently made on British foreign policy—to dispatch armies and navies to oppose the rise of nationalist forces—were threatening, if heeded, to turn Shanghai into "the Ulster of the East." The Chinese, for their part, were habitually misled into believing that the opinions of the Shanghai press, dominated by the British business community's viewpoints, coincided in any meaningful way with British foreign policy. "Just as we at home are apt to think of them as English," Ransome concluded dryly, "so the Chinese, in China, make the same mistake."[6]

In reform-era Shanghai, the Japanese were the largest expat group (almost a third), but it was the Americans (at about 12 percent) who had taken over the role the British once held as the alpha business community, and it was U.S. foreign policy that held the key to the regional balance of political and economic forces. There were no gunboats on the Huangpu, though command ships from the Seventh Fleet made irregular but strategic visits to the port in the name of military-to-military diplomacy. Modern communications had virtually eliminated the information gap between the two countries, and the economic interests of the American community were part of an interconnected global network. So was there anything that resembled an updated American version of Ransome's "Shanghai Mind"? If so, was it a factor in the play of forces that determined how China's economic growth was affecting American and Chinese workers—or those of other countries, for that matter?

The Rainbow's Mouth

Like its British counterpart, so keenly satirized by Ransome, the positions taken by the American Chamber of Commerce in pre-Liberation Shanghai increasingly reflected the parochial interests of its membership. From the mid-1920s onward, the chamber was inclined to see the emergence of the nationalist movement for Chinese self-determination as a threat to be put down with force, if necessary. Unlike the univocal British, however, there were other powerful elements in Shanghai's

American community with quite different views. One was the influential voice of the *China Weekly Review,* which, in the maverick editorials of William Powell, hewed more closely to the official U.S. policy of neutrality.[7] Though the Americans in China had long enjoyed the benefits of a junior partnership in Britain's "informal empire," Washington could not afford to be aligned too closely in Asia with the more belligerent mind-set of European imperialists. Besides, there were many who believed that a Free China, under Nationalist rule, might turn out to be an American asset, especially after its potential ruler converted to the Methodist faith of his Wellesley-educated bride, as Chiang Kai-shek did in 1931, four years after marrying Soong Meiling.

The Christian factor was key. Among the other thorns in the side of the chamber's leadership were the missionaries, whose claim as China stakeholders dated back to the 1830s, when evangelists first set out to save the Chinese from their heathen ways. For over a century, friction between the missionaries and the merchants was a visible outgrowth of the divided U.S. sentiment toward Chinese affairs. At first there was little conflict of interest. Indeed, Shanghai's own American Settlement had its origins when William Boone, bishop of the American Church Mission, purchased or leased land in 1848 in an area north of the Suzhou Creek, in Hongkou (the "rainbow's mouth"). The official boundary of the rapidly growing community was not settled by the U.S. consul until 1863, by which time the Americans were on the verge of formally amalgamating with the British to create the International Settlement, while the French, even more beholden to their Jesuit missionaries, went their own way. None of these agreements were officially confirmed by the U.S. government, which was preoccupied, at the time, with the more pressing matter of the Civil War.[8] Yet Washington's de facto neutrality—if that is how the non-response should be interpreted—would become a habit until the Japanese, armed to the teeth with American weaponry, invaded China and forced the United States to take sides.

As elsewhere in the world, the activities of the early missionaries often helped open up trade opportunities for merchants, and, since they were legally persona non grata, most had to operate from positions held within American trading houses.[9] A wave of zealous sentiment for overseas evangelizing swept the United States in the 1890s when the leaders of the Intercollegiate Student Volunteers for Foreign Missions chose China as their great cause. After that, and partly as a result of the traumatic anti-foreign Boxer Rebellion, the prevailing missionary spirit was liberal and humanitarian, and increasingly leaned toward sympathy for the nationalist aspirations of the Chinese. The far-flung network of American missionary schools, colleges, and hospitals laid a foundation for many of the modern educational and medical institutions in operation today, as did the tradition of encouraging Chinese elites to pursue degrees in the United States.

Yet the efforts of the missionary community to persuade Washington to support the nationalist cause were repeatedly dashed until the late 1930s, when Chiang Kai-shek emerged as a potential strategic ally in regional politics. By then, Washington was on a crusade of its own, which would propel it eventually down the path of the anticommunist religion. Missionaries on the ground were all too aware of the Generalissimo's corrupt ways (as was almost every U.S. government official in China). But they could not persuade the United States to break ranks with Chiang, even as he launched an ill-fated campaign of liquidation, with the Japanese driven out, against his wartime Communist allies. Washington's role as Chiang's paymaster would poison regional politics for the next three decades. By the time the PLA marched into Shanghai in 1949, many American missionaries, especially those who had seen the Communists win peasant support in the north, were openly sympathetic.[10] The enthusiasm of the foreign business community in Shanghai was more expedient by far. The *China Weekly Review* welcomed the troops, and the American Chamber, in a miraculous deathbed conversion, actually expressed optimism about the future under the new rulers of the city, sending a detailed, upbeat cable on the topic to President Truman.[11]

Over a century of fractious intimacy between the servants of God and the agents of Mammon left a curious legacy. When AmCham reopened for business in Shanghai in 1986 (the first foreign chamber to do so), the missionaries had long since left town. But some of the strains of that evangelical spirit had worked their way into the mind-set of the business community. Not that there was any lack of fertile soil.

Americans abroad have long carried with them a self-image as reformers. It was powerful enough to be considered a secular theology. One former AmCham board member put it quite succinctly: "That's what Americans do. We tend to want to make things better, wherever we go."

Regardless of whether the results mirrored the belief, no one could naïvely maintain this credo for very long in China. It was too useful by far in the game of power and influence. For one thing, the latest spectacle of China "opening up" to Western trade was of much more direct interest to Washington than the last effort, in the mid-nineteenth century, had been. The crusade "to change China"—which had seen a centuries-long procession of foreign experts—was now much more than a matter of opening the door to U.S. business.[12] With the winding down of the Cold War, it had become the last great political challenge on Washington's anticommunist agenda. For those who were hungry for the challenge, trade was viewed as a way of opening a door to U.S. influence over the measured process of political reform in China. Memories of the Cold War debate about "who lost China" had only been consigned to a very shallow grave.

In addition, the notion that Americans were *natural reformers,* promoting, among other things, better conditions for employees, opened other kinds of doors. Jeff Bernstein, owner of an import logistics company, and AmCham's president in 2005, observed that "U.S. companies here treat their workers well because they think that's the right thing to do. They also abide by the same type of environmental practices that they would anywhere overseas, even if they're in excess of what the Chinese government requires." Yet, as Bernstein acknowledged, there was also a utilitarian side to this. It wasn't just the right thing to do, it was a practical strategy for prying open the market. "AmCham," he explained,

> has a huge interest in the enforcement of proper working conditions, because in many cases, competitors of U.S. factories on the ground are locally owned factories, who might not abide by all the rules, and who might not be paying the right social benefits. So obviously it's in the interest of these American companies

to make sure the rules are enforced, and there's a fair playing field here. . . . If they are trying to compete and sell their product back to the Asian market, a place where people really don't care about the sweat-free label on the product, it's critical that there's a level playing field.

In the current business environment, where China's labor laws were routinely ignored, it was customary for domestic companies to factor in the cost of punishment in the event of a government inspection that uncovered violations. They still came out ahead. As Bernstein saw it, "the local entrepreneur says, 'there's no way that I could meet that bar, so I'm just going to run at whatever practice I want to, and then I know if I get caught, I get caught, and it's just a matter of how much money I have to pay in fines.' " For foreign firms competing locally, then, there was a strategic advantage to observing China's labor regulations. Much more than a moral reward, it gave them leverage to demand that the regulations apply across the board to their domestic as well as foreign competitors.

In the export trade, there was a different calculus to consider. The shaming of Kathy Lee Gifford, Nike, the Gap, and others (exposed by North American anti-sweatshop activists for the atrocious conditions suffered by Asian and Central American workers supplying their clothing lines) had cast a long shadow. No company wanted their precious brand names sullied by headline-seeking revelations about substandard pay, forced overwork, hazardous workplaces, or brutal managerial practices.[13] In reality, it was all too easy to bury these conditions deep in the subcontracting chain, where suppliers—these "local entrepreneurs" who couldn't "meet the bar"—operated sweatshops that were not directly associated or identified with the household brand name.[14]

AmCham members expressed little doubt about the superiority of working conditions in their own factories. As Charles Browne, regional director of DuPont and AmCham's 2003 president, put it:

I really wouldn't be a good guy to say what happens in the local Chinese companies. But I think it's fair to say that the foreign companies—the American companies being among them—are held to a higher standard, and indeed do operate by a higher standard on labor issues than likely would a local company. We have a lot of government officials who come over with the impression that the labor standards inside of American companies in China are different than they would be in the U.S., Europe, the Philippines, Brazil, Chile, wherever. And that's simply not true. . . . It's just the wage scale that's different.

Browne added, however, that Chinese government officials generally expected a higher standard from the Americans: "Sometimes it would seem as if that law is being applied more strictly, more precisely, than it is to local companies. In other words, the playing field isn't exactly fair. Not that American companies complain that the bar is too high in China, that's not the issue at all. We'd just like the bar to be the same level for everybody."

Browne's comments, however, had glossed over one of the major differences between the U.S. companies in China and those elsewhere. The workforces of their China affiliates were largely non-union. If they hosted Chinese-style unions, they were not adversarial in the Western sense, and so they differed quite significantly from their domestic counterparts in Michigan or Delaware. Because of their roots in a socialist economy, where workers' interests were not, in principle, at odds with those of employers, China's trade unions have mostly functioned in a social capacity, to organize picnics or film screenings, or take a pastoral interest in workers' domestic welfare.[15] In the event of disputes, union stewards invariably took the side of managers, and for many unions, established simply to comply with the national labor laws, the firm's manager or deputy manager acted as the director of the union. Indeed, the tendency for employees to retain their compliant relationship with managerial authority was one aspect of the Maoist work-unit (*danwei*) mentality that foreign companies were more than happy to inherit.[16] Yet for many multinationals, even a compliant "yellow union" of this sort was too much to contemplate. By 2004, the 123-million-member All-China Federation of Trade Unions (ACFTU) was threatening to blacklist foreign firms that refused to allow unions in their Chinese plants. The list included names like Wal-Mart, Kodak,

Dell, Samsung, McDonald's, and KFC.[17] These companies, and many others, were all in clear violation of national labor law, which stipulated that any enterprise with more than twenty-five workers was required to establish a union. The notoriously anti-union Wal-Mart, with 190,000 employees directly on its mainland payroll (and untold others in sub-contracted companies producing for the retail giant) had been an ACFTU target since 2000. The retail giant held out in the face of wide-spread bad publicity for fear of setting a precedent that would encour-age its 1.3 million workers in nine other countries.[18] In the fall of 2004, under intense legal pressure, the company finally conceded: "Should associates request formation of a union," the firm announced, "Wal-Mart China would respect their wishes and honor its obligation under China's Trade Union Law."[19]

When it came to making a noise about weaknesses in the rule of law, the foreign business community displayed a clear double standard. Intellectual property rights and contract law were one thing, but no business lobby was clamoring for China to strengthen its labor laws to include the right to form independent unions or to collectively bargain in any meaningful way. This was one of the few features of interna-tional business practice that the chambers of commerce would rather not see China adopt. In light of the domestic perception that all Chinese factories were sweatshops, Western managers counted them-selves fortunate that their counterparts from Hong Kong, Taiwan, Korea, and Japan had a worse reputation than they did for harsh labor exploitation.

The smaller East Asian investors were always cited as the worst offenders when it came to squeezing workers. "I don't want to sound racist," observed one American HR manager, "because I know some very good Taiwanese and Korean managers. But there is an overall per-ception here that Korean and Taiwanese companies are badly run, not very good working conditions, below average salaries, and the bonuses and promotions tend to be promised but don't materialize."

According to Diane Long, VP for sourcing at Liz Claiborne: "The Taiwanese companies would have to be very big and famous to treat their people well, or to follow the ethical standards that we follow. I'm not saying Americans are perfect, but we are definitely on a different road. We are scrutinized differently. The Chinese are watching us. Can you imagine working for IBM and taking a bribe? They would just love to have that story to show all the world. I feel that I have to stand on a different platform." Yet, despite their reputation for driving workers to the limit, I found in my interviews that the Taiwanese had one local advantage over the other foreign employers. Their Chinese employees felt they were likely to be there for a long time, and so, although the Taiwanese work discipline was feared, the companies enjoyed a little more loyalty. In the mid- to long term, the Westerners, always on the lookout for more squeeze elsewhere, could not be counted on to stick around.

The Art of the Doorknock

If anything resembling an American "Shanghai mind" did exist, then it was best evoked in the phrase "raising the bar," which I heard repeatedly in AmCham circles. This was a common code word for the belief that U.S. corporations were bringing reforms to China—in economic fairness, primarily, but also in matters related to the rule of law, human rights, and liberal conduct. One of AmCham's Old China Hands, who had been in Shanghai since the late 1980s, had seen waves of newcomers exhibit this quality: "Americans come over with such a mentality for change—a predisposition to believe that you can change individuals. It's a very evangelical drive. After a while in China, you learn to temper that." He acknowledged that this kind of zeal did not seem to have an equivalent in any of the other foreign business communities; it was more or less unique to the Americans. No less than the missionaries of yore, the more fervent U.S. corporate expats had convinced themselves that setting a model example was an intrinsic part of doing business in China.

According to James Green, AmCham's full-time officer for government relations,

> a lot of U.S. businesses that operate overseas feel like they are
> bringing more than just a job to the company that they're run-

ning. They can impart U.S. values of fairness and hard work and decent pay and safe working conditions to the workforce, and in some way influence the society overall through being a good example in their businesses. . . . My guess is American companies in particular, when they go overseas, often have that view of themselves. I don't know whether or not that's actually had an impact on other countries' labor laws or the way that they manage the economy, but I think the perception is that, yes, in a way we really are changing the social environment of China, slowly.

Green, who attributed this belief to native optimism, was appointed in 2004 (from a diplomatic career in Beijing) to beef up AmCham's capacity to "influence the policy decisions being made in Shanghai, Beijing and Washington." Most of the city's expat managers had a technical background and therefore lacked the diplomatic skills that the company's representative offices in Beijing had traditionally offered. The relaxation of central government control over foreign capital required more and more involvement in local politics, which was now part of Green's job. Though it was an organization with considerable power and influence in the Yangtze Delta economy, AmCham had no official, registered status until 2005. Until then, it could not send a letterhead document to the Chinese government, and its officers had to be received instead as informal representatives of the American business community. In theory, the numerous meetings and social events it organized were illicit, at least under a little-observed Chinese law forbidding congregations larger than twelve. Unlike the other Shanghai chambers of commerce—German, British, Japanese—AmCham was not a sub-branch of a parent organization based in Beijing. Green's appointment not only confirmed AmCham's own aspirations, independent of Beijing's officially registered chamber, it was also a sign that the organization intended to play an increasingly ambitious role in international lobbying.

The lobbying had actually begun after 1989, when the Tiananmen Square crackdown sparked widespread skepticism among corporations and policymakers about the wisdom of investing further in China. The Shanghai and Beijing AmChams organized twice-yearly lobbying trips to Washington (called "doorknocks") in order to rally the fainthearted on Capitol Hill. The visiting delegations called upon key congressional committee members and members of the executive branch to remind them not only of the needs of the U.S. corporations in China, but also of the political uses that could be made of their presence. In addition to agencies like the NSC, USDA, USTR, and departments of Commerce, State, Homeland Security, and the Treasury, the visitors were also accustomed to meet with China business consultants, like Kissinger Associates and the U.S.-China Business Council, along with powerful academic advocates at centers like the School of Advanced International Studies (at Johns Hopkins University). These links were cemented, at the other end, when senators, senior administration officials, and other figures of influence in the U.S.-China trade lobby made the respective chambers an integral part of their visits to the PRC.

In return for a hearing in Washington, the doorknock delegation offered valuable information that would ordinarily be obscured to Washington insiders by Beijing's lack of transparency on a host of trade issues. It was a cozy network of relationships that required special attention whenever a crisis in Sino-U.S. relations occurred. The notion that AmCham was "raising the bar" in China was an especially effective card to play when Congress had to be persuaded to stand firm in supporting the China trade. The preferred line was that U.S. corporations were not there simply to harvest profits, they were helping to liberalize China's political system, and to introduce American values that would not otherwise penetrate the thick filter of diplomacy.

But with the upsurge of anti-outsourcing sentiment and the ruckus around currency revaluation, cracks had appeared in the normally solid chain of influence that connected U.S. corporations in China with legislators on the Hill. For one thing, the assertive position adopted by the National Association of Manufacturers meant that the Department of Commerce, which was accustomed to serving a more unified constituency, was faced with a business community split down the middle on China. So, too, lawmakers who were usually reliable supporters of free-trade measures were holding back, mindful of a potential revolt among their constituents over job displacements.

Even the business wing of the Republican Party was drifting. At a September 25, 2003, hearing of the U.S.-China Economic and Security Review Commission, Senator Lindsey Graham (R-SC), co-sponsor of a Senate bill to impose across-the-board 27.5 percent tariffs on Chinese imports, testified: "The growth of the Chinese economy is not being shared with its people, because one of the reasons we are losing jobs is . . . you can build a plant in China and people work for a dollar a day. There is no OSHA. There are no minimum wages. China is taking advantage of trade regimes. They are cheating and they are taking the money to build up their military. It's a lose-lose."[20] It wasn't the inaccuracy of such assertions (minimum wages exist in all townships and cities in China) or the political grandstanding that worried multinational beneficiaries of the China trade. It was the growing sense that their allies were straying from the "approved" script. The Republican senator's "lose-lose" was way off-message. The China trade was only supposed to be described as a "win-win," or what some free-trade economists more gracefully referred to as a "virtuous circle."

One of the doorknock delegation members explained: "Normally, we are all joined at the hip, but currently there are divisions where there used to be unanimity on free trade. We are on 'higher ground' and are right, but we appear too 'self-interested.' We need to have people over there and elsewhere to present our case better in the press and on the Hill—we need more hired guns. We want to appear as an honest broker, rather than an apologist for China, which would be very bad at this time." James Green underlined the need for others to make the case. "One of the upsides of this debate is that virtually no economist is against free trade—one of the key tenets of economic theory, as it's taught in college, is that free trade is good. But how do you get that message to people who generally haven't studied the Ricardian model of economics? I think it's probably better to come from people in the academy, or from somewhat independent voices, as opposed to coming from us, when it can be dismissed as clearly self-serving."

The Ladders of Mobility

Whatever the shape of its policies, the Bush administration could not be counted on to be perceived as one of these "independent voices." Nor did its efforts at economic diplomacy prove to be very well crafted. When Gregory Mankiw, chairman of the White House Council of Economic Advisers, released the annual Economic Report of the President in February 2004, he asserted that outsourcing was just "the latest manifestation of the gains from trade that economists have talked about at least since Adam Smith," and that it was "probably a plus for the economy in the long run." His comments were slammed on both sides of the aisle, and some Republican members called for his resignation. Even those who agreed with the free-trade fundamentalists could see that public statements like this were highly insensitive at a time when job loss was a front-burner concern with voters. George Bush was obliged to distance himself from the comments.[21] Soon enough, however, he struck back at critics of his own tax-cut-driven schemes for job creation. Those who had been scolded before as "protectionists" were now given the more ominous label of "economic isolationists."[22]

The Bush administration's record of job creation remained abysmal. Its much-vaunted tax-cut package, known as the "Jobs and Growth Plan" (which took effect in July 2003), not only failed to produce its projected 1.4 million additional jobs in eighteen months, but also fell far short, by 1.7 million, of the total expected without the tax cuts.[23] By the time his second term began, he was presiding over the longest post-recession slump on record. The sorry reputation of his fiscal policies was not helped by what seemed to be a chronic pattern of bungles. For example, his much-ballyhooed appointment of a manufacturing-jobs czar had to be withdrawn at the last minute when it was revealed that Tony Raimondo, the Nebraska businessman in line for the position, had laid off his own workers and was building a factory in China to replace them.[24] Shortly afterward, Bush's fund-raising and vote-seeking campaign was revealed to have outsourced its telephone solicitation work contracts to call centers in New Delhi suburbs. More than 10 million registered Republicans were solicited in a calling process that was automated to prevent the recipients from recognizing a foreign-accented voice on the other end of the line.[25] Nor did it help matters that his appointees at the Commerce Department routinely co-sponsored conferences at high-profile locations like the Waldorf-Astoria Hotel that encouraged American companies to move their operations to China. Unavoidably, these events attracted critical press coverage.[26] Indeed, whenever Bush or his appointees tried to address the public hue and cry over outsourcing, they invariably put their foot in it. With friends like these, the free-trade lobby hardly needed enemies.

More-convincing arguments for offshore outsourcing would have to come from voices who were willing to agonize out loud over wind shifts in the direction of their own opinion. Foremost among them was the *New York Times*'s foreign affairs columnist Thomas Friedman, whose much-vaunted ten-day visit to Bangalore in March 2004 offered him an opportunity to test his faith as an apostle of corporate globalization. In the first of a series of columns, later incorporated into his book *The World Is Flat,* Friedman confessed to having "missed the revolution" in business process outsourcing (BPO), because he was so focused on 9/11 and the war in Iraq. "While I was sleeping," he wrote, "the world entered the third great era of globalization." Now it seemed inevitable to him that "in a networked world," where "work-flow platforms" could chop up any white-collar service job, distribute the parts globally, and reassemble them seamlessly, such jobs would be dispersed from the United States. The consequences were a grave cause for concern, however. What worried him was the speed and scale of the changes, rendering their impact "enormous and unpredictable." Because of the potential of technological networking, virtually any job that could be done at home, including many that carried high salaries, could now be transferred overnight.[27]

Friedman initially sidestepped the position adopted by free-market fundamentalism and mused instead about various public-policy responses. He took care, however, to allow someone else—Robert Reich, Clinton's former labor secretary—to voice them. "Job training, lifelong learning, and wage insurance" were vital, Reich said, adding that "perhaps we need to welcome more unionization in the personal services area—retail, hotel, restaurant, and hospital jobs which cannot be moved overseas—in order to stabilize their wages and health care benefits." Calling for government action was not Friedman's bailiwick, and so in the third and fourth of the column reports from Bangalore, he revealed the silver lining of outsourcing. The upgrading of jobs in India, he argued, had boosted the volume of U.S. exports to that country. Everything being used in the Bangalore call-center office he visited was an American-branded product. Friedman failed to mention that very few American workers were any longer likely to be employed in their production or, increasingly, their design.

Later in the week, he profiled a Bangalore engineer who had read about a laid-off American making "all kinds of money" from the sale of a T-shirt emblazoned with "I Lost My Job to India and All I Got Was This [Lousy] T-Shirt." " 'Only in America,' she said, shaking her head, 'would someone figure out how to profit from his own unemployment.' " A country, she concluded, that is so creative and innovative need not fear outsourcing to the developing world. Friedman went on to spin this comment into a parable about how "America is the greatest engine of innovation that has ever existed," and why the conditions that made it so are still the envy of the world. Tom Tomorrow, the widely syndicated cartoonist, promptly tracked down the pink-slipped entrepreneur in question, and discovered that, despite the offshore threat, he still had his job, and also that he had reportedly made no more than ten dollars from selling the shirt. On his weblog, Tomorrow went on to point out that these details were immaterial; the more pressing issue, which Friedman had ignored, was that selling novelty T-shirts is not a replacement for a decent-paying job with health benefits.[28]

There was no empirical evidence that the United States would continue to enjoy a comparative advantage in industrial innovation over its competitors. Even if it did, such an advantage was unlikely to translate into a sufficient volume of well-paying jobs to replace those lost overseas. East Asian countries with a significant economic stake in the high-tech industries—Korea, Singapore, Taiwan, Malaysia, and now India and China—were all steering their economies more singlemindedly, and more cheaply, toward the capture of the same pool of innovation jobs in design and R&D. Friedman's brand of blithe boosterism was neatly summarized by his fellow *Times* columnist Bob Herbert, who described advocates of offshore outsourcing "as sounding more and more like the hapless Mr. Micawber in *David Copperfield* who could never be swayed from his good-natured belief that something would 'turn up.'" It was a sign of their desperation that boosters settled on the belief that the good jobs would appear "in the long run." For the time being, and throughout the period of recovery from the recession, the new opportunities continued to show up in those low-wage job categories that had been seeing consistent growth for two decades: food preparers and servers, retail sales clerks, customer service reps, security guards, janitors, cleaners, nursing aides, and cashiers.

At the same hearing at which the wild-eyed Senator Graham had testified, Chuck Schumer (D-NY), his co-sponsor of the Senate bill, went on record as having second thoughts about the free-trade agreements he●ad hitherto supported. He estimated that the adjustments needed to offset job dislocation would indeed come in "the long run": "in about three generations when the wealth of America and the wealth of all these other countries is about even."[29] Later in the day, Paul Craig Roberts, former assistant secretary of the treasury under Reagan (and prized convert from the free-trader camp), testified that once the "factors of production" were entirely mobile, free trade would no longer exist in the sense in which Ricardo imagined it as a system of mutual, comparative advantage between trading partners. If the result today was an ominous "substitution of American labor out of American production functions," then "the ladders of upward mobility are collapsing, along with the growth of income."[30]

A year later, the commission held its fall field hearing in the electoral battleground state of Ohio, which it described as "ground zero in terms of the impact that trade has had in our nation." One in five of the state's manufacturing jobs had been eliminated in the past three years, and there was a firm consensus among those testifying about the causes and results. Witnesses spoke of trade policies that exclusively favored large corporations, and, in some cases, tax and financing incentives that actively encouraged offshoring. The U.S. Export-Import

Bank, for example, had been financing exports of equipment to China in industries where American manufacturers still domestically produced. In effect, the commission concluded, "the U.S. Government has effectively paid China to create production capabilities that will compete with U.S. producers."[31] Stark testimony about corporate greed alternated with poignant firsthand accounts of the debilitating pain of workers laid off summarily after thirty years of service—"I am too old to work and too young to die." In destabilized Ohio communities with decimated tax bases, the few companies that held on were being asked by multinationals to match the offshore price—"the China price"—of suppliers.

A Little Pain, Lots of Gain

A choice place to sample expat opinion about offshore outsourcing's impact on the United States was at one of AmCham's regular social mixers, often held in the city's swankiest locations. It was at such an event—in the lavish fortieth-floor penthouse of the Tomorrow Square Marriott, overlooking the brilliant sparkle of downtown Shanghai's night lights—that a middle-level manager in a U.S. multinational told me the joke that I cited in the introduction to this book: "Pretty soon, lawyers will be the only people left with jobs in America." As far as lawyer jokes go, it wasn't a bad one, but it was also an unusually honest spin on the jobs crisis at home. Nor did he exempt his own job from the fallout. "I know that my company is looking for a local replacement for me," he added blithely.

These mixers were ideal networking occasions for new arrivals—adventurers, mostly, looking to make a fast buck. But they often attracted job seekers from the United States whose jobs had migrated to Asia. Jack Lemisch was one of those who had been purged from the Bay Area software industry. "I'm not following my job," he insisted. "I don't know where it actually went to. But I had no alternative except to come here if I wanted to stay in the industry." He said he felt a little bad about being in a country whose employees his former company had exploited, "at the low end of the food chain," but he was desperate to try his hand at any reasonably priced position. When I first met him at the mixer, he had not found a job after six weeks of interviewing. Dismayed to discover that IT companies were already thinking about moving inland in pursuit of a cheaper workforce, he lamented, "Can't companies ever make some commitment to a community? What happened in California shouldn't be happening so quickly here." Tall and handsome, and mindful of the attention he was getting from across the bar, he was unlikely to go home alone. AmCham mixers were carefully staked out by a coterie of old hands and locals who saw a fresh opportunity in each newcomer.

Casual conversation at networking events organized by AmCham's industry committees was also a reliable way of gauging the economic climate from the perspective of Shanghai's foreign strivers. Managers complained incessantly about the cost of doing business, especially about the loading of social security benefits, which could double the expense line on a base wage. So, too, Chinese employees regularly featured in their conversation as overpriced and lacking in qualities. But the attraction of Shanghai itself offset these shortcomings. Quite simply, it was the place to be. Whether it was your career prospects or your entrepreneurial game, the city held much the same existential appeal as Manhattan. As one small investor put it, "You meet your match in Shanghai. Whatever issue you have not faced in your life, it will come flying at you and you will have to deal with it." She was equally philosophical about the difficulties of making a smooth exit with your loot: "Easy to get in, tough to get out; they have ways of keeping foreign investors captive." Every adventurer, except the greenhorns, knew how difficult it was actually to make money, but the effort was part of the high. In comparison with their own daily struggles, the troubles they heard about in the job market at home were a negligible concern.

In my formal interviews with AmCham members who worked for large corporations, I found evidence of a more deeply divided psychology. Most were emotionally sympathetic, on the one hand, to the pain suffered by individuals and communities devastated by job flight, and they were generally unable to offer any solutions to the related problems faced by the U.S. workforce. Few were conversant with the proposals being thrown around at home to protect jobs or reform the corporate tax system to discourage offshoring. On the other hand, their exposure, within the business community, to the belief system of free-market fundamentalism allowed them to rationalize the pain. Indeed, the vast majority were attracted to the ideology that the market had its own providential way of delivering benefits to everyone. All that was required was an outlook most often described as "no pain, no gain." For the dislocated, the benefit was always envisaged in the long term. Short-term gains, without any of the pain, could be collected by employers who ordered the transfers. It was the natural economic order of things, and to oppose nature was to invite retribution.

"No one should feel entitled to a well-paying job," observed Mark DiBattista, who had grown up in blue-collar Pittsburgh, and was the Asia-Pacific director of a U.S. technology company. "My father and his union buddies picked up forty grand for doing jobs that should have gone overseas years before. If the market had prevailed then, the elastic would not have snapped back so painfully." In the interim, Americans had "learned this lesson," he believed, "and now the white-collar folks who have been handed pink slips can adjust quicker. They had it too easy in the 1990s, and so I think some good will come out of the experience of losing their jobs. America will be stronger and more creative as a result." Like so many others, he preferred to imagine a "win-win" situation: "Through bringing our technologies and our business skills here, we're helping the Chinese in all sorts of ways. Our profits will also help people back home," he added. Though, when pressed, he could not quite say how or why.

Others were more determined to put a patriotic face on their opinions, detailing all the ways in which they believed their companies were advancing the national interest. The most commonplace argument was that U.S. consumers were benefiting from the lower prices of processed goods imported from China, though some acknowledged that reduced prices at the local Wal-Mart superstore could hardly compensate for the loss of a livelihood. Others insisted that their profitable China operations made it more likely that key employees would be retained in the United States. One even pointed out that the revenue from China trade would help pay the pensions of domestic employees who had been let go.

Even more popular was the argument that American business in China was creating wealth that would be repatriated. Statistics, drawn from a variety of econometric studies, circulated informally within AmCham. These analyses all showed that only a fraction of the export earnings from China reflected domestic value added by Chinese producers. The figure ranged from twenty cents to thirty-six cents of every dollar, with the onshore country taking the lion's share of the value.[32] Another well-cited study by the McKinsey Global Institute estimated that for every dollar American companies spent offshore, as much as $1.46 in new economic value was created. The offshore country gained thirty-three cents on the dollar, or 22 percent, while the U.S. earned $1.13, or 78 percent.[33] These kinds of figures were widely touted in articles in the business press, and became a staple of arguments in defense of outsourcing. Yet none of the studies could say anything about how this value was distributed. Which investors' or stockholders' bank accounts were fattened, and who saw theirs drained? In fact, the same calculation used for the McKinsey estimate of a fourteen-cent net gain from offshore spending showed a twenty-six-cent net loss for onshore workers (as opposed to investors), illustrating the lopsided distribution of benefits.

Every so often, one or another of my interviewees acknowledged that it was probably the wealthiest Americans who benefited, and that it was unlikely that any significant share of the earned offshore value would ever find its way into the pockets of those whose jobs were being migrated. Despite the perception that more and more U.S. citizens had a stake in the stock market through pension funds, the Congressional Budget Office reported that more than half of corporate profits go to the wealthiest one percent of taxpayers, while only about 8 percent go to the bottom 60 percent.[34] Nor did the long-term economic statistics do anything to dispel the belief that the economic impact of the boom in offshoring was pulverizing the middle-class wage structure and reinforcing the steady polarization of domestic income. Economists have attributed a full 25 percent of the increase in U.S. wage disparity to corporate-led globalization.[35] As for taxes on repatriated profit, every offshore accountant knew how easy it was to defer taxes on profits earned abroad for a lifetime. Since 1960, the share of federal taxes paid by American corporations has dropped by nearly two-thirds. Between 2001 and 2003, one-third of those in the Fortune 500 paid no federal taxes, even though their pre-tax profits were up by 26 percent.[36]

On occasion, an interviewee spoke in favor of the various "protectionist" measures—higher import tariffs or bans on outsourcing state and federal jobs—that were being contemplated by U.S. legislators. One company owner, directly involved in the IT outsourcing business, professed support for the legislation, even though he acknowledged it would be bad for his own business. "Maybe it is useful to put some barriers in place to slow things down. But you have to be careful of building a dam that water starts backing up behind. A speed bump is a good thing, it gives people time to readjust to what the new environment's going to be." He could say this, however, because, like the others, he knew that the chances of such measures succeeding in Congress were next to zero. Like virtually everyone else in the AmCham community, he preferred to see the outcry at home simply as part of the election-year cycle, a storm to be weathered until it blew over after the election ballots were counted in November. "If America suddenly becomes protectionist," he concluded, "then another country is going to become free, because that's how you make the most money. The nature of our beings, as biological organisms, is that when there's a little bit of an advantage to be had somewhere, some organism's going to go get it. It's just the way it is." In this way, trade liberalization was perceived as a force of nature, rather than as a process directed by corporate-driven institutions like the IMF and the WTO with no democratic mandate. To change it was, in his words, like "trying to hold back a river—you can hold this spot back or this spot back, but you can't hold the whole thing back."

Steering the Gravy Train

It was AmCham's job to steer that river in a direction most beneficial to its members, and so its officers picked up and circulated the most strategic arguments, pressing them upon policymakers in Beijing and Washington. In this respect, it played a critical role in the channeling of the Bush administration's often heavy-handed dealings with China over trade issues. Pushed by domestic pressure to "do something about China," the administration engaged in some high-level brinkmanship beginning in the fall of 2003. Citing the brouhaha at home, including the sentiment for revaluing the yuan, U.S. delegates on a series of trade missions pounded Beijing over the bilateral trade deficit. AmCham's job was to provide ammunition, which it did primarily in the form of its White Paper, an annual report on the business climate aimed directly at influencing commercial relations between the two countries. The 2003 report offered negotiators an especially well-crafted stick with which to beat their Chinese counterparts.[37]

According to the report, which drew on a membership survey, Beijing had made slow progress in implementing many of its WTO commitments. While appearing to fulfill its obligations on paper, the relevant ministries seemed more committed to "creatively finding new ways to restrict market access of foreign firms in order to protect domestic constituencies."[38] In areas such as financial services, agriculture, and distribution, progress had been especially scant, and foreign firms were still disadvantaged by what the chamber's member companies perceived as the glacial pace of reform of state-owned enterprises, capital markets, the banking system, intellectual property rights, and the rule of law.

Hammering Beijing on these specific points was seen as a win-win. It benefited U.S. corporations seeking market access, and it helped the administration garner some public approval for appearing to take a hard line on China. In reality, no one in the U.S.-China business community had much of an appetite at all for revaluing the yuan. For one thing, it would increase the cost of the multinationals' own China-processed exports, and its impact on business as usual was far too volatile to risk. Accordingly, the Bush administration's commitment to the issue proved to be remarkably inconsistent. Treasury Secretary John Snow gave lip service to the idea throughout the summer of 2003, and floated the prospect during a visit to Beijing in the fall of that year, but, in his semiannual Treasury report to Congress in October, declined to include China on a list of countries that manipulated their currency unfairly. Indeed, each time congressional and public pressure for firm economic action on China mounted, the same kind of retreat was executed. This pressure was being applied in order to appease domestic constituencies. But when push came to shove, the administration was more than willing to sacrifice, or buy off, these domestic interests— including the Fair Currency Alliance, spearheaded by NAM's small businesses—at the altar of the multinationals in China. Nor was the administration's acknowledged concern over job loss at home any more than a rhetorical gesture to build up face in the negotiations with the Chinese. Allowing China to enter the WTO had been sold at home as the best way to get American-made goods into the China market, thereby boosting domestic manufacturing jobs. But it had become clear that the real agenda was to boost the returns of corporate invest-

Tupperware teaches Shanghainese how to be consumers,
Nanjing Road, Shanghai

ments in China itself through access to the China market for their own China-made products. The scapegoat in this scenario was Beijing's own efforts to salvage domestic industries and jobs.

Accordingly, the basic themes of the White Paper got a good airing in successive visits to China by Commerce Secretary Evans, Treasury Secretary Snow, Secretary of State Colin Powell, and U.S. Trade Representative Robert Zoellick. Each official brandished threats of retaliatory trade sanctions, and even a full-blown trade war, if Beijing did not facilitate broader market access to U.S. corporations. China watchers could see that the threats were mostly bluster. The tough talk was designed to give voters at home the impression that Bush was somehow addressing the links between job loss and the China trade. The threat of a trade war, if followed through, would have been disastrous for U.S. interests in general. China's massive investment in U.S. government securities was directly financing America's current-account deficit. By purchasing Treasury bonds to the tune of hundreds of billions of dollars a year, Beijing was keeping down interest rates, and funding a domestic economic recovery that was allowing Americans to go on consuming products made in China. In turn, Beijing had to be reassured that the saber-rattling was simply election-year politics and that any follow-through would be much less consequential than it appeared.[39] The Shanghai and Beijing chambers helped to run interference on both sides, smoothing relations and directing the conversation toward the interest of their corporate members.

By the time the presidential election came along, the chambers were sitting pretty. Beijing had agreed to extend retail and distribution rights to wholly foreign-owned firms, and had opened up the country's banking and insurance sectors to foreign investors.[40] It had also taken significant first steps to protect intellectual property rights. A slew of other reforms, mostly mandated by the WTO commitment, had been moved up the pipeline. With all eyes on the election and the war in Iraq, the storm over China had subsided on Capitol Hill. None of the more threatening bills had passed, and the few measures taken by the Bush administration to penalize select imports—brassieres, dressing gowns, and knit fabrics—were pawns in the larger chess game of trade negotiations with China. Even the laws, proposed in almost thirty-five states, to ban the outsourcing of state-contracted work, had been watered down, or effectively neutered, by opposition from groups like the Economic Growth and American Jobs Coalition, which represented more than 200 trade groups and large companies.[41] NAM's rebellious smaller members had been paid off with some $76.5 billion of corporate welfare, as part of Bush's sweeping overhaul of corporate tax policy in October 2004. Compensated for their losses by the taxpayer, they toned down their insurgency and fell in line behind the free-trade agenda favored by the association's global players.

Of course, the outcome of the election did not vanquish fears about the impact of the China trade on onshore economies. Fear is much too valuable as a political commodity to jettison lightly, and the "China problem," insofar as it had been built up in the public mind, could still be spun every which way. Publicly, Washington continued to push for

Under foreign pressure to protect intellectual property rights, government warns against counterfeiting, Xiangyang Market, Shanghai

the revaluation of the yuan, largely because it was one of the few face-saving options available to the Bush administration for addressing the runaway trade imbalance with China. But the actual agreements reached with Beijing were all primarily aimed at facilitating U.S.-China business interests.

In July 2005, Beijing finally announced that the yuan would be released from its decade-long peg to the dollar and allowed to fluctuate (against a select basket of currencies) within a daily trading band of 0.3 percent. The symbolism of the decision had high visibility, but its economic impact was carefully designed to be minimal. The value of the currency would still remain firmly in the discretionary grasp of the People's Bank of China, and little was likely to change in the cost of goods, flow of investment, and balance of trade. Yet both administrations, in Washington and Beijing, salvaged valuable political credit from the announcement, and the heat on U.S. firms offshore was eased. Business could go on as usual.[42] Two years' worth of high-energy debating and politicking had been effectively channeled into policy outcomes that could not have been more beneficial to corporations with vested interests in China. Just as in earlier years of crisis—the storm over the renewal of China's MFN status in 1994, and the larger battle over PNTR in 2000—the U.S.-China business lobby showed it could prevail over the opposition of the most powerful coalitions and the most widespread public disgust over offshoring and outsourcing.

A century before, the British residents of the "Shanghai Mind" had used their trade associations to peddle their mercantile policy to their own home government, but their interests were judged too insular to merit action on the part of Whitehall. Today's American counterparts had their minds just as firmly fixed on extracting local profit, but they were tuned to all the key global wavelengths, and their interests happened to reside at the pivot of the world economy. Indeed, the fierce public and political scrutiny of the China trade had been a test of their ability to activate far-flung channels of influence, while keeping local ones well-lubricated. When AmCham threw its annual Government Appreciation Dinner just after the U.S. election in November 2004, there was lots to give thanks for. The American ambassador and more than sixty Shanghai government officials in attendance celebrated an outcome that the business community in the Yangtze boomtown had never seriously doubted. No one was going to upset this gravy train soon, least of all the grandstanding senators on the Hill, and their constituents whose jobs had been shipped out.

The Sent-up Generation

Corporate globalization has left its footprint on cities all around the world. Many of the contours are similar, but each city hosts a unique variant. Shanghai is a good example. It has its share of global capitalist enclaves, where the multinational brand names and the supporting services are as familiar as the franchises of a chain store. But some of the foreign money filters deeper into the commercial entrails of the city, triggering new hybrids of traditional and modern economic life, all the way down to the storefronts and street markets. No less unique is the precise mix of public and private. Shanghai's economy, for example, is no longer centrally planned in every detail, but it is still being steered by officials with a strong hand to play. Foreign investors take their cues from industrial policies set by the city's Communist Party authorities, and they stow their capital in the preferred, or "pillar," industries, most of them technology-driven and skill-intensive.

It was in IT services, the city's freshest industry, and one highly favored by the government, that I decided to begin my interviews inside companies. This was a sector in which offshore outsourcing from the United States, the EU, and Japan had made some of its most visible inroads, and its local employees were a new breed—urbane, aspiring, and none too patient. Though inexperienced, they were not absolute beginners. As I would discover, the attitudes they brought to the workplace had already been molded by several factors: the socialist-era career experience of their parents and grandparents; expectations about their role as minor-league pioneers of the nation's high-tech future; folklore and business literature about market capitalism; and the steady pressure to forge their own way in a world without guarantees. Though their bosses would have preferred it, they were not unformed, raw material, waiting to be processed into ideal corporate citizens.

One of the easiest and most revealing ways of seeing these new workers was to watch them eat together. On any day of the working week, the employee cafeteria at Shanghai Pudong Software Park (SPSP)—a high-tech zone at the pastoral edge of the new city—was a prime viewing site. The central dining hall seated about 1,500, and was usually packed by 12:10. In the main canteen area, heads were quickly lowered over the bowls with a sure sense of purpose. Mobile phones sounded off at every other table, and at some there was a light conversational buzz, even a little hilarity. But the general goal was not to linger. By 12:45, the crowd was thinning quite rapidly. Most of the diners were at a courting age, but there was no flirting or cruising, indeed very little socializing beyond the small groupings that entered and left. Many of them carried ID badges around their necks, and some were wearing the branded jackets of their companies. Clothing style ran on a spectrum from student scruffy to business casual. Quite a few of the young men wore suits, though this was not necessarily a mark of corporate belonging—it was a common male wardrobe choice among all of Shanghai's classes. Among the women, those with accessories, advanced hair care, dresses, and distinctive fashion sense were few and far between, which put them in a category quite apart from the street-style standards famously associated with Shanghai women. Like techies anywhere else, they carried the air of being preoccupied, and distracted from the world at hand.

If these were the foot soldiers of a new industrial army, their individual insecurities belied their collective presence and sense of discipline. At the time of my first visits to SPSP, in early 2004, most of the 200 companies in the park had a small- to medium-sized payroll (the largest was Bearing Point's "global development center," with almost

A new rice bowl for the foot soldiers of China's IT army,
Shanghai Pudong Software Park cafeteria

400 employees). Their products and services were customized for small niche markets or clients with special needs. Consequently the individuality of their skilled employees was a potential selling point. Yet the mass dining-hall experience told another story. It was a stark reminder to employees that their new urban industry might still be in its infancy, but it already had a seemingly populous labor supply. Shanghai's IT services sector was far from competing with India's, but the rate at which it was growing was comparable, and it had received lavish support from the central government. Even in this relatively bucolic spot, where the well-spaced buildings—far removed from Puxi's downtown throng—only reached four or five stories, the park's agglomerate workforce was 6,000 strong, and ballooning by the month. "Every day," observed Emily Zhang, a programmer for a private Chinese company, "I look around and I can see hundreds of people who can take my place. China has no shortage of people, and IT is not really much dif-

ferent from a traditional industry. It puts a little more anxiety into my life, so I feel very lucky to have this job."

Zhang had a little more perspective on the matter than did her freshly graduated peers. She had worked in various jobs before enrolling in college in her late twenties. By the time she graduated, a college degree was no longer an automatic meal ticket. Her graduating class of 2003, numbering 2.12 million students (40 percent larger than the previous year), took several months to find jobs. When they did, they found that their average salaries, which had been climbing quite steadily since the mid-1990s, had dropped from the year before. Also on the decline were the salaries of returnees, who had studied abroad and had gotten used to claiming a handsome reward for their English-language skills and exposure to Western ways. "The cost of human resources," concluded a salary survey by the global management consultancy Hewitt, "has peaked."[1]

This momentous news was toasted in corporate offices from one end of Shanghai to the other. When the 2004 results began to come in, the toasts continued. The national graduating class had swelled to 2.8 million (3.4 million were expected in 2005), and salaries of graduates had fallen even more, averaging from a quarter to a third less than the 2003 national figure of 1,550 RMB ($187) monthly. One national survey reported that those who already held jobs saw their salaries drop by as much as 14.7 percent over the course of the year.[2] The official 2004 figures for Shanghai had fallen to 1,680 RMB ($203) a month. Average starting salaries in multinational companies were a good deal higher. In these firms, a fresh graduate could earn a 2003 average of 2,650 RMB ($320) in first-tier cities such as Shanghai, Beijing, Guangzhou, and Shenzhen, yet only slightly more in 2004, for an average of 2,850 RMB ($344).[3] Wage inflation among skilled employees had been a standard complaint among those raising their glasses. Did these figures indicate that this problem was coming under control? Not exactly, and not yet.

For most foreign HR managers of China operations, recruiting freshly graduated students was not the number-one concern. They hardly needed to consult statistics to know that the real difficulty lay with finding skilled employees who had a few years' experience under their belts. If they could find such employees, retaining them was at the very top of their list of daily challenges. As Huan Benyin, a manager at the Chinese unit of Radiall, a French electronics company, lamented, "It's difficult to get the right people in the first place. But what really hurts is when you give them the benefit of training and then they leave for a better salary somewhere else."[4] So far, this charmed pool of employees seemed to be unaffected by the downward wage pressure of China's vast oversupply of labor. Annual salary increases of 15 to 20 percent were typical, and even more for key operational employees.[5]

Engineers' ease of mobility, in particular, was a source of acute frustration to foreign firms itching to shift more of their technology-intensive business to China. Because of a severe shortage in their ranks, the bargaining power of these employees was not likely to peak until the graduate harvest of the last few years had seasoned. In short, it was their moment to eat well.

Each to His Own Rice Bowl

Where, what, and how you eat is hardly a matter that Chinese take lightly. No matter what the circumstances, you can be sure that eating expresses some important pattern of relationships between those sitting at the table. Whether to reflect this fact, or to ensure proper nutritional balance, the component dishes of Chinese meals are planned to be eaten by groups of diners, rather than by individuals. The spoken language is peppered with stock phrases and metaphors that draw on food and eating to convey the loftiest thoughts as well as the most mundane. A common greeting, on the street, for example, is not "How are you?" but "Have you eaten?" (*Ni chi le ma?*).

In the SPSP cafeteria in Pudong, the high-end engineers and project managers were more likely to be found, locked in discussion with team members, in a smaller, roped-off section at the far end of the canteen. There, waitstaff serviced the pink-cloth-covered tables, each protected from the food fallout by a thin layer of cellophane. Their working lunches were more leisurely than the chop-chop in the main dining section. Even so, the distance between the two was slight compared with the gulf observed by their bosses, the senior managers who ate their rice across the way in a restaurant called Tiramisu. This pretentious European boîte, boasting elaborate flower arrangements, was separated from the main refectory by an artificial pond stocked with a small but energetic shoal of red fish. The eclectic menu offered lobster bisque, escargots, prawn tempura, and rib-eye steak, with bottles of Château Bardoulet, to suit a generous expense account. On any given day, the staff seemed to outnumber the diners.

These three dining areas were a direct reflection of the employee pecking order. But the manner in which the diners ate also said a lot about how different kinds of employees worked. The bulk of the lunchers ate on an individual basis, but they did so en masse, and took their limited choices from a set range of dishes. For the most part, their work routines followed a similar pattern. Most were coding and programming from a fixed set of instructions, and their combined effort resulted in a product of quantifiable value. Factors of cost and punctuality governed their work and lunch alike. The higher-skilled or more experienced were working and eating in teams. Value was derived from their cooperation with each other, which released the kind of input unavailable from individuals alone. If they ate from the same bowls, figuratively speaking, it was because the resources allocated to their jobs were estimated on the productivity of their teamwork. The upper managers ate by themselves, with clients, or with their peers at other companies, either to update their knowledge of the business environment or compare their common problems and challenges. Even though I offered to go to the canteen with them, all of the company managers I interviewed over lunch chose to eat at Tiramisu. "It suits my needs perfectly," as one of them plainly put it, adding pointedly, "My employees shouldn't have to see me eat."

Emily Zhang, at the lower rungs of her company ladder, had grown up around the state-owned factory where her parents worked—both of them were machinists—and remembered going to the canteen of their work unit. "It was much larger, but the food was about the same. There were over 20,000 workers, and the factory had a hospital, a movie theater, housing, schools, everything. Here where I work we only have a few facilities—basketball, and a gym—but we use them to reduce our stress." For her parents' generation, who were beneficiaries of the iron rice bowl, all of their needs were bundled together. Their work units had been self-sufficient urban villages, and the workplace was just a passport to other social services.[6] In the SPSP, by contrast the rec facilities were there to service the workplace. Employees' bodies got run down and had to be toned and recharged at the gym. "For people of my age, working hard is more important, we have to earn our life by ourselves. My parents had a hard time in their lives, but not where they worked. That was the easiest part, they have never had to worry about that."

Before she left the cafeteria, she advised that a visit in the late evening was the best way of seeing what the park was all about. "I'm often here until ten p.m., when the company pays for a car to take me home. When I leave, the lights are still on in a lot of the offices around here." Long working hours were hardly new to a technology industry famous for workweeks that could easily stretch beyond seventy or eighty hours. "I knew that tech was like this when I chose my major." Zhang shrugged. "It's just something that goes with the job." But the nighttime shift to which she alerted me was something quite specific. The employees in many of these offices were doing business process outsourcing (BPO) for clients in other time zones, sometimes halfway across the world. The timing of their work shifts was a significant factor in the development of a project or delivery of a service that required global input on a daily basis. If multinational companies utilized their far-flung contractors efficiently, they could have all engines firing twenty-four hours a day. Nothing ever needed to wait until the next day, because the sun never set on their empires. In this kind of environment, where clients who called the shots could be in Sydney, Singapore, Yokohama, London, or Chicago, the standard nine-to-five workday was a rapidly vanishing luxury. If they were very lucky, employees might still only put in a forty-hour week—they just may not know which forty hours they would be working.

Wesley Wu, the park's business investment manager, confirmed that East China's slot in the twenty-four-hour global schedule was one of the selling points he used to attract business to SPSP. In fact, he reported that firms engaged in outsourcing had seen the biggest growth—150 percent—from the previous year. This booming sector was likely to drive Phase Three of the park's construction, slotted to expand to almost five times its current acreage over the next two years. All of the big Indian IT companies—Satyam, Mphasis, TCS, Wipro, and Infosys—were already there. SPSP also housed American multinationals like Citibank and Bearing Point, along with a host of smaller custom IT companies, some of them working directly for American clients.[7] The bulk of the outsourcing work was for Japanese corporations, but Wu estimated that American contracting would increase substantially over the next few years.[8]

In addition to the outsourcing cluster, SPSP had chosen to focus on two other industry groups: information security and microchip design. These choices revealed the strong hand of the government behind the park's creation and conceptualization. SPSP was the result of a collaboration between Shanghai's municipal government and the new Ministry of Information Industry. As part of the big push to establish China's presence on the global high-tech landscape, it had been designated as a National Software Industry Base and a National Software Outsourcing and Export Base. These portentous titles were intended to resound with privilege; they were used to impress foreign investors who knew that government backing could make all the difference between a good and bad investment in China. Government support for an industry sector devoted to information security would also help reassure investors about the protection of their intellectual property. As for the presence of chip design companies, with skilled local employees, it was a surefire way of broadcasting that China had the native talent to create its own high-tech intellectual property.

In common with all such enterprise zones, SPSP offered lucrative terms for its prospective tenants, including massive tax exemptions (for up to five years after a company showed profits), some of which applied specifically to advanced technology enterprises. Rents were substantially cheaper than for the office space used by corporations in Shanghai's central business district, or in Pudong's own downtown Lujiazui.

Elevated view of the Shanghai Pudong Software Park

"Software companies need lower prices," Wu pointed out, "because they are basically like factories, with employees who are low-cost coders. Clients also need high bandwidth and connectivity, which downtown offices can't provide." In addition, the park offered a range of support services and facilities—a data-sharing center, a software component bank for reusable technology, an export service platform, an open lab center, and an integrated circuit design platform—all cherry-picked to cater to tenants' needs. Since Shanghai's electrical utility was a 50 percent shareholder, there would be no worries about the power shortages, or rolling blackouts, that plagued the region's businesses and became a major factor in Beijing's 2004 efforts to slow down an "overheated" economy.

Wu acknowledged that there was a turnover problem among SPSP's companies (data for Phase One showed average turnover of about 20 percent, though my informal surveys put the figure at between 25 and 30 percent), but he played it down. "Companies have accepted it as part of the cost of doing business here. They invest a lot in training employees, but they accept the fact that other companies will pay more for that experienced employee." His nonchalance was not shared by managers I interviewed. They were more likely to get worked up about this topic than almost any other, though they were reluctant to criticize new companies who set up shop by poaching their people at higher prices. Instead, they blamed the employees themselves as too selfish by far.

Communication Difficulties

Guaranteed to set managers off were the inflated aspirations of college graduates in particular. No one, they lamented, was content to commit to a stable career track at the technical end. Such craft professionals as engineers were unwilling to apply their occupational skills for very long. They all wanted short work contracts, and expected quick promotions, steep salary upgrades, and managerial responsibilities well before their time. Billy Yep, operations manager at Bearing Point, suggested that China was going through its version of the "Me Generation"—and pointed to the nation's one-child policy as a contributing factor. "The whole culture expects a single child to show improvements and attainments every year. So everyone wants to be a project manager in at least two years." He had seen job-hopping in SPSP escalate to a rate of every two months in some cases, a turnover that contrasted sharply with the stability of the staff he had worked with in his native Singapore. Melding such self-seeking individuals into a team was his daily challenge. James Jasper, an HR manager at a U.S. software firm, pointed out that "these kids have never seen a downturn, they will be spoiled until it comes along."

Yep's and Jasper's comments reflected a consensus view shared by HR managers of foreign firms in Shanghai, who bewailed the work mentality of the city's Brat Generation. In rapidly changing economic times, generational complaints like these are not uncommon. In this case, the youthful offenders appeared to have acquired their bad habits from Shanghai's boomtown culture. Because of all the new career opportunities, the city's pampered youth had lost its chance of learning the kind of work ethic—distinguished by patience and loyalty—that is favored by most employers. But what had triggered this environment of rampant self-interest? Who, exactly, had spoiled the crop? Almost certainly, some of the causes lay with opportunistic investments on the part of those same foreign companies. Their managers were reaping a harvest sown, in part, by corporate adventurism. The disloyal mind-set of their job-hopping employees, always on the lookout for the main chance, could not easily be distinguished from the ravening mentality of the investor, always on the lookout for the best returns.

When it came to finding employees with just the right fit, managers were seldom happy with what they got. As often as I heard the complaint about the excessive individualism of Shanghainese youth, I also heard managers bemoaning their lack of personal initiative. Mark Cavicchia, managing director of everse, an L.A.-based software developer with offshore sites in SPSP and in Bangalore, offered a common perspective: "The Chinese think collectively. They have no concept of personal space. They are not into individual-type thinking." For the kind of position that required analytical skills, this shortcoming could be a real obstacle. Ramesh Govindan, a technology manager at a U.S. multinational, whose job was to effect knowledge transfer to local employees, assessed the consequences: "They also are not up to 'thinking outside the box,' which is not good in the IT industry. You tell them to do something and they will do a good job, but they are not likely to deviate from those instructions. In high tech, you are supposed to exploit the technology, to stretch the limit. You need to say 'It's taking me ten steps to do this, can I do it in five steps?' You probably don't see that happening in Chinese technicians."

An even greater source of managerial frustration was what they experienced as an opaque communication style on the part of their Chinese employees. Govindan put it this way: "There is a difference between what they mean and what they say. When you tell them something, they nod the head and say, 'Yes, we understood,' when they haven't. So I ask them to say it in their own words to see if they really understood." Even worse, in his view, "Chinese technicians may also know what is being asked, but they don't want to tell you the answer—they know, but they won't tell you." His comment reflected the general perception of foreigners that mainland Chinese people were not in the habit of speaking directly, especially to their bosses. Chris Grocock, a regional director for a British head-hunting firm, offered a precise diagnosis: "Culturally, Chinese don't like to be bringers of bad news, or they don't like to say no. So the common answer to questions is either to skirt them or answer a different question. . . . Or they pretend they didn't hear the question at all."

Govindan, Grocock, and Cavicchia were echoing the opinions of at least fifty managers whom I interviewed for this book, whether in IT services or in manufacturing. For each of them, what they saw as "Chinese characteristics" was an obstacle to rational corporate conduct, and a frustrating challenge for the would-be managerial reformer.[9]

- Mainland Chinese obey whatever a boss tells them, but they are at a loss when asked to think for themselves.
- Because of the pervasive influence of "face" in the culture at large, they will not risk bringing shame on others, especially bosses, by pointing out errors.
- They learn quickly, but only if they are shown how.
- China's educational system is top-heavy on drill and routine, and so Chinese workers have to be retrained rigorously to think and act in a creative fashion.
- If they revert to "the boss is always right" conditioning when they become managers, they are more likely to train sycophants than good performers.
- They have little sense of loyalty, and are liable to walk out with corporate intellectual property.
- The single-child policy has made them unduly pampered, and so they are self-centered and incapable of relating to others in teamwork.

Nearly all my interviewees expressed similar views about the work mentality of mainland Chinese employees. Most seemed comfortable about offering such sweeping generalizations, even those who had only been in China for a matter of months. This chutzpah was compounded by the fact that non-Chinese-speaking foreign managers usually only communicated with employees through a local middle manager, in a relationship not unlike the compradores of Old Shanghai. After a while I began to suspect that they had all read the same book in the airport lounge. Indeed, the most popular business literature around town was aimed at preparing foreigners for the cultural differences they would likely encounter. Volumes of such tips sported titles like the corporate consultant Laurence Brahm's *When Yes Means No!*[10] These books had absorbed several centuries of Orientalism, and so they were often updated Western stereotypes of Asian behavior, masquerading as insider information from old China hands like Brahm. Like all such trading in stereotypes, they left the reader believing that seemingly contradictory perceptions were, in fact, just the flip sides of the same mentality. In this way, the "Oriental" was both obscure and transparent to the Western eye, both exotic and all too knowable, not "like us" and yet also capable of conforming to our ways.

Take the topic at hand. The managers I interviewed had accepted the notion that mainland Chinese thought and acted in lockstep, and that individualism was an alien property of the culture, whether from several centuries of the dynastic "horde," or from decades of socialist collectivism. Drawing on a long legacy of Western distrust of the Chinese, they could also believe that their employees, given half a chance, would take advantage of any cross-cultural confusion to further their own self-interest. The first belief explained their employees' aversion to risk as if it were a culture-bound condition of blind Confucian obedience. The second explained their employees' minor acts of enterprise as a reflection of their ethical blindness. If the two beliefs seemed contradictory, they could always be rationalized in the following way. The former distilled the worst of "Asian despotism"—mass conformity with authority. The latter extracted the worst of "Western individualism"—look out for number one.

In truth, however, when managers made such comments, they were not describing their Chinese employees at all. They were justifying to themselves why they did not have a workforce of ideal corporate employees who would be all things to them, and who would also come at a discount price. The inability to access such employees at will was the real source of their discontent. It was one of the reasons, for example, why there was so much interest among HR managers in personality tests for local employee aptitude. Several Shanghai IT firms were developing software programs responsive to cross-cultural differences, which would aid in recruiting the fittest Chinese employees.[11]

Some of the managerial frustration came from the extra pressure placed on offshore sites to perform. In IT services, there were many occupational tasks, for example, that merely required employees to follow a process laid down in a manual, or a template provided by a project manager. Indeed, for many BPO tasks, the process had to be written down in this way to ensure seamless communication between the client and the offshore site worker. To complete such tasks barely required any more mental variation than an assembly-line or data-entry job. Work moved along mechanically, with each phase of product delivery guaranteed by a streamlined process. In addition, however, there were tasks that could only be accomplished through individual problem-solving, and that required some degree of personal initiative. In traditional companies with a workforce of scale, these tasks might be broken down and allocated to different divisions with different pay scales. But, increasingly, managers, especially in the knowledge industry, demanded more flexibility from employees who were expected to switch in and out of roles as required, regardless of their salary level. This was particularly true of smaller firms that eked out profit margins from a limited human resource pool, but it was no less the case with multinationals hoping that the cost savings from offshore sites could be spread across more and more of their operations.

How did employees respond to these multiple demands? Lu Shilun, an engineer at one of SPSP's American multinationals, used a digital metaphor to describe the result: "It's just like opening different programs or applications in your brain. The one you use for half the day is only for input, and the other one is more interactive, where you feel you are competing against the program, like in a game, or that you are making up new rules to make the program compete for you." Lu explained that the general manager had told her that the goal in IT was to "work smarter, not harder," but she confessed that it was often quite difficult to interpret exactly what her boss wanted, other than that "we're not supposed to overrun on the project schedule or go over budget." Even her project manager admitted he had given up listening very closely to his superior, who often issued contradictory requests. Some employees, especially those with experience in both Chinese and Western companies, were quick to acknowledge that the cultural differences did not always help matters. Lu's housemate Albert Chang, a programmer at an Indian company, explained: "Usually, at a Chinese company, the boss is always right, and so there is no confusion. I prefer the foreign style, where you can have open speech, and participate in decisions. But this means that my manager is also more open about what he wants. Sometimes," he added with precise diplomacy, "I think he wants a little too much."

From the perspective of their Chinese employees, the foreign managers were the ones who were difficult to read. Their demands were more likely to be enigmatic, especially since they were trying to translate a faraway corporate policy into directives for an inexperienced local staff. Most offshore sites were established initially to cut the costs of low-skill operations. But because they were the cheapest link in the chain, the pressure to expand them by taking on higher-value operations kicked in quickly. If local wages rose—and in Shanghai's IT industry, that had been the case—managers had to deliver better profit and productivity figures, often while using more or less the same workforce. Consequently the demands made on employees multiplied, and they were asked to take on many different kinds of tasks. Under such circumstances, communication deteriorated, and employees had one more reason to jump ship for some more lucrative opportunity, or one that carried less pressure. The resulting high turnover bequeathed additional burdens to those left behind.

In a bid to stem wage inflation, employers had begun to use the threat of moving to cheaper locations. Coding, programming, and other rote operations seemed destined to migrate inland, or to northern locations like Dalian. For IT service companies that did not share the logistics needs of manufacturers, the lure of cities in the far west was considerable. Officials in Chengdu or Xian were promising them the world. Chang, who wanted to run his own company as soon as he could, had already sized up the possibilities. "Maybe I'll get there before my employers do," he quipped. He and his peers had watched foreign companies bail out of other locations in East Asia after less than a decade. They knew their time to be passed over would come, so they had no incentive to stick around. "My knowledge will go with me," he said firmly. "It won't be transferred by anyone else."

The Great Chinese Engineer

Because private-sector employers would generally not hire anyone over the age of thirty, all the engineers whom I interviewed in the software park were in their twenties, but their family histories were central to the story of modern China. Most of them had parents or grandparents who had been "sent down" from the city to work in inland rural areas or towns. Skilled and well educated, their elders had been delegated to share their expertise with the population of underdeveloped regions. In some respects, this was a socialist variant of what corporations today call knowledge transfer. Unlike the corporate version, it was undertaken to equalize, rather than to exploit, the gap between the coastal cities and the countryside. This forced relocation of millions of skilled technicians to help set up factories in inland cities and on rural communes was one of the most controversial policies of the Maoist period. The full brunt of this rustication campaign was borne most famously by the "sent-down generation" in the years during the Cultural Revolution. But the practice dated from the 1950s and continued even after 1978, when almost 800,000 Shanghainese were sent to other provinces, while those who stayed served as "Sunday engineers," or weekend consultants, to rural and township enterprises and cooperatives.[12] Of course, the policy was also exploited over the years; political dissenters were regularly sent to China's mountainside equivalents of Siberia. Eventually their numbers included the student Red Guards who were deemed too subversive to remain in key urban centers after 1968, and were ordered out to "learn from the peasants" in whose name they had shouted their slogans.

It was many years, sometimes decades, before the sent-down generation found some way to return to the city. Those who resented their involuntary transfer were the loudest critics of the policies, demanding the return of "ten years deducted" from their age.[13] Bureaucratic planning had often delivered them into circumstances where the noble goal of bridging mental and manual labor proved impractical. Yet there were many others who made the most of their sacrifice in the spirit most famously summarized in the saying of Lei Feng, the most fêted of the "model workers" used in party propaganda: "I will be a screw in the locomotive of the Revolution." China's nation-building needs, they concluded, were greater and more urgent than their personal career ambitions, and so they made their homes in far-flung provinces, engineering the country's industrial infrastructure all through the Mao years. When their children, or grandchildren, returned to the Shanghai region in the 1990s, it was in response, once again, to China's industrial needs. In a sense, the new generation of technically skilled were being "sent up." They were being channeled and steered either by the state or by an embryonic labor market. This time around, the industry was high-tech—computers, telecommunications, microchips, automotive, and biogenetics—and the locations were the most, not the least, developed regions in the country.

Foreign managers often cited the loss, during the Cultural Revolution years, of the younger generation's parents' college education as one of the primary reasons why China lacked seasoned, managerial talent in their forties and fifties. As for the older generations of Shanghainese, the city's park benches were still occupied by veterans who had learned their English in the 1930s and 1940s, and retained some of their natty dress sense from that period. They spoke a faintly archaic English with a period accent that had been preserved in linguistic amber. In the Shanghai Library, they were also conspicuous in the foreign language section, reading magazines of opinion or specialized journals in their former fields. At the same library tables, readers of their grandchildren's generation were scanning the *Wall Street Journal* or cramming business or management textbooks. Business literature was widely read among Shanghainese youth, more voraciously consumed than any other form of Western popular culture, though self-help literature—from classics like Dale Carnegie to more-contemporary volumes like Stephen Covey's *The 7 Habits of Highly Effective People,* or Laurie Beth Jones's Christian-based *The Power of Positive Prophecy*—was gaining ground.

It was at the library that I met Liu Hongjian, and, sure enough, his reading material consisted of business guru books with titles like *In Search of Excellence: Lessons from America's Best-Run Companies.* As it happened, he worked for a software company in SPSP, so I could just as easily have met him during my visits to the park. His family history was shared by many of those I had already interviewed there. His engineer parents were both educated in Shanghai in the 1960s and then sent down, along with their chemical company, to a small city in Hunan province, not far from Mao's hometown. Mao, Liu acknowledged, "was a great hero for them. They met him once in Hunan, and they followed his example, even in bad times when everyone was struggling to survive." Liu himself felt no debts to the Great Helmsman: "He had no economic sense. Bill Gates is my hero. Like Mao, he is a monopoly, he succeeded in dominating." Sure enough, the English name he had chosen for himself was Bill.

Like many of his peers, Liu's parents had determined his choice of major in mechanical engineering. By the time he entered Dalian University in the late 1990s, the government no longer allocated students to their majors or their jobs, but there was still little information to guide prospective students, especially those from the inland provinces, in choosing their careers. Liu was happy, initially, to follow his parents' career advice, but in the course of his training, and partly under the influence of his namesake, he developed a passion for computers and an awareness of how an IT career might bring him prosperity. "The dot-com boom was still going strong," he recalled, "and China was getting wired faster than anywhere. Everyone said that Shanghai was the best place to be." Securing a place in a computer science master's program at East China Science and Technology University brought him to the city, where, because his skills were in demand, he was virtually assured of a much-sought-after residence card that gave him full access to the city's housing, schooling, and welfare benefits.

His education and relocation meant that he would never have to "get dirty hands from manufacturing." Somewhere along the road from Hunan, he decided that "the workshops and the assembly lines are not a good environment for me. They are limited opportunities, and in China, there is some stigma attached to manufacturing jobs. Software is much more prestigious. If you want to produce value, it's not in manufacturing, at least not in the simple things that China makes, like toys, clothes, and lighters." What about his parents? Had they not dirtied their hands for a good cause? "Yes," he acknowledged, "they contributed to China's development, but the country had simple needs, and so they also had simple needs and simple lives. Now we have to aim higher."

His parents, as it happens, were both lucky to have retained their jobs, after their company, in common with thousands of other state-owned enterprises, was forced to shed a third of its workforce. Liu got a taste of their work culture when he took his first job at a state-owned company. Although the firm had revamped itself, and pared down its "surplus labor," the low-pressure expectations on the job had not changed all that much. "There were many days when I did nothing useful. Or, at least, not for the company. I took the opportunity to work on my English and computing skills." Liu's tour of duty lasted a little over a year. "I can only learn by working hard, and I don't feel comfortable unless I am working hard. When you are young, you need to be engaged and active." His most enduring memory of that work-place was of his manager's deficiencies. "My boss only thought about himself," he recalled, "and did not look out for the company. Unlike before [the firm's restructuring], he consulted with us about some things, but I don't believe it made any difference to his decisions. He did not see us as a resource for him."

Liu's criticism of the manager was not a response to any abuse of authority, nor was he judging from the point of view of an overworked employee. On the contrary, he was identifying with the boss and, by extension, with the company's fortunes, in order to judge him by the standards of managerial efficiency. Liu was already thinking about how he himself would be a more effective manager. His desire, then, to be a "resource" for his manager was not in quite the tradition of Lei Feng's spirit of self-sacrifice that had captivated his parents. Chinese of his parents' generation, he said, "had no choice but to be obedient. . . . Nowadays we have a choice, but we don't yet know where the choice will lead us."

This wannabe managerial mind-set shaped how he would approach his next job, as a software engineer in an American IT service company providing services directly to multinationals in China: "My American manager speaks to me directly and wants results. Chinese managers have to show some appreciation for your efforts before they ask you for a result, like asking for a favor. They praise you, and then they ask you for the favor. Because foreigners ask directly, employees can also be more direct with the manager. In China, this is not very polite, but it is a better way of doing business. I want to learn this."

As an engineer with a little job experience under his belt, Liu had some choices about where he could work. Given his aspirations, he sought out a line of work where he could maximize his contacts, even though his current employer paid him less than he could get elsewhere: "I wanted the experience of an IT company to have more opportunities so that I can get involved in business. Business applications in software are where all the good contacts are. In this job, I have contact with people in many domains—manufacturing, banking, and retail. I can learn from the diversity of these domains." Ten years down the road, he fully expected to be running his own company. For the time being, he was picking up tips from working with clients and with managers—one American and one Singaporean—who cracked the whip much faster than his old bosses. Did he respect them more if they drove him harder? He smiled, and deflected the question. Like Emily Zhang, he knew that working in the tech field meant long hours, but he had not expected to be putting in a twelve-hour day, with regular stints in the office on both weekend days. "I would like more balance in my life," he finally acknowledged. His wife, also Hunanese, who worked in sales for a British multinational, did ten-hour days on average, but always had weekends off, and wanted him at home more often.

Liu's attitude was typical of employees who expected to rise quickly. When he dwelled on his own situation, it was from the perspective of his managers, and his self-analysis drew on the managerial truisms of the New Economy about the golden virtues of risk and flexibility. These were things he had read in the business books at the library, and he had no reason as yet to question them. Ultimately, however, his choices were limited by what he described as "pressure," the most common term used by my engineer interviewees to describe their economic situation. Like Emily Zhang, he was conscious of the many others who would line up to take his job, even in a city with a soaring cost of living. As a country boy who still felt disoriented in Shanghai after four years, he believed that the odds were somehow stacked against him. Nor was IT a very stable industry. "These days, customers," he observed, "just want to have their problems solved, they are only focused on value, and they don't care what technology you use to get it for them."

Technology had lost its thrill for clients, but employees like Liu still had to work overtime to stay abreast of new IT applications. Like almost every engineer I interviewed, he spent several hours of his own time every week surfing technology sites just to keep up. Though they did not include this in their rough estimates of working hours, this time was very much a part of their workweek. Even if he did not have his business ambitions, Liu was aware he might have to move into a manager's position soon enough. Younger technologists always know the new technology better, and employers overwhelmingly favor them. In addition, several engineer friends had already quit the private IT sector to move into a healthier work environment. Dismayed with the overwork and performance pressure, they had job-hopped for a while in search of a more balanced kind of work life. Now they were doing network maintenance or system support in a traditional industry or a state-owned company. Though they had taken a pay cut, their daily lives were much easier and they saw their families more. Liu had already decided this option would be his safety net if his more entrepreneurial dreams came to naught.

In between our two interviews, Liu took advantage of the long May holidays to visit his family in Hunan. The government had extended these national holidays in order to stimulate mass consumption, and he joked that he "had been a bad patriot" by eschewing the shopping malls. But the visit had reminded him of his roots. "My life really is divided into two different parts," he acknowledged. "In my work team, I must think in Western ways, but in my family I must keep my Chinese ways. We have to learn things from the outside, but my personal life will not change. I want to be very Chinese." Is this what being a modern Chinese person means? "Maybe," he answered, but he also thought that this combination was "not so new in China, and certainly not in Shanghai."

Liu's comment evoked a century's worth of debate among the Chinese about how to "learn from the West" while preserving native culture. It is a history worth reflecting on briefly. While China's nationalist movement was born in the nineteenth century of the desire to rid China of both the Qing rulers and occupying foreign powers, it was not aimed at returning the country to insular ways. Looking to the West for new technologies and ideas became a deeply ingrained habit for nationalists of every stripe. But the capacity to spread the benefits equitably was thwarted by the concentrated power of the treaty-port economy. Despite, or perhaps because of, their peasant base, China's new Communist leaders never turned their backs on technological modernization. If anything, their ardor for bringing modern industry to the provinces ran in advance of what was practically possible. Mao's efforts to mechanize the new rural communes, and the messianic goals behind the Great Leap Forward ("Overtake England in Fifteen Years!") were examples of premature or wishful thinking that cost many Chinese dearly.

Mao himself earned a reputation abroad of being a fervent pastoralist, trusting peasant knowledge over and above the expertise of educated technicians. Contrary to this image overseas, Mao never ceased to encourage rapid industrialization, and was adamant about the need to learn the most advanced technologies from other countries. "We must walk on two legs," he exhorted, meaning that China must embrace both modernity and traditions, both technology and self-reliant, indigenous ways.[14] Given the colossal obstacles that China faced, few could doubt the remarkable advances that were achieved. Indeed, if Maoism had not built a strong modern society with a technologically advanced base, the Western powers would not have had to ask to come and bargain, as President Nixon did in 1972. For foreign investors, China's robust infrastructure (today it has a more extensive highway system than any country but the United States, and a much-envied high-tech infrastructure) remains one of its chief comparative advantages over other developing countries.

In fact, Beijing had been steadily importing technology in arm's-length transactions from the 1950s onward. Initially the technology transfer was from the Soviet Union and Eastern Europe—including hundreds of turnkey plants complete with blueprints and specifications. In addition, 10,000 Soviet technicians came to China, and up to 15,000 Chinese trained as engineers in the Soviet Union. After the Sino-Soviet split, the deals were with Japan and Western Europe. By the time that the Four Modernizations (in agriculture, industry, technology, and defense) were adopted into China's constitution in 1979, the pivotal decision to admit foreign investment as well as foreign technology had been made. If China was to achieve its modernization goal, an Open Door policy was needed to absorb Western funds, along with professional skills, including managerial and marketing know-how.[15]

The Open Door policy left little room for the political considerations that had driven the late Mao's thinking about national development. Where before politics was "in command," now "technique" would be in the driver's seat, a view often summarized in Deng Xiaoping's famous dictum, "It makes no difference whether the cat is black or white, as long it catches mice." How did the government's execution of this pragmatic philosophy (in addition to engineer leaders like Jiang Zemin and Hu Jintao, nearly all members of the Politburo have technical degrees) impact the role of engineers like Liu Hongjian? Gone for good was the Maoist principle of being both "red and expert." According to that credo, technical knowledge was not neutral, and its holders were guided in their application of expertise by their political orientation. Under Mao's doctrine, it would be impossible, for example, to simply sell your skills to the highest bidder, as the new generation of technicians was doing.

There was no longer an obligation to share knowledge with the less educated masses, though the act of becoming a party member was not insignificant—it could still help your career, especially if you worked in the public sector. Nation-building, on the other hand, had not declined as a way of life for many Chinese. If anything, it had become more pronounced in the course of the 1990s, when the government introduced a heavy diet of patriotic campaigning into the educational system. Propaganda with Marxist content dropped off, and the doctrine of strident nationalism took its place.[16] For engineers of Liu's generation, who were not in any case inclined to hold ardent political views, the strong gravitational force of their patriotism was more than ever the key to China's status as an ascending power. Technological modernization still came in a package from overseas, stamped with the managerial demands and expectations of multinational capitalism. But their enterprising ability to open the package, reengineer its contents, and rapidly diffuse the result presaged a day very soon when the nation would stand entirely on its own two feet.[17]

To play this role in nation-building, the new sent-up engineers had to be as modern as possible. They had to familiarize themselves with the ways of international business practice, whether they worked in IT services or in precision manufacturing. This involved speaking English, communicating directly, absorbing the habits of the marketplace, and understanding how technologies, commodities, and knowledge circulated from country to country. All of these belonged to the package of Western business skills that fell under the rubric of "knowledge transfer." The knowledge in question wasn't just technical skills or content, it was a whole mentality, rooted in the customs of capitalist expansion.

Yet, outside of the market culture evangelized in their Westernized workplaces, the impact of this rage to be modern was far from predictable. Early on in my research for this book, an American manager at a Suzhou plant proudly informed me that his workforce was made up of what he called "modern Chinese people." When I asked the firm's operations manager, who was Chinese, what this meant, he pulled his brow into a deep furrow and exclaimed, "But no one knows what a modern Chinese person is." From then on, I asked all my interviewees how they felt this concept applied to their lives. A vast majority

Luxury consumerism and the drive for modernity,
Huai Hai Road, Shanghai

described themselves as much more traditional than modern, including many who had been raised in the dizzy orbit of Shanghai's downtown heartbeat. This gave rise to an equally interesting question: In this kind of environment, what was a traditional Chinese person? For most of my interviewees, "tradition" seemed to be a nationalist code word. It was an opportunity for employees who might have been regarded as would-be Westerners to express their loyalty to native ideals.

The Rise of Gray-Collar

One such employee was Sean Chen (named for Sean Connery), who had grown up in Jing'an, one of the most urbane of Shanghai's downtown districts. His parents, an English teacher and a city planner, had fully exposed him, from an early age, to the new climate of openness. With his unusually sharp command of English, his light gray polo-neck sweater, and designer glasses with thick black frames, he could have been at home in any hip precinct of Hong Kong, Toronto, or Manhattan. For a while I was lulled by his familiarity with a music scene that cast deeper shadows than Celine Dion or the Backstreet Boys. He affirmed that he had been an Outkast fan from the beginning, and he had a taste for acid jazz that would have even been uncommon in its heyday several years before. I would not have predicted his retro passion for Nicholas Ray films. But there was another side that didn't quite fit the profile: "I'm not in favor of casual sex. Having different partners is wrong." In a town where pricey, exotic lingerie, fully loaded mobile phones, and A-one brand names were the social currency of youth, the fashion consumer parade along Huai Hai Road, with its share of *linglei* (subcultural style renegades) was not his cup of tea. "I don't feel comfortable with the brand culture. It's like a disease. Besides, there is nothing new there that we Chinese have made, it is all copied or imported."

Even worse, he declared with some disgust, was the nightclub scene on Maoming Road, memorialized in over-the-top chick-lit by club kids like Mian Mian (author of *Candy, La La La,* and *Acid Lover*) and Wei Hui (author of *Shanghai Baby*). He had come of age when these novels were defining the breathless image of Shanghai's new youth hedonism, in sync with Western codes of faux-rebel decadence. The government censor had moved quickly to ban the books as corrosive examples of foreign influence, and I got the impression that Chen might have done the same. If this kind of lifestyle was the epitome of modern, "it is not going in a healthy direction. I don't want to exchange it for the life we have always had in China. Our traditions are what keep us strong inside. Family and friends are number one, and we will no longer be Chinese if we forget that."

Chen did not attach much importance to his own role in the national economy. "As a software person, I do not feel very special," he mused. "If I were an aerospace engineer, or a physicist, maybe I would. But people like me are not national heroes." Nor did he believe that his comparative advantage as an educated urbanite would endure. "I guess we were always typical, arrogant Shanghainese," he joked, "looking down at everyone in the rest of the country. When the boom came," he added with a grin, "we had the opportunities which they all wanted." Permission to register (*hukou*) for urban residence had always been a passport to a better life, but Shanghai's residence card became the most sought-after in the years following the 1992 opening of Pudong. Like Zhang and Liu, Chen was anxiously looking over his shoulder at the multitude of job-seekers. "I've been quite lucky," he observed, "but I don't assume my luck will last. The pressure is growing, and besides, they say that employers consider you old in China by the time you are twenty-four."[18]

Aside from the task of easing the soaring general unemployment, government cadres were especially animated about the shortage of skilled technical workers. By the spring of 2005, Beijing was acknowledging that for every experienced skilled worker, there were eighty-eight vacancies, and for every factory technician there were sixteen vacancies.[19] If growth fueled by foreign capital was to continue unobstructed, then this scarcity had become as much of a problem as the energy shortages that required staggered production in many Delta factories. In early 2004, the Ministry of Education launched a drive to train an additional million workers in occupations that labor authorities were beginning to label officially as "gray-collar." Short-term training would also be offered to 3 million technician-level students as part of a national program involving more than 500 professional training schools and 1,400 companies and enterprises.[20] Gray-collar was a rather broad category, covering everything from fashion designers to software engineers, from ad writers to numerical control technicians. Recruits were expected to fill the gap between unskilled blue-collar jobs and the white-collar professional and managerial positions to which most college graduates aspired.[21] Alongside the ubiquitous lingerie and mobile-phone ads, Shanghai's metro stations hosted billboards that described these occupations and broadcast the need for recruits.

Chen recognized himself in this niche. "I am definitely not a white-collar worker. Their work and lives are more regulated than mine. Even though I am a low-level programmer, I have more creative control of my environment." Some of the designated gray-collar occupations were the sweet ones favored by every large city looking to promote its "creative industries." But the less glamorous ones were just as essential if China, courtesy of its foreign investors, was going to be able to sustain its long march up the value chain. Every manufacturer in the Yangtze Delta needed skilled technicians, not just to maintain production levels but to upgrade plants from assembly and testing to accommodate higher-grade operations like product engineering and design. In Shanghai's IT service sector, the effort to scale up from the industrial routine of "code farms" to the knowledge-rich realm of business strategy consulting required a similar injection of skills. Without an oversupply of these skills, wage inflation and high turnover would continue to blight the offshore expansion plans of foreign investors.

Naturally, corporations had turned to the government to solve their problem. In this case it was a problem not ordinarily associated with China—a dearth of labor. Yet, unlike anywhere else in the world, China's government could deliver in huge quantities. Though not exactly on the scale of building the Three Gorges dam, the gray-collar initiative for training talented workers amounted to a massive HR recruitment effort. It was also a sobering addition to the list of favors that government officials usually offered to investors who still considered themselves beneficiaries of free trade—virtually free land, oodles of tax exemptions, and a soft guarantee that labor laws (on paper, some of the best in the world) would never be properly enforced.[22]

Largely because he wanted to work with engineers and managers who had experience in the software industry, Sean Chen had taken his first job at one of the Indian IT companies in SPSP. He was made aware, from the first day, of the factors that drove the competition between the two countries: quality of infrastructure, labor and social security costs, the potential of the China market, language and other skill sets, and the comfort level of clients. "Chinese are cheap, but, in this case, not the cheapest labor," Chen quipped. "Knowing this makes a big difference to the way we do things in my workplace." Despite the pressure, he was not putting in the extra-long hours that were typical in the IT sector. In the Indian companies, employee time was flexible, but I found that employees were not generally expected to work more than an eight- or nine-hour day. Still, they talked about how their minds were often preoccupied with "unsolved problems," even when they were not on the job. For knowledge workers, there was no escaping this occupational hazard. After a year, Chen's monthly salary was 3,000 RMB ($362), which was slightly below the IT market average in Shanghai, but he felt he was getting a training from the people with the best experience in the field. Most of the company's clients were Japanese, but it had one U.S. customer with a large presence in China, and had just signed a contract with another that was moving operations to the Yangtze Delta. Chen would soon be working directly with this client on U.S.-specific business.

Given that he would be doing work that had previously employed an American, how did he feel about "taking away" the job? "Maybe this job would have been done in India," he replied rather evasively. When pressed, he acknowledged that Americans would have a hard time holding on to this kind of work: "They will have to retrain and find something with more value. They are more creative anyway. But I can do this kind of job just as well as an American. Even better if I am dealing with Asian clients. These days no one owns his job." Even so, he thought the comparison with India was the more relevant one. His manager, a native of Mumbai, regularly told him that the Chinese would never be able to match the software advantage India had built up over the past fifteen years. Chen was more optimistic about the prospects for his country: "We are fast learners, and we are desperate for work. Since we started later, we have to work harder to catch up. China will win in the end." Needless to say, IT managers in Shanghai were all too aware that appeals to the patriotism of employees like Chen were an effective way of stimulating their productivity.

Even with higher productivity, Shanghai would still be at a cost disadvantage with India. Chen's own manager saw a simple solution: outsource to inland locations. "My ideal business model," he declared, "would be to have one or two hundred engineers in Shanghai as a basic design workforce, and maybe two or three thousand in Chengdu to do the implementation—coding, programming, product development, testing, lower-level work."

An Entrepreneur's Plan

Eric Rongley, the managing director of Bluem, an IT start-up with offices in downtown Shanghai, had more or less the same plan in mind: "What I see happening with my company is ending up with about fifty people in the States who are going around for different projects, about 200 people here in Shanghai—project managers, business analysts, some teams—and then about 2,000 people out there in Xian or Chengdu. I'm saving about half my costs right there." For a while the names of these two cities were on the lips of most IT company managers in Shanghai. Their low labor costs, high-quality technology colleges and institutes, and existing software clusters made them a natural choice for job transfers. That they were thousands of kilometers from Shanghai mattered no more or less than the distance from Pudong to Los Angeles.

Bluem's Rongley was quite open about the cost advantages of recruiting talent from the far west over local employees:

> If they are local people, that means they are about twenty-five, and they probably still live with their family. The market here is so hot that it's a seller's market, as far as talent is concerned. Joe is coming home at eight o'clock every night, and the neighbor comes home at six o'clock. The parents start talking, and Joe's parents start giving him a hard time. "Why you gotta come home at eight? Our neighbor doesn't come home at that time." Somebody who's not from Shanghai, they don't have their parents giving them this weird pressure. Shanghai people have come to expect everything easy. I'm not impressed with the work ethic in Shanghai. You would think, "Third World country, they've got to work like hell." There are people here who work hard, but when you look around and say, "Wow, that guy really works hard," check into it, he's not from Shanghai. He's from Xian or Chengdu.

Rongley, who was serving, at the time, as chair of AmCham's Info-Comm Committee, was the Shanghai poster boy for U.S. software outsourcing. He had garnered several years of industry experience in Bangalore before moving to Shanghai to set up Navion—"China's first mature software shop," as he put it. After building that company for Capital One (it was subsequently sold to the Indian IT giant Mphasis), he gathered enough funds to start up Bluem. Initially geared to tap the China market, the firm was burned by some ruinous encounters with local businesses—either ripped off, or accused of espionage when deals turned sour. "Chinese customers try to squeeze all the life out of their vendor and then move on to the next one," Rongley reported. "You'd think they would say, 'You're making a system for me, so I want to try to help you.' But that's not what they do, they fight with you. . . . Bribery and thievery is the thing. They're all crooked. It's all the same culture." With these cutthroat dalliances behind him, he focused on growing Bluem into an offshore development center (ODC) for multinational banking and insurance firms. The most fully fledged species of outsourcing, an ODC will normally have forty or fifty employees fully dedicated to a client—to all intents and purposes, they are de facto employees of the larger company. A bank, for example, cannot work IT employees as efficiently as an ODC, and therefore not only does it save huge costs by outsourcing, but it "acquires" a drastically reduced workforce that can be cut at any time without serving termination packages.

With the BPO boom in full swing, a company that presented itself as a slick mix of American-Chinese-Indian was well placed to pick up outsourcing business from the United States, though it could not yet compete with the multinationals in town, like HP, IBM, EDS, Bearing Point, and Citicorp, which were taking the largest of the corporate outsourcing contracts. Rongley hired some high-level Indian engineers to come over to Shanghai to do knowledge transfer with his Chinese employees. In addition, Bluem was one of the IT companies where employees told me that they were pressed to work harder precisely because their counterparts in India earned less than they did. Before long, Rongley was operating two ODCs for American clients, a third was on the way, and he was thinking of establishing an offshore center in Thailand. After the company achieved CMM 5 (the highest level of certification in the software industry), he set the optimistic goal of becoming China's first billion-dollar software service company.

Because Bluem's position in the outsourcing industry was umbilically linked to the U.S. economy, its prospects (and its employee wages) ebbed and flowed in response to developments onshore. Did Rongley feel that his company was contributing to U.S. job loss? At first he offered the customary free-marketeer response: "Market forces will have their way, they are unstoppable. . . . Everyone is going to have to adjust, and whoever adjusts first is going to win." But then he gave his own analysis of the hollowing-out of the IT industry. The real culprit in his view was the H-1B technical visa program, which had depressed IT salaries by bringing in an "artificial supply" of cheap Indian programmers in the 1990s. As a result, he said, American students "chose to become lawyers instead of programmers. Now there's a lower supply of programmers in the U.S. than market conditions require." When the program was cut back, "you then had excess demand without the supply." In Rongley's view, he was "temporarily" and "artificially" filling the gap by providing offshore employees. In other words, his employees were not taking jobs from Americans. At best, they were replacing Indians who had been bodyshopped to the United States through the H-1B program without having a specific job contract.

Rongley was on firm ground in his estimate of the H-1B program. It is widely agreed that employer groups like the Information Technology Association of America conspired to create the illusion of an IT worker shortage in the 1990s.[23] As a result of their lobbying, the government's H-1B program allowed them to enjoy cheaper Indian employees and lower the wage floor. But there was little statistical evidence to support his view of the subsequent depletion of homegrown supply. Even during the tech boom, U.S. technology firms turned their backs on employees approaching middle age, in pursuit of a younger and cheaper workforce. When the Nasdaq crash took its toll on the industry, a large surplus pool of skilled employees was readily available for work. Nor was Rongley's own business model all that different from the employment plan behind the H-1B program. When all was said and done, bodyshopping, permatemping, outsourcing, and offshoring were birds of a feather, each offering a slightly different method for companies to avoid paying a market wage and a responsible amount of social security for their "fully loaded" employees. The root of the problem was much simpler than Rongley's analysis of supply and demand.

In a free-trade economy where capital enjoyed limitless mobility, investors also expected to be able to move their human resources around at will. Whether you relocated to the most convenient employee pool or enlisted the government's aid in importing workers made little difference. China's burgeoning call-center industry was a case in point. Overshadowed by all the attention garnered by India's English-language call-center sector, China was effectively capturing the business of Japanese, Korean, Taiwanese, and Hong Kongese clients. Some local firms also catered to Chinese-speaking customers in the United States. Most of these language centers, along with many other BPO operations for Asian clients, had set up in Dalian, a northeastern port formerly occupied by Japan, which hosted a limited supply of Japanese-speaking Chinese. The region also harbored a large population of ethnic Korean speakers. Shanghai had no such language pool to draw on as a cheap local resource. Shanghainese who could speak these languages would have access to well-paying jobs in businesses that serviced Japanese and Korean clients. Some firms had lured migrant Korean speakers from the north only to find that their accents and communication skills were generally not up to the job of conversing with angry customers. A more ingenious way of importing cut-price native Japanese and Korean speakers had to be found.

Next Focus, a U.S. consultancy based in Asia, had solved the problem by creating a work-and-study program that took advantage of the current vogue among Koreans and Japanese for learning Chinese. Jean Min, a company executive, explained: "Students are brought over for a year. We provide them with the learning opportunities here, while we have them work for us. So they will be learning Chinese half-time as a student, and working half-time as a telephone operator, and we will be providing them with tuition and accommodations and airfare." The students, who weren't quite ready to take their first real jobs, were able to add a crucial business language to their résumés, while the company acquired its perfect workforce—highly dispensable, low-cost employees with native accents, whose vulnerability in a foreign country made them extra-pliable in their employers' hands.

The *Xiaojie* Comes of Age

With the advent of white-collar outsourcing, the legacy of colonialism on the world's language map surfaced as a major factor in the global redistribution of jobs and capital investment. Formerly it had made little difference which language was spoken by offshore workers in the export assembly platforms of the world. In fact, it was generally better for business if workers could not understand the language of their employers; their workplace rights and the end products of their labor were obscured to them as a result. The new kind of white-collar outsourcing was quite a different matter. Countries like Singapore, Malaysia, the Philippines, and Hong Kong, but especially India, were in the ambivalent position of taking economic advantage of their previous encounters with Anglo rule and cultural influence. The customer-service call centers, for example, depended on an available army of cheap but accomplished English speakers. But even factory technicians increasingly had to be able to read the foreign language instructions in operating manuals for imported technology. The English language was becoming a source of pure labor power. Mainland Chinese were at a disadvantage in this regard ("They think in Chinese even when they speak in English" was a common managerial lament), but they were taking herculean steps to close the gap. Widespread local government campaigns of bilingual education were being designed to produce a nation of English-speaking infants.[24] The crusade had gone so far that it sparked a backlash from nationalists. The huge public investments in English-language training, they pointed out, were unnecessary for the bulk of the population, and the mother tongues, far more venerable languages, were being neglected.[25] Ammunition for their cause was supplied by extreme anecdotes about South Koreans who submitted their children to surgery that snipped the membrane under the tongue in the belief that near flawless English would result.[26]

For a decade and a half after the reforms kicked in, English skills were an automatic passport for educated youth to move into foreign firms—among the more lucrative and attractive reaches of the Chinese economy. Those who made the biggest impression on popular culture were the "white-collar misses" (*xiaojie*) of the 1990s. These were secretarial employees of foreign firms in urban centers, and they became famous for their fashion sense, their cosmopolitan airs, and the social independence afforded by their salaries. In Shanghai, as James Farrer argues, they were "the newest incarnation of the Shanghai Girl," heiresses to the legacy of the sexually liberated and "thoroughly modern" Jazz Age film actresses (and prostitutes) of Old Shanghai. Partly as a result of that legacy, Shanghai had retained its reputation of being a "women's city," where the strong will of women held dominion. Indeed, as Farrer points out, the prevailing stereotype of the weaker Shanghainese male was that of the fully domesticated husband, coveted by every Chinese woman, who spent all his spare time shopping, running chores, and minding the child.[27]

Corporate version of a famous statue of the
liberated "Shanghai Girl"

Foreign managers needed local floor managers to supervise their Chinese workforces. They also needed administrative aides—eyes and ears—who could mediate daily life in China for them. The latter, who were entirely indispensable, invariably started out as personal assistants and moved into managerial positions. Here is a typical job description (taken from the popular *zhaopin* job website): "You'll provide general routine and nonroutine clerical help for your assigned area . . . along with the 1,001 things that are vital to the smooth running of our business. As you progress through the experience levels, you'll use your knowledge of business issues, key customers, company practices, procedures and processes to coordinate and manage processes, projects and, at team leader level, people."

My visits to companies were almost always arranged and handled by a ranking office *xiaojie,* and I regularly met and interviewed administrators who had been promoted from *xiaojie* positions. Their career stories were a poignant archaeological journey through reform-era China: "I was a *xiaojie* when it meant something positive," recalled Wang Ying, a manager at a British composites company. "We had respect, because we had been selected from many applicants, and so we were proud of the name. Then they made a popular TV show about us, though I didn't do any of the wild things they put in the show. After that, people used *xiaojie* to refer to something less polite." The *xiaojie* appellation was her reform-era generation's first exposure to a gender-specific label in the workplace. "Before that, everyone was called *shifu* [artisan or comrade], whether they were male or female, young or old. As *xiaojie,* we stood out, we were the Chinese face of the foreign-invested enterprises before they started to localize everybody, so we were women with a new kind of status."

The prestige, she recounted, was worth savoring for a while, but as soon as the firms started turning their expat positions over to locals, she noticed that women, in general, did not enjoy equal pay. Even more obvious, however, was the bamboo ceiling, "though no one," she observed, "really acknowledges it. But Westerners, or ABCs, or returnees with a foreign education, occupy the higher slots, and if these jobs are converted, and turned over to Chinese, it will be at a much lower salary. It's not a glass ceiling, men are affected by it too. Since we're not allowed to compare salaries [she had been told that, at foreign companies, employees would be fired if they told each other their salaries], there's nothing we can do about it."

Wang was in a good position to compare job experiences, since she had worked at a state-owned enterprise and a joint venture before joining her current firm, which was a wholly owned foreign enterprise. Each had its distinct work culture. She had come of age at a time when students were still allocated majors on the basis of their performance on entrance exams. On the strength of her degree in inorganic chemistry, which she "hated from day one," she was allotted a technical job at a state-owned electronics enterprise. On the job, she was only expected to work for a couple of hours a day ("three people's tasks are done by five people" was the popular saying), so she had lots of time to fulfill the social tasks required of her elected role as the director of the company's trade union: showing movies, visiting female employees who had given birth, attending funerals of former workers, organizing holiday parties and social outings, and resolving family quarrels of union members. "We did not bargain over wages, no one did. Your salary was based on your educational background and how many years you have worked, and that was it. If you worked for five years, your salary was 100 RMB, if you worked ten years, 120 RMB. It didn't matter if you did more work or less work, or nothing at all, your earnings were the same. So why bother to work really hard?" The question was in no way rhetorical. Wang had been raised to value learning, and she viewed her work experience primarily as an opportunity to learn from others.

When the company bought a production line from the United States, and needed language support, her command of English made her indispensable, and a VIP. Once this advantage became apparent, it was a short step for her to move on, this time to a joint venture between Chicago investors and a Chinese auto parts company, where she was an assistant to the general manager: "I think my working efficiency improved a lot, simply because every day I had so much more work to do. Also, I felt I was given the chance to make some decisions by myself, which my boss encouraged. Not like in the Chinese factory, where I knew every day what I would have to do, and none of it involved any fresh thinking, or new stuff that makes your life colorful." Wang neatly described the difference in management style and status of her respective bosses. In the previous company, "employees were vocal, but not because they wanted to improve something. They just wanted to let the boss know they felt uncomfortable, so they just complained. But in the joint venture company, if they saw something which could be improved, then they reported it to the boss, and efficiency got better." Of course, they could also be fired, so they were careful about what came out of their mouths: "Whatever the boss said was the last word." The manager of the state company had no such authority, and was often the target of contempt or personal threats. "Once," she reported, "I saw workers beat the director."

So, too, the union was even weaker at the joint venture. "I never heard of a union settling a labor dispute," she recalled. "Union chairs are usually 'nice guys,' and they always side more with the bosses than with the workers. They never argue with the boss, and they try to persuade the workers to accept the situation. Chinese also have difficulty with direct conflict. They will try to avoid it to save face, or they may say something three days later. This is not good for a real labor union that has to be critical of management." With her new employer, where she ran the office, Wang had mastered Western management skills enough to feel that the Chinese traits made for less efficiency in business, though she herself believed that "face" was a more humane way of dealing with people. "I appreciate both ways," she said, yet, like most of my interviewees, she found it hard, but necessary, to "balance the Western and the Chinese ways." Indeed, while foreign managers discouraged Chinese characteristics like face and *guanxi* (the art of personal connections) in most skilled positions, these traits were considered somewhat advantageous in sales, marketing, and other client-facing jobs. As Wang observed, "customers need to be deferred to, and Chinese have a long training in such skills. We know how to make people feel important and welcomed."

As far as office administration went, Wang felt that women still had a big advantage in the Shanghai area. Their people skills were more developed, and if they had the ability to make foreign managers comfortable, from a cultural perspective, they also met the more traditional gender standards of Chinese managers. The onward march of localization meant that some of them could climb quicker and higher. Among the younger administrators I interviewed, I found that the choice of working for an enterprising manager was more and more preferable to the lure of a brand-name firm. Foreign businesses had been around for long enough that certain individuals now had a local reputation from their own entrepreneurial profile. Jenny Lee, for example, chose a position at a Chinese-American start-up over a job at GM, because she "wanted a shortcut to success by learning from a successful boss. I can't afford to wait for promotions, I should take the knowledge I can get from my boss and use it to make my own way."

With fighting words like these, she spoke for a more confident, even aggressive, generation than Wang's. Yet her plucky attitude, she explained, was entirely a result of peer pressure or circumstance, and not part of what she considered her own personality. "I am not at all interested in materialism, but everyone I know is very anxious about the future. They feel that the opportunities maybe won't be there for long. Perhaps it's because of Chinese history, or maybe because companies move around so quickly. It's already much more difficult now for my friends to get a good job. Competing ruthlessly," she felt, was "not how we want to live, we want more balance and harmony." Job-hopping was no less prevalent among office employees like herself than in other sectors. According to one survey, a third of all office workers moved their jobs in 2003, 21 percent moving twice, and over 8 percent more than twice.[28]

Unlike most of my interviewees, Lee, a native Shanghainese in her early twenties, had been to some of the city's famous nightclubs. With her 6,000 RMB ($725) monthly salary, she clearly had been able to indulge her eye for fashion. On the day that I talked to her, she was wearing a flat tweed cap and a sumptuously ornate cashmere shawl. But, like Sean Chen, her outward display of up-to-date taste concealed a distaste for the quicksilver currents of consumer modernity. "I'm not an 'in' person," she assured me. "To me, modern means superficial, it's not the real me. I prefer writing my own fiction to reading all the glossy magazines, and I'm happiest when I'm doing traditional Chinese painting." As for China, her patriotism was unequivocal—"of course I love my country"—but she felt no personal obligation to contribute to nation-building. "The government gave my parents a blueprint for the future and then the Cultural Revolution destroyed it. The promise was broken, and I can no longer trust them." Nor did she see any reason to trust an employer, especially foreign firms that had used her city as a way station. "We can only afford to be loyal to our family," she joked. "This is the story of Shanghainese, what we learned from our history."

Lee had ample reason to be skeptical. Urban Chinese like her had been asked to reprogram their attitudes to work four times in the past half-century: first, to direct their minds toward serving the new communist state; second, to reduce the gap with the peasantry; third, to question the authority of their bosses during the Cultural Revolution; and, most recently, to learn the ways of Western business. Given this experience of rapid changes in orientation, who could question their caution, or the instinct to feather their own beds? They were serving now as foot soldiers of globalization, but this did not mean they were blinded by necessity. On the contrary, working on the value chain gang was a way of preserving their own will and their separate sense of destiny.

Mister Tata Comes to Town

In the years after the 2001 recession, the bulk of white-collar outsourcing from the United States and the United Kingdom made its way to India, especially in IT-enabled services (ITeS). This new investment flow was clearly driven by the corporate bottom line, but it also served Washington's geopolitical designs. When it came to a choice between New Delhi and Beijing, the former was much more likely to be a compliant U.S. ally. Among hard-line neoconservatives, China was considered a strategic rival that had to be contained by encirclement. When Secretary of State Condoleezza Rice declared, during a visit to Delhi in March 2005, that "the U.S. policy was to help India become a major world power in the twenty-first century," the clear implication was that one of the two emerging Asian mega-economies would be used to counterbalance the influence of the other.

No member of India's elite was likely to miss the significance of this policy reorientation. Rivalry with China had been a regional way of life for several decades, and had lately become a source of acute economic anxiety. But the outcome of Washington's wooing of India was by no means guaranteed. Just two months after Rice's declaration, the announcement that China and India would, for the first time ever, hold joint military maneuvers was an indication that the China containment policy might have a rocky future.[1] Indeed, a new era of Sino-Indian cooperation had already been marked by extensive bilateral trade relations in several industry sectors. By the time of Rice's declaration, trade between the two Asian countries had increased to $13.6 billion annually, and both governments were busy signing new agreements that would open up new sectors to commerce.

This trend had even surfaced in ITeS, the main target of foreign investment within India's economy. After the first flush of the ITeS boom, the industry talk in India was all about the coming rivalry with China. Indeed, in the summer of 2003, a research report from the respected Gartner consultancy estimated that China would outstrip India's global lead in software development and ITeS by 2006, pulling in up to $27 billion in business.[2] This mercurial growth rate (at more than 600 percent annually) would apparently be stimulated by China's entrepreneurial returnees, the nation's accession to the WTO, and its hosting of the 2008 Olympics.

Predictions like this were guaranteed to generate alarm among Indians accustomed to viewing their Chinese neighbors as deadly rivals in the military sphere. NASSCOM, the national trade association for India's software companies, took the opportunity to conduct research of its own. It concluded that "the China threat" was real, but that it represented a clear business opportunity—a "China challenge"—for its member companies, among them some of the world's leading software service firms. After all, the Gartner report had also estimated that Indian companies could eventually control as much as 40 percent of China's ITeS trade.[3] Part of NASSCOM's job was to encourage an Indian invasion, and the results were quickly felt in Shanghai. All of the major Indian IT companies—Satyam, Mphasis, Wipro, NIIT, Infosys, and TCS—flocked to open offshore offices in a sector that had already attracted such U.S. multinationals as IBM, HP, EDS, and Bearing Point. The Chinese government did its part, establishing a Sino-Indian Cooperative Office to ease the way. The rush to set up shop inevitably added a new round to an old spectator sport, devoted to comparisons between the world's two most populous countries.[4]

Both nations, after all, had broken free from colonial dominion within two years of each other in the late 1940s, and each had taken drastic steps to reduce its economic dependence on foreign capital. At

Indian IT managers outside Tiramisu restaurant,
Shanghai Pudong Software Park

the time they embarked on their own distinct paths to modernization,
both countries had similar demographic imbalances between huge,
impoverished rural populations and much smaller, developed urban
populations. Their respective efforts at nation-building were driven,
for several decades, by state-led industrialization and autarkic policies
aimed at import substitution. Each had recently been opened up to
foreign investment and trade liberalization—China beginning in the
1980s, and India since 1991, when over-indebtedness effectively placed
the latter's economy under the jurisdiction of the World Bank and the
IMF. For most of this history, however, India had trailed China in its
record of achievement in public health, life expectancy, literacy, education, land reform, poverty reduction, and real GDP per capita. In
almost every index of development, the communist state registered
better results than the multiparty democracy of its neighbor.

Since its emergence in the mid-1980s, India's software services
industry had made its mark on the global information economy, yet

the country barely had a national IT infrastructure to speak of. Computer penetration was very shallow outside of the big cities and the high-tech-friendly states of Maharashtra, Gujarat, and Andhra Pradesh. By contrast, China's installed PC base was three times as large, and its Internet usage was eight times greater. China was already the world's third-largest technology hardware supplier, after the United States and Japan; it had moved aggressively into microchip manufacturing, and its government had poured money into a national infrastructure that extended to all the provincial cities. This dynamic combination sorely tempted not just foreign investors in the IT sector, but also those in technology-driven manufacturing. China's networks were uneven, and its rulers' censorious instinct to retain control over the country's intranet—the "Great Firewall of China"—slowed the data flow along its backbones. In principle, the government could sniff every Internet packet of information entering or leaving the country. But, in almost every other respect, it was a more reliable technical environment than India for the kind of global communications that offshore operations required.[5]

Hardware was not everything, however. The Indian software industry was driven in part by native innovation, and its national boosters never missed an opportunity to promote the ingenuity and brainpower of their engineers as the secret of its sauce. "Building a mind," as one Indian IT manager put it to me, "takes much longer than building an infrastructure. In India, we have built a human infrastructure."

This human infrastructure was also cheaper, at least for the time being. The going rate for engineers in the big Indian cities was lower than in their counterparts in East China. This was not a widely known fact, and the international business press, accustomed to seeing China in general as the lowest wage floor, regularly reported the opposite.[6] By contrast, the most common estimate of the cost of manufacturing labor in India was more than 60 percent higher than in China. Even in the ITeS sector, knowledge about such wage comparisons was spread unevenly. Yet in the first few years of the twenty-first century, competition between these two low-wage countries began to emerge as a factor in shaping how and where white-collar jobs were finding their way to Asia.

Inevitably, the rivalry showed up in the workplace as a way of putting pressure on employees. In India, for example, employees were told they must work harder or they would lose their jobs, like everyone else, to China. In the IT companies operating in Shanghai, I often found that employees were told they must work harder, because their Indian counterparts were paid less. "Every so often, my manager reminds me that the company pays me more than it pays a programmer in Mumbai," reported an employee at one of Shanghai's Indian offices. "I am sure he thinks it will make me work harder. And, to be honest, it probably does." Employers had long used such intimidation to speed up the work rate, or win concessions, in labor-intensive industries. Now these threats were being applied in white-collar services that were split between different locations. The outcome was bound to have a decisive impact on the division of labor all across Asia. It was difficult to see how it would not also affect the balance of power in the region, endlessly complicating U.S. realpolitik aimed at courting India and containing China.

The Ghost of the Merchant Princes

The Spring Festival season was officially over, and a mild breeze from the Yellow Sea was threading its way through Pudong's corporate towers and across the Huangpu River when we boarded the cruise boat for the Tata welcoming party. Jumbo neon hoardings on our side of the river—Epson and TDK—jeered loudly at the brand names on the Pudong side—Canon and NEC. Our guest on board was a mogul whose name was itself a household brand. Ratan Tata, the genteel chairman of the Tata Group, India's leading industrial conglomerate, had come to Shanghai. So had the group's CEO, and a bevy of executive officers from the Asia-Pacific region. Existing and potential clients of the firm had been invited, along with a sprinkling of bankers and business bigwigs. A select group of ranking company engineers filled out the guest list. The Indian consul-general and the director of the China branch of the Confederation of Indian Industry were gracious co-hosts, the former speaking Chinese to whoever was listening, the latter welcoming each visitor on board with regal warmth. From their perspective at least, a visit from India's most famous businessman was not unlike a state occasion. Indeed, it had been foreshadowed by Indian prime minister Atal Vajpayee's landmark visit, in June 2003, to ink a new milestone agreement on economic and political cooperation between the two countries.[7]

Tata came to East China to cement Tata Consultancy Services' (TCS) ties in the local IT sector, though, like Vajpayee, he had a diplomat's itinerary that included calls on the vice-mayor of Shanghai, officials in Beijing, and the mayor of Hangzhou, who conferred on him the status of honorary economic adviser to the city. Indeed, his brief remarks on board the cruise boat had an ambassadorial ring. The world's two population giants, we were told, had a unique opportunity to work together as a powerful new force in the global economy. This was a line Tata had been pitching recently in a little more detail: "I ask myself quite often what would happen if India and China could themselves create an economic bloc of their own with two billion people," he had told a CNBC reporter, adding, "China being the factory of the world and India perhaps being the IT or high-end services of the world, could [we] together do something that would be formidable?" To Chinese ears, it may not have been the most flattering proposition—India would provide the brains, and China the brawn—which was probably why we were spared this particular version at the Shanghai event.

Later that week, in the course of a long interview on CCTV's *Dialogue* show, Tata reiterated that Indian companies "look at China as an opportunity, not as a competitor." Lamenting that Indian labor laws had been an "abnormal manifestation," making it "difficult for companies to modernize and be globally competitive," he also expressed regret that Indian businesspeople "pay a price for our type of democracy"; it is a "great drag on investment," he explained. His inference was that no such obstacles to business existed in China, where politicians could clear any path with minimal resistance, and where regulatory laws were all too lightly implemented. Tata's call to work together was not the only one in the media that week. Brazil's iconoclastic president, Luiz Inácio Lula da Silva, had just returned from Delhi, where he had been pushing India to join with China and Brazil in forming their own economic bloc. Lula's blueprint for cooperation was driven by a political agenda for the global South to break free of the North's economic stranglehold. By contrast, Tata's vision for China and India was one of sheer economic expedience—let's make a deal.

As our boat plied the river waters, the managers and bankers started networking on these deals, exchanging cards and shuffling around the long buffet table. The lesser ranks filled their plates and sat down around the tables on either side. Presently we slid past the floodlit buildings of the Bund, the original site of the godowns and wharves where Ratan's ancestor Jamsetji Tata, the founder of the Tata empire, had entered the China trade 145 years before. The story of his exploits offers an instructive lesson in the history of trade between India and China.

Setting up branches of the family's trading firm in Shanghai and Hong Kong had been Jamsetji Tata's first business venture in 1859.[8] Subsequently the Tata house maintained a mercantile presence in Shanghai, where a small but influential Parsi community flourished until the late 1940s. The Parsis claimed descent from the fabled group of Zoroastrian Persians who fled the Muslim conquest of their homeland to exile in Gujarat several centuries earlier. In time, most of the community moved to Bombay, and after a period of competition with the East India Company, many of them took on roles as mercantile intermediaries between the British and Indians. They were thus in a position to profit royally from opium exports to China, both before and after the British moved to control the trade.[9] Although he came too late to match the opium profits of the other Parsi "merchant princes," such as Cowasji Jehangir and Jamsetji Jeejeebhoy, Tata's ventures in China earned the family firm a tidy sum from selling the narcotic. A greater fortune came from speculation in Bombay's cotton boom during the U.S. Civil War, when India temporarily replaced the American South as the chief supplier of cotton for Lancashire mills.

Jamsetji Tata's most significant act, however, was to bring back some dismantled textile machinery from Manchester and resurrect it in 1874 as India's first fully mechanized textile mill, the Central India Spinning, Weaving & Manufacturing Company. This was the origin of the Tata reputation for promoting native self-reliance in industry. After all, the future of a free India would rest in part on the building of indigenous manufactures, and the house of Tata was ever in the forefront of this endeavor. Tata's second-most-heroicized act was the building of Bombay's opulent Taj Mahal Hotel in 1903. The formation of Tata Iron and Steel in 1907 pushed the country into the steel age, and was followed by the firm's industrial pioneering in almost every sector of the economy: electric and power utilities, consumer goods, printing, chemicals, air travel, locomotives, cosmetics, engineering, tea, consulting, publishing, computer hardware and software, vans and trucks, telecom, and IT services. In 1998, the company launched the Indica, India's first indigenously (*swadeshi*) designed, developed, and manufactured car. It is safe to say that no other company anywhere has dominated the history of its national industry as the house of Tata has done.

Their record contrasts with that of their great rivals in British Bombay, the Sassoon family (the "Rothschilds of the East"), whose flight from the Middle East was more recent. Among the Baghdadi Jewish traders who left the rotting Ottoman Empire for the Asian hubs of the British Empire in the early to mid-nineteenth century, the Sassoons proved the most successful. They established commercial branches all over Asia, and had a hand in virtually every cargo of silk, spice, wool, silver, and, above all, opium, that crisscrossed the region. After the Scottish firm of Jardine Matheson relinquished its dominance in the opium trade, the Sassoons, along with their Parsi partners, exercised a near monopoly. Indeed, the Sassoon name was stamped on the bags of opium that Commissioner Lin Tse-hsu seized on Canton's wharves in 1839, sparking the onset of the Opium Wars. The Sassoon trading operations would play a significant intermediary role in the subsequent forced "opening" of China by Britain and other Western powers. Trading from its Bombay portal, the Sassoon Dock, the family amassed one of India's largest fortunes. Yet the fourth-generation heir, Victor Sassoon, elected to move the company base to Shanghai in 1929 in anticipation of easier profits. The firm's textile mills in Bombay were beset with strikes and worker agitation, and Sassoon was faced with the prospect of ever stricter factory laws to regulate working conditions. In

Shanghai's International Settlement, there was little prospect of such legislation being passed, nor indeed any regulations that would put a damper on profits. The Settlement's Municipal Council even rejected a 1925 proposal for a law prohibiting the routine employment of child labor (for up to sixteen hours a day).[10] Nor would Sassoon be subject to British taxation in the extraterritorial business haven of Shanghai.[11]

For those who think of corporate flight as a relatively recent development, Sassoon's transfer of operations to Shanghai was a transparent example of an employer moving overseas to avoid any restrictions on his ability to freely exploit labor. In a letter explaining his departure from India, he explained: "China offers a better field to the foreigner because the Nanking government realizes the necessity for foreign finance."[12] Indeed, by the 1920s, Old Shanghai was nothing if not a premier offshore site. The foreign powers had seized the right to open factories after Japan officially extracted the privilege through the 1895 Treaty of Shimonoseki. China's first and biggest industrial center quickly sprang up in Shanghai in the areas north of the Suzhou Creek and east of the Huangpu River. Under treaty-port provisions, the products of the city's foreign-owned factories enjoyed the same low tariffs extended to Western imports, even though they were manufactured in China itself. Labor laws and workplace regulations were nonexistent, and compradores could take advantage of an inexhaustible supply of rural laborers, many of them indentured, streaming into the shanty-towns of Zhabei, Hongkou, and Pudong, or the sampan colonies along the Suzhou Creek. Though it had many other infamous competitors, Shanghai could claim some of the world's worst working conditions for the 200,000 workers who sweated their lives away inside the factories, while even more coolies worked the wharves, warehouses, and rickshaw circuits until they dropped.[13] It was no coincidence that resistance to these conditions on the part of China's first proletariat helped give birth to the Chinese Communist Party in Shanghai in 1921, and fueled its rise through a series of large industrial strikes.[14]

While the firm invested in some factory holdings, Sassoon quickly saw that the best returns lay in real estate, and he rapidly amassed a property empire. In the rosy annals of Old Shanghai, he is most lionized for the erection of the Chicago School–style Cathay Hotel (now the Peace Hotel) on a prime Bund site at the corner of Nanjing Road. Much like Tata's Taj Mahal Hotel, it was a highly visible representation of the outsider's triumph in a society of insiders. Like the Tatas, the Sassoons (along with the other prominent Baghdadi Jews and Parsis) were self-styled entrepreneurs, even though they emulated the colonial's ways—some even picked up British titles along the road. So, too, their roles in the business world were quite apart from the Chinese compradores who guaranteed the squeeze of daily profit to the foreign taipans, or even from the native entrepreneurs who put up half the capital for China's first joint ventures. For one thing, their non-insider status obliged them to redistribute a portion of their wealth through a steady stream of benefactions, both to their own co-ethnic communities and to the public at large. As a result, the Sassoon name could be found attached to a long list of synagogues, public buildings, education and welfare foundations, and other charitable institutions both in Shanghai and India. The Tata name is even more widespread today among charitable foundations in India, many of which benefit handsomely from annual Tata stock dividends. This philanthropic activity was quite typical of the noblesse oblige of "benevolent capitalists" who amassed wealth from nineteenth-century industrialization. But in the case of the Parsi and Jewish entrepreneurs, their social standing as outsiders only reinforced the obligation.

Hotels like the Cathay and the Taj Mahal advertised their respective owners' proven record in serving as successful intermediaries between powerful Westerners. As social hot spots, they were ideal locations for hosting the needs of foreign elites and for lubricating the circulation of their investments. When first the Japanese and then the Communists took control of the city, the Cathay's main bar, the Horse and Hound, became a refuge for throngs of Shanghainese lamenting their upcoming exile, and the loss of their local fortunes. Sassoon himself soon joined their number, moving his assets to the Bahamas (in anticipation of another property empire), and quipping, with pitch-perfect colonial insouciance, "I gave up on India, and China gave up on me."

The Sassoons never returned, but the Tata name, like others from the old days, reappeared in Shanghai. Now a player in a new kind of global trade—supplying software services to multinationals—the firm would once again prove a reliable intermediary for powerful foreigners looking to extract profit from Chinese labor, and perhaps even the domestic China market. This time around, some of the most important clients hailed from Asia itself, and Japan in particular. But Indian entrepreneurs would be approaching with some caution. After all, there was a long tradition of mutual distrust between the two neighbors, which came to a head in a full-blown 1962 border war. The wounds had only recently closed over, and Indian companies that entered China were virtually obliged to help jump-start the renewal of diplomatic relations. As far as trading volume went, software was not the most important industry sector; iron ore, steel, and pharmaceuticals accounted for a greater share of the $13.6 billion bilateral trade between India and China in 2004 (making the latter India's second-largest trading partner). But the names of Tata and the other Indian ITeS companies that came to Shanghai had a luminary ring. They brought the allure of high tech, they generated headlines, and they helped to embellish Shanghai's status as an information industry hub.

The Boom in India

In their day, the purveyors of opium had stirred up no end of revulsion. In the United Kingdom especially, the public outcry against the "poison trade" was heard consistently from the 1840s until 1913, when an international campaign finally pressured the British government to prohibit its nationals from importing the narcotic. The more recent wave of business process outsourcing to India sparked a different kind of revulsion, some of it with racist overtones, among service-sector employees faced with job loss. This response had a backdrop in the IT sector, where, throughout the 1990s, Indian engineers who had come to the United States on H-1B visas (for skilled professionals) were subject to a variety of abuses and forms of discrimination. Because companies employed them at reduced salaries, they were invariably regarded, and treated, by fellow employees in a manner akin to labor scabs.

The engineers themselves were often swindled by employment agents (bodyshoppers) who promised them the world when they were recruited in India. When they arrived in the States they were often assigned to the worst jobs: graveyard shifts, no overtime pay, and demeaning office tasks. Since deportation was the potential cost of protest, their passive acceptance of these conditions was the most likely response. This quietist attitude hardly endeared them to U.S. colleagues weaned on the tech industry's house style of fearless open speech.

When the IT outsourcing boom took off, Indian employees in the United States had even more hostility to contend with.[15] But the brunt of the ill will was borne by workers on the subcontinent itself. Much of the resentment arose from the fact that some of the jobs being transferred were top-end positions. Almost overnight, it seemed, Indian programmers, engineers, and designers were doing R&D for Western technology firms in India. In the IT sector alone, R&D outsourcing was estimated to grow by 32 percent annually, from $1.3 billion in 2003 to $9.1 billion in 2010.[16] A similar pattern soon emerged in other professional fields; Indian accountants were preparing U.S. tax returns, financial analysts were writing brokerage reports for Wall Street, doctors were offering diagnoses and second opinions for HMOs, medical and drug companies were conducting trials and lab research, and lawyers were providing all sorts of counsel. These professional services made up a knowledge process outsourcing market for India that, in one estimate, would grow from $720 million in 2004 to $12 billion in 2010.[17]

But the bulk of the new jobs called on Indian employees to perform back-office work—routine housekeeping duties for multinationals, such as processing applications and bills, preparing invoices and payrolls, tending to accounts, or responding to a host of customer inquiries. Out of all proportion, however, it was call-center employees who attracted the most press and the most enmity. Their jobs, which paid from one-eighth to one-tenth of the going rate in the United States, required them to have direct contact with American and British customers who often personally resented their domestic inquiries being redirected to a voice on the line that was thousands of miles away. It only sharpened the sense of outrage that the voices had been accent-trained to emulate the regional twang of customers (to assuage local racism), including up-to-date slang, or that employees often had a better grasp of the affairs of the home country than the caller did.

In India, the call-center jobs were promoted as plum opportunities for fresh college graduates with a yearning to become world citizens. The workplaces were advertised as ultramodern, dot-commish fun-houses, buzzing with clever hipsters—a world apart from that of the employees onshore who were vacating the jobs. A typical job ad (from Daksh eServices) for Customer Care Specialists, and Voice and Accent Trainers, offered applicants the chance to be a " 'designer' of your own future" by "interacting with the finest companies in the world," in an environment of "fun@work" which included "ultra-cool cafeterias, attractive incentives, stress-busting games rooms." Such jobs paid well above the average salaries for white-collar trainees, and they had a celebrity cachet. In select urban centers, college graduates took the night shift to answer calls about U.S. infomercials, offering information and advice about diet pills and George Foreman grills. Delinquent customers were urged to pay their bills, and were invited, in flattened American accents, to Have a Wonderful Day. Employees were also obliged to master the British obsession with weather details, and some were encouraged to invent personal family histories for themselves to garnish the customer-service relationship. Yet the conditions were far from ideal. Though this was a service industry, which required quality social skills, and a certain level of computer literacy, the organization of labor on the job was brutally industrial. Employers preferred rapid turnover to ensure a docile workforce, and so job attrition was sky-high. Career paths in the industry were non-existent, and stress on the job acquired some notoriety.[18]

Most striking, however, was the controversy over the industrial personality required of call-center employees. For many customers, the employees' mimicry of accents was perceived as dishonest, even offensive. To Indian critics, the mimicry was a bitter reminder of a colonial legacy, most infamously summarized in Thomas Macauley's 1835

"Minute on Indian Education." Announcing that it was the responsibility of the British colonial authorities "to educate a people who cannot at present be educated by means of their mother-tongue," Macauley proposed the cultivation of a dual identity among Indians who could act as reliable intermediaries in this endeavor: "We must at present do our best to form a class who may be interpreters between us and the millions whom we govern; a class of persons, Indian in blood and colour, but English in taste, in opinions, in morals, and in intellect."[19]

The call-center mimics were the latest in a long line of Macauley's dual-identity Indians, obliged to take on a Western voice and personality as a condition of career advancement. All over the world, access to English language skills and Western business culture had become a prerequisite for youth seeking employment in the globalized sectors of the economy. But the ignominy of the situation in India was an especially sensitive topic. Critics of corporate globalization, like Arundhati Roy, argued that the impersonation showed "how easily an ancient civilization can be made to abase itself completely. . . . Sushma becomes Suzie, Govind becomes Jerry, Adavani becomes Andy." Commenting on the nativism espoused by the right-wing Hindu nationalists in power, she described the call centers' mimicry of the West as the flip side of their religious fundamentalism.[20]

As the outcry increased in volume, call centers began to shift away from the policy of training employees in national accents. The new preference was for neutral, or "global English," accents. This had two advantages to employers. One was to cut the cost of voice training, the other was to ensure more internal mobility for staff who were increasingly required to take calls from different parts of the world, as business from new regional markets poured in. For employees, the shift removed the indignity of having to pretend they were speaking from Baltimore or Birmingham instead of Chennai. Yet was the mimicry qualitatively more degrading than any other service-sector job that required some kind of performance? After all, more and more in-person service positions demanded a training in emotional labor or theatrical presentation to enhance the personality of employees on the job.[21]

If the result was humiliating for college-educated youth in the Indian call centers, the employees who were losing the call-center jobs in developed nations experienced a different kind of humbling. The town where I'd grown up in lowland Scotland was a case in point. It had been in the forefront of industrialization in the nineteenth century, and was one of the first in the region to feel the impact of deindustrialization. At one time or another, firms had flourished in shipbuilding, potterymaking, engineering, ceramics, ropemaking, textiles, glassmaking, and brewing. The town was also surrounded by several coal-mining centers in an industry that was in decline by the 1960s, but still holding on. By the time I came of age, the majority of manufacturing jobs were gone, and to this day, little has come along to take their place. In the early 1990s, the call centers arrived, when there were few job ads for anything else. Skilled and semi-skilled workers learned how to answer the phones, with patience and obligatory good humor, but they hailed from communities where pride derived from making things, and it was almost impossible to feel comfortable in these new jobs. Consequently, when the call centers were shuttered, there was some satisfaction mixed in with the despair at the loss of a livelihood. This ambivalent reaction was common all across the rust belts of Western Europe and North America, where customer-service jobs had, for a brief while, succeeded the collapse of manufacturing and extractive industry.

On the Indian side, the BPO boom created hundreds of thousands of jobs almost overnight, with millions more forecast to come their way. Employment levels in the software industry had taken almost twenty years to reach the half-million mark, so this new job growth was mercurial. Even more uncommonly, the resulting controversy about outsourcing put India directly in the limelight, where it was unaccustomed to be. That celebrity came at a time when the national economy was enjoying up to 8 percent annual growth, and finance performance indicators had made it the latest hot spot in Asia. For the ITeS companies that raked in the outsourcing contracts, the boom was evidence of their providential position in the global economy. The ruling Bharatiya Janata Party government hired slick advertisers to concoct a national brand, India Shining, to capture the mood, and staked a large part of its political reputation on the growth in ITeS.

The vast majority of the country's population lacked basic literacy, yet India Shining's boosters had designated it as the knowledge society of the near future. This claim rested primarily on the high quality of the nation's engineers, on the strength of its training institutes—the justly famous Institutes of Information Technology—and on the reputation and growth of its software and ITeS companies. Indeed, of the world's software firms that had attained the industry's highest certification—CMM 5—half were from India. Yet their impact on the domestic economy was skin-deep and, in any case, was concentrated in a few urban havens—Mumbai, Bangalore, Hyderabad, and Delhi-Noida-Gurgaon. Eighty percent of India's software business was entirely dependent on exports—"end-to-end solutions" for overseas clients—and virtually all of its IT hardware was imported. By contrast, China's state managers were systematically throwing resources into creating an extensive national IT infrastructure, and were using every means to attract, absorb, and develop the technologies and skills needed to exploit it fully.

In common with China, the ballyhoo about the new outsourced jobs overshadowed the story about the millions of Indians who had become unemployed as a result of trade liberalization. Privatization of the public sector, supervised by the Minister of Disinvestment, Arun Shourie, a former executive with the World Bank, took a drastic toll. National assets built up over years with public money were sold off without public consent to the highest or, more often, the most corrupt bidder. Land reforms were reversed, and farmers stood by helplessly as foreign multinationals established control over crop patterns and seeds, patenting plants that had been indigenous staple foods for centuries.[22] Artisans and workers saw their work being casualized, and the informal sector mushroomed. Indeed, ever since India opened up its economy in 1991, its growth pattern in inequality had matched that of other countries forced into export-oriented development. In the cities that serviced global corporations, pockets of wealth had become increasingly visible, supporting skyrocketing real estate prices. As the informal economy flourished, the migration to these cities of desperate rural people, joining the plight of workers laid off from traditional state-supported industries, created a vast population of immiserated poor. Over half of Mumbai was soon consumed by slums, largely abandoned by public agencies whose service budgets had been slashed, while the information-rich basked in the warmth of India Shining's embrace of corporate globalization. The result was a familiar footprint that roving multinationals were leaving on selected national economies.

In the wake of the tech recession, India, like the United States, experienced a jobless recovery. Corporate profits and GDP figures rebounded and the service sector sizzled, thanks to all the offshore contracts. But the "transition" to a liberalized economy hurt many more than it helped. Only half of the 212 million workers between the ages of fourteen and twenty-five had jobs, and suicides among the victims of liberalization, especially farmers, became quite common.[23] Some regional states scrambled to produce the kind of workforce demanded by BPO work, devoting more and more educational resources to matching that employment profile. The result was limited spending on infrastructure and even less on raising the basic literacy and living standards of the general population. In the race to shine as a knowledge society, "knowledge" was defined narrowly as the kind of skill set that could be packaged and transmitted as a profitable export commodity.[24] Excluded from this definition were other, more sustainable, knowledge systems of a traditional society—techniques, beliefs, and values that had served peasants, artisans, and workers as survival mechanisms for generations.

Those who had been left behind or excluded got their chance to deliver a verdict in the general election of 2004. The Bharatiya Janata Party was voted out by a sizable majority of the nation's masses who had not benefited in the least from the free-market gospel of India Shining. The most significant losses came in the southern states of Tamil Nadu and Andhra Pradesh, which had been foremost in promoting an "IT revolution" sparked by the wooing of foreign technology firms. N. Chandrababu Naidu, the chief minister of Andhra Pradesh, who was best known for courting the multinational corporations and for pushing the software export economy at the cost of all else, was pummeled at the polls, losing three-quarters of his ruling party's assembly seats.[25] While farmers in this largely agricultural state suffered from drought, power outages, and increased rates for water, electricity, and agro-commodities, Naidu had insisted on bountiful water supplies to maintain the landscaping in the high-tech corporate parks of Hyderabad, and had offered discounted utility fees and virtually free land to lure the foreign firms into the region.[26] Computers, he insisted, should be introduced into every village to enable citizens to chart transparency in government.[27] As it turned out, Naidu's high-tech evangelism proved more than transparent to poor urban and rural voters who soundly rejected its tilt toward enriching those they regarded as an information aristocracy.

Tale of Two Cities

Media and government elites in India had long played down domestic protests against trade and investment liberalization. They were agitated, however, when U.S. legislators, bowing to public pressure, sought to pass legislation that would protect American jobs from being outsourced. For the most part, NASSCOM and industry leaders appeased foreign anti-outsourcing sentiment by arguing that Indian employees were providing quality, not just cost savings, and by echoing the free-trade mantra that the ultimate benefit would be to the United States and the UK. Editorials dutifully cited U.S. government reports alleging that job-loss numbers were overestimates.[28] However, the passing of a bill in the U.S. Senate in January 2004 to protect federally funded contracts from going offshore forced a blizzard of protest in the Indian media. Prime Minister Vajpayee lashed out at the "so-called advocates of liberalization," pointing out that the developed nations had specifically "asked the developing ones to liberalize their market economy" and that these unfair "laws are being enacted at a time when Indian youth are creating their niche in the IT and software sector worldwide."[29] Delhi now had an opportunity to echo long-held complaints from Beijing about the double standards employed by U.S.

politicians who insisted on liberalization policies from developing countries, while adopting protectionist measures, for political gain, at home.[30]

In addition, Indian BPO companies faced repercussions in the UK, where the Trade Union Congress president took an especially strong stand, pointing to the disadvantages of the Indian offshore sites, including "insufficiently spoken English skills, high attrition rates, rising wages, frequent power cuts."[31] British customer surveys showed that BPO was extremely unpopular, and Indian call centers began to receive an increasing volume of "backlash calls." Public pressure swayed several companies, citing concerns about "quality," to move their customer-support operations back from India. Littlewoods and Axa in the UK, and Dell and Lehman Brothers in the United States were among the more prominent returnees. Their decisions to shift operations overnight demonstrated not only the extreme sensitivity around offshoring, but also the starkly transitory nature of this kind of business operation—here today, gone tomorrow.

Anticipating widespread PR damage, publicly traded companies screened off any mention of their offshoring activities, even though publicizing the cost savings to investors would ordinarily have boosted their stock prices. To protect foreign clients from bad PR exposure, the Indian majors like Satyam, Wipro, TCS, and Infosys also stopped publicly identifying their new customers.[32] By contrast, publicity was lavished on the U.S. firms like IBM, HP, Accenture, and EDS, who were doing outsourcing work themselves, or benefiting from the boom by moving aggressively into the Indian market, and swallowing up domestic firms, as IBM did with Dasch and Bharti. But there was also evidence that the publicity generated by the backlash brought in even more business by promoting awareness of the cost benefits to firms, especially small companies, that would not otherwise have considered offshoring operations. One survey estimated that the anti-outsourcing brouhaha generated as much as $89 million of free publicity for the BPO industry.[33]

If individual companies often scrambled for PR cover, the business press was openly gung ho about the profits to be extracted from BPO.

Forbes magazine selected Karin Karnik, president of NASSCOM, as their 2003 "Face of the Year," and the magazine's readers overwhelmingly chose "white-collar outsourcing" as the most significant business trend of the year, with 44 percent of the vote.[34] Others, like *The Economist*, the *Wall Street Journal*, and *BusinessWeek*, went into attack mode, deriding those who claimed that white-collar America was being "hollowed out" by offshoring.[35] *Business 2.0*, the U.S. technology and business magazine, went even further by brazenly outsourcing the editing of a section of its August 2004 issue to a freelance team in India for half the normal cost. This decision helped to publicize the creep upward, into the "creative" sector, of jobs that were now vulnerable. Reuters announced a major shift of editorial personnel from the U.S. and the UK to Bangalore, and many major newspapers and presses began to move in the same direction.[36] The march into the professions was evident everywhere. In many corporations, in-house legal departments were relying less on U.S. counsel, and more and more on cheaper lawyers in India and other countries. HR outsourcing had ballooned into a huge industry, and sales divisions were following suit. Amicus, the British trade union whose membership included several thousand clergymen, even reported that religious services and prayers for the dead were being performed in India.[37]

From 2002 onward, the rise in BPO demand was so sharp that analysts almost immediately forecast a labor shortage down the road. With outsourcing growing at an annual rate of 50 percent or above, India simply could not produce the necessary supply of English-speaking employees with basic computer literacy. A NASSCOM-McKinsey study in the summer of 2004 showed a shortage of as many as 200,000 IT and ITeS employees. The deficit was estimated to grow to 3.6 million in the next eight years.[38] As the impact of the shortfall began to show up, wage inflation—from 10 percent to 40 percent annually—took a bite out of the cost savings from offshore operations.[39] Cost arbitrage and tight labor supply were only two of the many factors that might divert business to other countries. Very soon the geographical net cast by analysts' BPO forecasts went far beyond India. According to one Deloitte survey, second-tier countries vying for a share of the BPO market included Canada, China, the Czech Republic, Hungary, Ireland, Israel, Mexico, Northern Ireland, the Philippines, Poland, Russia, Spain, and South Africa. The third tier comprised Belarus, Brazil, the Caribbean, Egypt, Latvia, Mauritius, Singapore, New Zealand, Ukraine, and Venezuela. The Gartner group predicted that India's share in the BPO market would slip from 80 percent to 55 percent by 2007.[40]

Among the low-wage contenders in the second tier, China loomed largest, and the most visible reason lay in its advanced infrastructure. Denizens of India's business capital, Mumbai, looked enviously across at the transformation of its Chinese counterpart at the mouth of the Yangtze. Travelers, for example, who arrived in Pudong International Airport encountered no evidence to suggest that they had entered a developing country. The facility itself was built like a moonport, evoking space travel rather than mundane jogs across the East China Sea. The world's fastest commercial Maglev train beckoned for those with appointments to keep in downtown Pudong. The highways and overpasses leading toward Shanghai were smooth and spotless, and most of the cars were sleek and new. For foreign businesspeople, speeding past roadside billboards that advertised corporate parks, luxury villas, and high-tech services, it really was like landing in a capitalist Shangri-la, and the effect was carefully maintained. By the time they reached the city, the breathlessly modern skyscrapers made it easy to overlook the makeover of substandard housing on the ground.

Mumbai International Airport could hardly be more different. Stray dogs were known to run onto the airstrip, and the facility itself was cracked and grimy, surrounded by shantytown chowks that confronted the traveler directly. With no airport highway, and no filtered way into the city, the density of the traffic jams in every direction was unavoidable. The city's public transit system strained at the seams, its infamous though much-loved suburban trains carried two or three times their passenger capacity. Havens of corporate affluence were everywhere insulated against the ragged fabric of poverty that stretched across the city landscape. On the first day that I used the airport, in January 2004, job ads in the city newspapers fell into two major categories: employers were either recruiting for new call centers, or for able-bodied applicants to fill security guard positions. As my taxi driver, who was having a hard time making headway in the traffic, observed, "Only those who have stolen their money need armed guards to protect them." No local booster, he was a harsh critic of what liberalization had brought to Mumbai. "Lots of desperate people," he mumbled, "both rich and poor."

Despite the obvious differences in infrastructure, the two cities had much in common, each threatening, or promising, to be the largest metropolis in the world.[41] Like Shanghai, the Indian port was largely a nineteenth-century product of mercantile trade on the part of far-flung imperialists, and it served, then and now, as a cosmopolitan haven for refugees. The mix of Christians, Parsis, Gujaratis, Jews, Sikhs, Hindus, Jains, and a rich variety of Muslims, went against the grain of India's traditional caste patterns in occupation and lifestyle. Both cities had lived through boom times—in shipping trade, real estate, and textiles—and both were undergoing a painful transition from manufacturing hubs into would-be service centers for global finance. The conspicuous consumption that came with the new fast wealth contrasted sharply with a mass of ill-fed, underhoused, and underemployed citizens, many of them migrants from the countryside. As the financial centers of their respective nations, each had relinquished the business of politics and high culture to the capital cities of Beijing and Delhi. For several Cold War decades, Western popular culture was banned, and now it flourished garishly.

Mumbai's city managers had decided they wanted to be more like Shanghai. In 2001, Bombay First, a corporate task force, commissioned a report from McKinsey to show the way. The study, *Vision Mumbai: Transforming Mumbai into a World-Class City,* noted that, in 1987, Shanghai was "a dimly lit, unpainted financial wreck," but after its overhaul in the 1990s, "its roads, transport and telecom emerged as the best in the world." Outlining an eight-step program of conversion, the report recommended funding of $40 billion over ten years, most of it to be invested in Mumbai's infrastructure.[42] The Maharashtra state government began to implement parts of the plan in 2004. Even if the full funding became available, the authorities were hardly in a position to act with the kind of unilateral power wielded by Shanghai's government officials. Environmentalists and advocates for Mumbai's poor savaged the plan for its promotion of expanded privatization and real estate development. Their voices poured doubt on whether public investments of this size should prioritize the monetary gain and comfort of the city's finance sector and its motorized elites over human welfare and environmental well-being.[43]

Such conflicts of interest were topics for discussion at the event for which I had traveled to Mumbai—the World Social Forum, the yearly gathering of alternative globalization activists from around the world. The social inequities generated by Mumbai's courting of corporate multinationals made the city an appropriate host for the forum's vision of promoting globalization from below.[44] A flamboyant gathering of more than 100,000 showcased India's vibrant civil society. Sadly, however, very few participants made the trip from China. Was it even possible to talk about globalization without Chinese input? The perils of doing so were illustrated by a panel I attended about the new wave of skilled outsourcing. Toward the end of the discussion, a British trade unionist warned the audience that the outsourced jobs were here today but they would be in China tomorrow (exactly the same threat used by managers to intimidate their Indian employees). He cited the rapid erosion of the Mexican maquiladora economy as a case in point. The jobs transferred from the United States had only temporarily been hosted by Mexico until the factories were moved to China. It was quite likely, he argued, that this pattern of moving jobs from north to south, and then from south to east, would repeat itself in the service economy. In Europe it had been the same pattern in manufacturing; French jobs went first to North Africa, German jobs to Eastern Europe, and from both locations they were now moving to China. In what had become a familiar game, poor nations were being played against each other in the race to the bottom.

For the losers in this game, mutual communication and solidarity were the basic tools for changing its rules. Unfortunately, China's official labor federation was not in a position to offer much of either. As an

Forest Workers Union march against globalization,
World Social Forum, Mumbai

official arm of the state, its voice and its capacity to act on an international front were severely limited. Independent labor advocates walked a fine line to avoid censorship and recrimination. China had become one of the biggest links in the chain of globalization, but, for the purposes of building an effective international labor alliance, it was also the weakest. The absence of independent Chinese representatives at the WTO, and a hundred other similar international forums, only underlined the problem. While some party leaders recognized the need to appease international voices of conscience, others were quick to revert to repressive habits. For example, on the eve of AFL-CIO president John Sweeney's first planned visit to China in December 2004, Beijing abruptly canceled a meeting—long planned in cooperation with the OECD—of global business and union leaders who had agreed to come up with a plan to protect and improve workers' rights in China.[45] In the meantime, local labor organizers who mounted worker protests and strikes continued to face show trials and lengthy prison sentences.[46]

Going Mobile

For Indians, fear of China's growing economic power was built on forty years of paranoia about the military might and nuclear capability of their biggest neighbor. Yet anxiety about regional competition was not confined to Indian politicians and industrialists. The BPO boom generated oodles of concern in Beijing about the prospect of India displacing China as Asia's magnet for foreign direct investment (FDI). A February 2004 article by the economists Yasheng Huang (MIT) and Tarun Khanna (HBS) caused a stir by issuing the first of many forecasts about the coming preeminence of India. Though China reigned supreme in many of the standard economic performance indices, they argued that India's bank assets were composed of a much smaller volume of nonperforming loans: its capital market performance was far superior; its foreign exchange earnings rate was higher; and, unlike China, it had produced a considerable number of world-level private firms.[47] High-profile coverage of the article in the party organ, the *People's Daily* ("Will China Be Replaced by India?") was accompanied by an editorial exhortation that China, to avoid being overtaken, should "turn itself not only into the 'world's factory,' but also the 'world's office.' "[48]

Naturally, the major Indian ITeS companies hoped to garner official goodwill by insisting that their own newly opened offices in China were helping realize this nationalist vision. Even so, they had very little initial success in persuading Chinese clients to trust them with service contracts. Michael Mi, a Shanghainese with an MBA from NYU, who was put in charge of TCS's business development in China, described this problem as one of his biggest challenges. "They do not want to get invaded," he observed. "We are like a *Titanic* getting into the Chinese market, and everyone is scared. Otherwise," he added, "Chinese people do not understand India, India is familiar to them only from one or two movies and a few news pieces." Basically, the lack of trust comes from being "poor neighbors, despising each other." Employing Chinese returnees like himself in Indian companies was crucial to establishing trust, as he acknowledged, but such employees did not come cheap.

The other big challenge, of course, was holding on to experienced employees in a tight job market. "We try not to hire people," he reported, "whose résumés show that they have changed jobs after three months, we try to keep our best-quality training within the organization." TCS hired programmers fresh out of college to keep payroll costs down, but ran into the usual wall of wage inflation and shortage of supply when it came to more experienced positions. In the aftermath of Ratan Tata's visit, Mi was given a $5 million infusion to start up offshore centers in a string of Chinese cities. The forecasts of exploding IT business in China, like the infamous Gartner report, were proving premature, but TCS's competitors all made plans to expand their China presence beyond Shanghai. With cheaper cities to migrate jobs to, they would be in a better position to control labor costs. The managerial art of squeeze, after all, was especially acute for Indian companies. Unlike the Western multinationals, they were not bringing work to China because employees were cheaper; for them, at least, it was a more expensive wage environment.

Indeed, Girija Pande, the Asia-Pacific regional director of TCS, estimated that, compared with India, the company paid about 20 percent more for its East China manpower—even more if the higher social security outlay and the price of real estate were factored in. In Hangzhou, two hours to the south of Shanghai, where TCS had started its first offshore center (to staff a huge contract for GE Medical Services), salaries were lower than in the metropolis. But you would have to go inland or farther north, to Dalian, to find labor costs cheaper than in Pune and Bangalore. In the short term, however, overall salary growth in China (4 percent) was expected to be much lower than in the Indian industry (15 percent), struggling as it was to find recruits to meet the BPO demand.[49]

There were other reasons, of course, for the Indian decision to go offshore. Pande affirmed that his Japanese, Korean, and Singaporean clients felt much more comfortable working with Chinese employees at a China site. In some cases they were already bypassing Indian companies to outsource directly with Chinese software firms.[50] However, U.S. and European multinationals doing business in China, who wanted service operations on the ground, looked to the Indian companies with whom they were familiar. Finally, there was the looming problem of the trainee deficit in India itself. Offices in China were not just a backup contingency, they were also the future of the industry. TCS was not the only company in the Tata Group leaning toward the same conclusion. Tata Infotech, which specialized in a much harder tech version of outsourcing, was also eyeing a move. Prasanna Lahoti, the regional director, envisaged that the Chinese units would serve as "backup options, in case of difficulties, as in disaster recovery. If India goes down," he put it bluntly, "the customer doesn't go without service." In addition, he reckoned that his firm would be able to "deliver some of our reusable solution sets" in Chinese and other Asian contracts. But his primary concern was to keep his firm's big American clients happy, and his competitors were in the same boat, all steering toward Shanghai.

Lahoti, whom I interviewed on one of his research trips, had consulted some of his expat friends in Shanghai about the likelihood of finding the right kind of workers. The Chinese, they had reported, were "a very industrious, process-oriented community . . . once their training is established, then the job gets done." But wasn't his technology industry supposed to be based on generating creative ideas? "Creative people," he responded, "often come with a lacuna of being process-oriented. In any case, you only really need 10 to 20 percent creative people who are conceptualizing the solution. Converting that into an application is a process-oriented activity."

Lahoti wasn't just reporting barroom hearsay. This view of Chinese employees as process-driven and lacking in creativity was as firmly shared among Indian managers as among American and European business expats.[51] Prakash Menon, president of the Shanghai-Indian Business Association, and kingpin of the city's Indian community, offered his own detailed account of this consensus:

What we find is that the Chinese mind is outstanding when it comes to the problem-solution approach in methodology. The minute you get into concept application, there are issues. The Chinese mind is finding it exceptionally more difficult to take the concept and apply it to ten different places. Because what is required of an IT engineer—when it comes to application programming—is to solve problems. As the problem comes to him, he needs to see from his realm of knowledge, he needs to put it all together, synthesize, and therefore then be able to come to the solution. How do you do things that you don't know anything about? We find that to be an issue. Once a process is defined, the Chinese mind is an outstanding execution, top class. But if you want the guy to tell you what the specs for the program are, then you've got a problem. Therefore, the educational system must bridge that.

Menon's firm, NIIT, which had come to Shanghai as early as 1998, was making up for what he believed the Chinese educational system lacked. The company's regional educational centers—offering a three- or four-year training in IT skills—numbered 125, were placed in twenty-six provinces, and served as many as 30,000 students. Catering to those who had not gone to college or who wanted a career change, the courses were designed to introduce the kind of training that was required for networking and programming. Many local authorities were asking for the programs to be embedded in public educational curricula. In addition, the Shanghai center had initiated a program for training project managers and specialists in information architecture and product design. It was this kind of training, in Menon's opinion, that spoke to the difference between what he called the "Chinese mind" and the "Indian mind":

If you handhold the Indian to attempt to solve a problem, you won't get the solution. The Indian will expect you to keep holding his hand. The trick to the Indian mind is not to hold his hand, but to get him to explore and cross that wall. If you give him help once, then he keeps coming back to you. If you tell him nothing, then he flies, from the first problem onwards, and he doesn't need you at all. He knows. If you take the Chinese mind and try to adopt this, you will completely and wholly fail, because the Chinese mind works exactly the other way around. You have to hold his hand. If you don't, he's just going to sit tight. He will not want to explore. The reasons are unknown to me. We don't know if it's an old cultural thing of saving face, but the guy just doesn't move. You have to hold his hand, get him to cross the wall, give him that opportunity to fly on his own, and then he does.

By acknowledging his bewilderment at the ultimate cause of Chinese self-discipline, Menon was admitting that the "Chinese mind" might be unknowable to him.[52] But his comparison was aimed at a foreign manager's understanding of how employees respond to demands in the workplace. More bluntly, it was based on an assessment of the specific skills required in the IT service industry, some of them routine, others more attuned to problem solving and conceptual development. Since "the Chinese mind is a lot more disciplined than the Indian mind," its strength, according to Menon's comparison, lay in the execution of instructions and orders, while "the Indian is extremely weak in execution." But, for the higher-end tasks, what is most "valued in software is a very undisciplined mind—I'm using the word 'undisciplined' in a positive way—to be able to explore possibilities and probabilities."

Michael Mi, at TCS, agreed that "the Chinese people are traditionally more used to doing what they're told to do . . . which may actually be an advantage for the BPO, because you are told to do something. The most primary objective of outsourcing to somebody else is that first you want to make sure that things get done the way you want, strictly following the original instructions." Employees who followed orders were exactly what IT outsourcing required, given the need to operate at a long distance from clients. That was also one of the reasons why manufacturers had flocked to China. For all the tech industry talk about valuing ideas and smart solutions, the art of blindly following orders was the more mundane reality in most software service jobs. According to Allen Qian, general manager at Mphasis's Shanghai center, "In the software development area, we don't need too much creativity. Although they call this high-tech, it's not actually a very complex or difficult business. Actually, people only want us to do the kinds of things they want a computer to do. They already know how to do it, so it doesn't require much creativity."

Contrary to Mphasis's policy in India of seeking out experienced engineers, Qian focused on recruiting fresh graduates. "Their minds are so fresh I can educate them," he reasoned, and, besides, "they are also willing to do any kind of job." Above all, however, the newly graduated were "willing to compromise on salary." Qian, a native Shanghainese, bristled at the suggestion that Chinese employees did not stack up. "Compared to the Indian engineer," he insisted, "they are superior. The Chinese are always thinking of clever ways to reach a goal or solution." With the United States, however, there was no comparison. American engineers controlled all "the most advanced resources in software," in his opinion, and were "encouraged to do their own thinking." "All the other countries," he observed, were "just following U.S. technology. We are not inventing anything."

In this game of comparing national expertise, Indians and Chinese, inevitably, were played off against each other. At another Indian IT company, for example, I interviewed two managers back-to-back. The first, an Indian, delivered the customary bromide about his industry's worship of ideas and creativity. "That's what we are all about. We have to have outspoken employees, young people with free-flowing information and ideas." In India, he pointed out, "we have that kind of democratic, open environment." Stopping himself from pronouncing that Chinese engineers lacked this kind of initiative, he observed that "they merely followed instructions, and never stopped presentations, for example, to ask questions." The second manager, a Shanghainese with international experience, said exactly the opposite. "It's the Indian engineers who are almost entirely process-driven. They understand what code you want them to develop, and they never deviate from this or that kind of module."

Obviously, national pride influenced comments like these, but there was a lot hanging on such perceptions. Chinese and Indian skilled workers were about to be assigned new roles in the international division of labor. These roles had not yet been fixed, yet managers' perceptions about the respective strengths and weaknesses of the "Indian mind" and the "Chinese mind" were already feeding into decisions about when and where operations and tasks would be assigned. Given the expectation of easy mobility, short-term factors could make all the difference in such decisions. For example, this particular Indian manager's low opinion of his Chinese employees had not blinded him to one feature that all technology managers could surely appreciate: "The Chinese engineer," he observed, "hasn't yet learned how to hoard information. Techies everywhere else do some hoarding to boost their individual advantage, but as yet the Chinese are too naïve, they give it all up when asked to do so." Until they learned how to use their knowledge as a bargaining tool, their naïveté, from this manager's perspective, would make them invaluable in an industry prone to job-hopping and wage inflation.

They may have been naïve in some respects, but the fresh recruits whom I interviewed were fully aware of how their performance could make certain segments of an industry more locally attractive to investors. If the results favored them in the short term, they were also aware that the wind could change quite rapidly. They knew that employers and investors would always be looking elsewhere for a better return, that their offshore managers had to squeeze harder, and that their own skills and proficiencies were only a temporary match for their jobs. Johnny Lu, who worked under the Indian manager quoted above, described how this came across: "Chinese have little experience with foreign managers, and we just can't always understand what they want. Sometimes my manager wants me to follow the manual, and sometimes he wants a new problem fixed and then asks me how, but there are other times when I can't be sure. I like to learn new things, but I also like to be logical, and have the same approach to my work. He won't be my manager forever."

Alice Luo, a colleague on Lu's project team under the same manager, put it another way: "He doesn't know how to react to some of the new contracts, so we are affected by his confusion, and sometimes we joke about it to ourselves." Luo was also clear about the relative value of her skills. "I will never speak English very fluently, and so Indians will always have an advantage over me. But there are other areas where our training and our culture can deliver more value. An Indian company in China can get both, and so ideally this should be a good job for me for a long time. But the industry changes, and technology changes very fast. I am young, and I need to anticipate the changes for myself, or I will be left behind." Asked about the implications for the national economy, she smiled as she responded, "I don't think China will be left behind again."

Lu's and Luo's savvy estimates of their manager, the IT service industry, its international scope, and the need to protect the future of their own livelihoods were reminders that any workplace-based generalizations about the "Chinese mind" were likely to be crude and inadequate. Nor were they going to sit still long enough for managers to adjust these stereotypical perceptions. Though they both worked for an industry giant, strategically positioned in several countries to ensure its continued share of a growing global market, Lu and Luo were lukewarm about their own commitment to their employer. Each confirmed that they would be moving on, as soon as they had acquired enough training from the company, adding to the growing army of job-hoppers in the industry. Lu asked if I had heard of the expression "roadkill on the information superhighway" (originally from an AT&T ad). "I want to avoid being in that situation," he concluded.

The Suzhou Price

The "Made in China" label has become so ubiquitous that it will take a while before China is perceived as anything other than a manufacturing behemoth. Despite the growth of IT and other services in major urban centers, by far the majority of jobs being transferred to the mainland are still in manufacturing, but they are no longer exclusively labor-intensive. The rising volume of high-tech production depends on a workforce capable of upgrading its skills periodically to match the changing needs of foreign investors. From the time I had spent in Shanghai, it was clear to me that this dependence on skilled workers was absolutely central to the story about the continued growth of China's coastal regions. Many corporate decisions about the distribution of global investment hung on the potential availability of such a labor pool, as did the fate of the holders of valued onshore jobs. In addition, if the current skills shortage proved to be only temporary, it would embolden those in Washington and other political capitals who viewed China's rise to high-tech eminence as a serious threat to the balance of power in Asia and beyond. In some eyes at least, the freshly graduated Chinese engineer was the face of a new Yellow Peril.

To meet those skilled technicians in their factory workplaces, and find out how they were responding to these extraordinary pressures, I had to leave Shanghai and move upriver. Since the late 1980s, the municipal government had been shifting industrial facilities out of the city that had been the country's primary manufacturing center for more than a century. Investors who wanted cheaper land for their plants had to locate farther inland, along the Yangtze Delta corridor that had become the nation's center of gravity for technology-driven manufacturing. In the first quarter of 2004, the booming cities (Suzhou, Kunshan, Zhenjiang, Wuxi, Nanjing, Hangzhou, and Ningbo) in the Delta economic circle that ringed Shanghai accounted for almost 35 percent of China's foreign trade, including $40 billion of exports and $43 billion of imports.[1] FDI in the region reached $25.57 billion in 2003, up by 50 percent over the previous year, far surpassing the figures for the Pearl River Delta, at $13.74 billion, which was up by only 18 percent from 2002.[2] After being held back for the first decade of reforms, the Lower Yangtze was reasserting its traditional role as the economic pivot of China.

Traveling within this corridor, it was easy to see the impact on the ground. No open country was visible in the journey across delta land that had been worked for thousands of years. Instead of a landscape of urban sprawl, it was a busy jumble of all modes of production, from subsistence farming to high-tech manufacture. Because the land was among the most productive in China, orchards and field plots had survived, served still by a thick network of irrigation canals and pools irradiating an often garish color. Rotting sampans were moored near hamlets of thatched houses and shelters. Garbage was clumped quite randomly, and laundry was omnipresent, hanging out to dry between trees, fences, and barges and on any other horizontal axis that was available. Crumbling smokestack plants from the Maoist period pronounced their loyalty to national production in large characters on their compound walls. Pockets of willow-pattern China—humpbacked bridges, ponds, weeping trees, upturned eaves—were interspersed with new apartment complexes. Spotless, newly laid highways reached out in all directions. Crowding out all the other buildings were the industrial newcomers—fat, squat warehouses with high-tech roofs, rows of low factories as long as freight trains, and a multitude of shiny postmodern boxes that carried the brand of their corporate owners but said nothing about what was done inside their walls. Construction cranes busied their heads on every view of the horizon.

The ancient silk center of Suzhou lay about one-third of the way along this rich belt of industry and agriculture. Eighty miles west of Shanghai, it had cornered the lion's share of the manufacturing business in the region. Indeed, of the $52 billion in foreign investment that flowed into China in 2002, the largest slice ($10 billion) had come to Suzhou, even more than to Shanghai itself.[3] That same year the municipality (with a population of about 5.9 million) produced as much as $25 billion in GDP, making it the fifth-richest city in China after Shanghai, Beijing, Guangzhou, and Shenzhen, all with much larger populations. By 2003, its average annual disposable income had climbed to $1,271 (10,404 RMB), and its industrial output was the second highest in all of China. In February 2004, at the time of my first visits, the city hosted as many as 13,400 foreign-invested enterprises, with registered foreign capital of almost $47 billion, of which $31.55 billion was already paid up. In the first two months of the year, contracted investment had increased by 50 percent over the same period in the previous year. More than ninety Fortune 500 corporations had set up almost 250 enterprises in Suzhou, and others were rushing to follow suit.

These statistics were the envy of local government cadres all over East and South China, if only because the assessment of officials' performance was directly based on GDP figures. While Suzhou's officials had every reason to prefer this system, they shortly announced a pilot program to abandon GDP evaluation—almost a state religion—in some of the city's townships. It seemed like a very bold step, yet it was undertaken in response to new central-government policies aimed at sustainable development, and also at reducing the inflated estimates turned in by local officials.[4] The new performance yardsticks were aimed at fostering balanced growth, or what Beijing called a "scientific concept of development."[5] With its famous canals and UNESCO-protected gardens, the water-city of Suzhou was in a unique position to prove it could be a model environmentalist in addition to being a model producer. There was already a seven-story height limit on downtown buildings, and the city quickly jump-started recycling policies, light-rail and waterway transportation projects, comprehensive cleanup programs, and a trial plan to run local taxis on natural gas.[6]

Given the ruinous environmental degradation all across China's newly industrialized zones, Suzhou's plan for green development was a late, if welcome, response. Officials would be pioneering policies of urbanization that were equal, and in some respects superior, to those of metropolitan centers in developed countries. But commentators agreed that Suzhou could afford to do so only because it enjoyed a position of economic strength, earned primarily by the runaway success of its two best-known industrial parks—Suzhou New District and Suzhou Industrial Park (SIP), established in 1991 and 1994 respectively. The city's sweet location and its timely concentration of tech-driven manufacturing gave it resources and clout unavailable to many of its competitor cities. Its ability to graduate to a higher, greener plateau of industrialization without losing its foreign investors would be very closely watched.

For the time being, however, the investors' eyes were all on the overheated labor market created by Suzhou's manufacturing boom. Shanghai's turnover malaise was not unique among Yangtze Delta cities, and Suzhou had the worst case. An HR survey showed overall staff turnover in the city at 17.8 percent in 2003, as compared with Shanghai at 14.5 percent, and China as a whole at 13.1 percent. Overall salary increases, at 9.86 percent, were also higher than Shanghai's 8 percent, while the national figure was 7.5 percent.[7] Increases in both categories over the next few years would call into question Suzhou's status—and its future—as a model low-price haven for upscale manufacturers.

Humble Administrators

Such scrutiny was not new to Suzhou. Its first industrial life as a silk center boasted more than 2,000 years of continuous production. Even before China's ancient trade moved from the Yellow River valley to the Lower Yangtze, silk-making was distinguished by highly developed industrial varieties and a corresponding labor system. Visitors to the city's Silk Museum learned that a specialized division of labor, called "the hundred jobs," existed as early as the Shang and Zhou dynasties (1766–221 B.C.). This system was professionalized in Yangtze Delta cities like Suzhou, Hangzhou, and Wujian, and in each component of the industry—growing, weaving, spinning, dying, apparel-making, and embroidery. Nor was labor unrest unknown in the industry. The municipal Suzhou Museum displayed steles from the later Qing dynasty forbidding strikes by silk workers.

Suzhou's silk trade benefited, as Marco Polo observed during his visit to the city, from its supply of "capable merchants and skilled practitioners of every craft." But it also commanded an all-important strategic position on the Grand Canal, completed during the Sui dynasty (A.D. 581–618). The waterway could carry goods northward to supply the fabled Silk Road, a network of interconnecting routes that ran from Chinese cities like Xian, through Central Asian kingdoms including Bukhara and Samarkand, all the way to the shores of the Mediterranean. The traffic along these routes included precious goods and ideas alike. Those who had contact with the traffic were part of China's vital link with the West, and vice versa. Suzhou silk was among a profusion of Chinese goods that flowed west. What came east was predominantly silver and other precious metals. In some respects this trafficking relationship has been reprised in the last twenty years as foreign investment flowed into China in return for a mountain of exports.

Then, as now, China had an export surplus with most countries, and it was paid for by foreigners' silver, which was virtually the only Western commodity that the Chinese needed. For many centuries, China's exports of silk, porcelain, ceramics, and other worked goods dominated overseas markets, while the domestic demand for silver (China abandoned paper money in the mid-fifteenth century) had a huge impact on the world economy. Indeed, most of the silver and gold extracted from the Americas ended up in Asia, and especially China, where it was put to use in all sorts of industrious ways. Far from being hoarded and used for decorative purposes by the aristocracy, the money was used to stimulate production. Consequently, productivity and population growth increased at rates far greater than in Europe in the period up to 1800.[8] Of course, great profits were made in the West from the money trade, but only because merchants could meet the demand for silver by paying for exports distinguished by the high productivity and low competitive cost of China's manufacturing industries.

Was this picture of the old China trade similar to the balance of trade today? In some ways, it was not so far off the mark. One of the major differences, of course, lay in the role of technology. Since cheap labor was plentiful, labor-saving technology was not considered especially important to the economy of medieval and early modern China. Indeed, the Western powers had to develop such technology to compete with Asian manufactures in the first place. This was the underlying story of the Industrial Revolution in Europe. To compete in today's global economy, Western industrialists began transferring their labor-saving technology to China in order to save costs at home.

Suzhou had not lost the craft industry that made it famous. It still contributed greatly to the nation's silk exports; China alone accounted for as much as 70 percent of the world demand. But silk-making in Suzhou had been dwarfed by the flood of investment in other industries—electronics, pharamceuticals, chemicals, machinery, and microchips. Once again the city's location paid dividends. This time the winning factor was its orientation to the financial center to the east. If Shanghai was the "dragon's mouth," Suzhou was the sturdy "neck" that connected the coastal metropolis to the hinterlands. In addition, the city's three Yangtze River harbors, ringed by heavy industry (iron, steel, energy, papermaking, automobiles, and grain and oil processing), afforded direct access to international shipping. By road or rail, there were express routes to Beijing, Guangzhou, and Hong Kong, and export-processing centers allowed firms to clear customs while the goods were still in Suzhou.

Local government officials had learned how to handle the many needs and expectations of foreign investors. Mike Barbalas, managing director of Andrew, the U.S. telecom multinational, and one of SIP's earliest investors, described the relative advantage of the business environment: "In Guangdong, everything is possible if you have the right connections. In the north, everything is impossible, because of the rigid bureaucracy. Here in the Yangtze region, American companies feel comfortable, because local governments are very professional. They know the regulatory laws, and they let you know how you can operate within them." The result, as he put it, was that "government is pro-business, not pro-Chinese or pro-Western, just pro-business."

From the early 1980s, Suzhou's township enterprises began to flourish, and the population shot up. As market reforms proceeded, local officials opted to promote foreign trade to help these enterprises connect to the global economy. Initially, investments were scattered, and land was badly managed, so Suzhou followed the model of creating development zones with fully loaded infrastructure. The Kunshan zone came first, operating in a legally gray area until its burgeoning GDP was rewarded with official recognition by the central government. Kunshan attracted a steady flow of Taiwanese investors, many of whom saw themselves as returning from exile, as did the children of Shanghainese who had been sent up to staff mountain companies in the west, and who provided the first pool of skilled talent for the Taiwanese employers. By 2002, six out of the top ten Taiwanese notebook makers were producing out of Kunshan, enjoying a notoriously loose regulatory haven for low-cost production.[9] Suzhou's next two zones— Suzhou New District and SIP—were to develop a famous rivalry, often cited within the foreign investment community as a case study in the perils of doing business in China.

SIP was conceived in the early 1990s as the mother of all joint ventures by Singapore's premier Lee Kuan Yew. With a treasure chest of foreign exchange to invest, Singapore's economic managers were looking for a low-cost production haven to retain their competitive edge at home. Suzhou officials pitched the town to Lee, who then proposed a plan, approved by Vice Premier Zhu Rongji, to build "a miniature Singapore" or, more precisely, a version of Singapore's flagship Jurong Industrial Township, which had successfully combined industrial and residential areas on a large urban scale. In Lee's words, his brainchild was to be "a government-to-government technical-assistance agreement to transfer our knowledge and experience [what we called 'software'] in attracting investments and building industrial estates, complete with housing and commercial centres, to an unbuilt site of about 100 square kilometers in Suzhou."[10] The project, backed by a consortium of foreign companies, would take more than twenty years to complete, and the mainlanders would learn how to develop foreign trade from fellow Asians with whom they had a close cultural affinity. As one SIP official put it to me, "Singaporeans have yellow skin, but their minds are Western."

With backing from the very top layer of Chinese government, the Singaporeans had good reason to think their investment would be carefully protected. But SIP fell afoul of the gap that often existed between Beijing and ambitious local authorities. From the first, the Suzhou mayor's office zealously promoted its own locally operated industrial park, Suzhou New District, to potential investors, undercutting SIP's land and infrastructure costs. Even multinationals like Motorola, which had its regional headquarters in Singapore, were persuaded to opt for the New District. The competition between the two parks grew untenable, and SIP's losses (about $24 million annually) piled up. By 1999, the Singapore government stepped back and decided to reduce its share in SIP from 65 percent to that of a 35 percent minority partner. "It was a chastening experience," recalled Lee in his memoirs:

> Each side expected the other to behave like itself. Unfortunately, while language was no problem, our business cultures were totally different. Singaporeans take for granted the sanctity of contracts. . . . For the Suzhou authorities, a signed agreement is an expression of serious and sincere intent, but one that is not necessarily comprehensive and can be altered or reinterpreted with changing circumstances. We depended on laws and systems. They were guided by official directives; often, these were not published and their interpretation varied with the official in charge.[11]

Lee was recounting an experience that became quite familiar to many foreign investors in China whose faith in agreements was regularly undermined by the whims of government officials. For Singaporeans as a whole, the result proved to be a massive loss of face. It was by far the country's largest single foreign investment, and it had fallen flat.

After the 1999 restructuring left China with a majority share in the park, the government made sure that SIP turned in a profit. To secure much-needed *guanxi,* the park hired as its new director Wang Jinhua, the party's deputy secretary in Suzhou. He was none other than the former manager of the New District, who, as vice-mayor of Suzhou, had been a frontline combatant in the investment wars between the two parks. Overnight, SIP's industrial rents were slashed from sixty dollars to fifteen dollars per square meter, with even better deals offered to the plum investors. The park quickly attracted a critical mass of top-brand European, American, Japanese, and Korean multinationals predominantly in high and new technologies (several even jumped ship from the other park). According to SIP's investment promotion manager, the park's annual investment target jumped from $1 billion to $5 bil-

Floral legacy of Singapore's biggest overseas investment,
in Suzhou Industrial Park

lion. It became the only foreign trade entity in China that had no upper limit for foreign investment approval from Beijing. This power alone exceeded that of municipalities like Shanghai. More important, the park's history was supposed to showcase how the Chinese, when they were left in charge, could successively manage a business venture on this mammoth scale.

By the time I began my visits, the park's core area of 70 square kilometers (known as the China-Singapore cooperation zone) hosted almost 100,000 employees. The larger 260 square-kilometer area (which included five existing townships under its jurisdiction) held more than 200,000 employees and as many as 230,000 residents. SIP had attracted 1,300 foreign companies, fifty of them in the Fortune 500 (contributing FDI of $15 billion) and more than 600 domestic firms (with an investment of $3.8 billion). According to the park's administrators, a quarter of the companies in operation had already recovered their investment, and exports totaled $5.96 billion in 2003. All of the industrial land in the core area was contractually committed, and gleaming new plants were rising every month out of vegetable fields and reclaimed land. Chasing their dream of an IPO, there was strong pressure from many of the park's administrative investors to expand its size to make way for new investment, but the decision was still under wraps. "Everything about SIP," an official warned me, "is politically sensitive." As part of its effort to cool down economic growth, Beijing had taken steps to arrest the rampant conversion of arable land into industrial zones, and had closed down as many as 2,500 such zones that had sprung up without official permission from the central government.[12] Despite this nationwide retrenchment, SIP was given approval in October 2004 to add another 30 square kilometers, confirming its privileged status as a national development priority at the highest level.

Just as the industrial rents came down, Suzhou city's housing prices began to rise sharply. SIP's residential division, aiming to eventually house 600,000 residents within the core, began to contribute more and more of the park's profits.[13] Before long, SIP residential land that was previously worth $70 per square meter was fetching up to $3,000—a sum 200 times higher than the price of industrial land.

With its mix of high- and low-density housing for sale or rent—some of it luxury, some of it subsidized for administrative employees—the park boasted amenities that included several international schools and kindergartens, an arts center in the making, a colossal central lake, a five-star hotel, lavishly landscaped parks and gardens, tree-lined boulevards, a 40 percent greenery ratio, and the overall feel of a well-ordered and rigorously zoned environment. In the rush to secure manufacturing contracts, officials had forgotten that the SIP project was originally named Suzhou Industrial Township, after its Singaporean garden city prototype. The vision of a modern urban town with values that reflected the needs of the corporate class proved a magnet for expats, returnees, and upwardly mobile locals, many of whom used it as commuter housing, returning to their family homes in the provinces on weekends. A manager in a Singaporean company described its appeal to expats: "It doesn't look anything like China, they can feel safe and comfortable, and they don't have to deal with the messiness of Suzhou." For locals, it was a version of the future City Beautiful. "One day, all of China ought to look like this," observed one of the

Scale model of residences and industry in the Suzhou Industrial Park

Singaporean manager's employees, who had recently placed a down payment on an apartment not too far from the central business district near the lake.

The Welfare State Park

As it happened, the opportunity for employees like him to buy was practically built into his contract of employment. All SIP employees and employers contributed to a Social Provident Fund (SPF) on which employees could draw to purchase or rent housing in the park. Employers and employees both paid 22 percent to the SPF, which was then divided into a consolidated public account and a personal account. Unemployment, along with major illness and maternity, was covered by the former, while employees drew on the latter, larger portion for their housing, and also to pay into retirement and medical policies of their own choosing. In addition, employers paid a smaller portion to the SPF to insure against work-related injuries and diseases. In effect, SIP had its own welfare state, and it was one in which the government had little responsibility other than administering the fund through its SIP authority.

Like the park itself, the SPF was based on a Singaporean model— a social security savings fund that is compulsory for all citizens and permanent residents of that island state. Providing for everything from retirement pensions to children's education and housing purchases, this fund enshrined the principle of personal self-reliance, which governments around the world have adopted in order to reduce their primary commitments to a welfare state. Indeed, the origin of the Singapore fund lay in the desire of the British colonial government to limit its own commitment to social security outlays. While it had succeeded, over time, in guaranteeing Singaporeans' high rate of savings, the liberalization of the savings options had encouraged participants to indulge in high-risk investments—perilous, in general, as a long-term social security plan. In China's case, the SPF (unique to SIP) was one end point of the long march toward privatization that had begun in 1978 with the breakup of the rural communes and the introduction of the responsibility system in the countryside. It was a self-contained system designed to benefit those who were in a position to enjoy stable employment. Participants were given ready access to portions of funds that, in a government-administered system, would ordinarily have been stowed away in long-term social security accounts.

From the perspective of the rent-seeking SIP administration, the scheme directly encouraged employees to buy into the real estate from which the park itself drew huge profits. Under the terms of the SPF, employees could not use their account to buy an apartment outside the park. So, too, the fund had obvious advantages for employers. For one thing, their contributions were much lower than outside the park. In Shanghai, for example, a typical social benefits load for an employer included 22 percent for pension costs, 2 percent for unemployment, 12 percent for medical, 7 percent for housing, and 1.6 percent for disability insurance.[14] This combined sum of 44.6 percent was twice as much as the SPF contribution of 22 percent. SIP employers were also absolved from contributing to the social security of the citizens of Suzhou, or the county as whole. Special breaks were always being brokered. In the case of unskilled operators, some employers could opt to pay as little as 14 percent into the fund. In addition, the SPF was promoted as a way of creating a stable workforce. If a worker left SIP, he or she would forfeit a portion of the fund's personal account. There was a real financial incentive to staying put, and so the system helped to address managers' fears about employee retention.

Beginning in the mid-nineteenth century, many American firms decided it was in their interest to provide housing and personal welfare for a captive pool of their workers. This was the concept behind the company town, and it became synonymous with corporate control over every aspect of their employees' lives, including morality and personal conduct. Inevitably, the restrictive environment resulted in widespread labor unrest and uprisings throughout the United States. When further repression proved impractical as a long-term solution, many employers reasoned that the best way of pacifying workers would be to allow them to purchase their homes.[15] In time, mass suburbanization made the company town obsolete, but the principle of worker pacification through ownership persisted. As William Levitt, the developer of Levittown, famously put it, "No man who owns his house and lot can be a Communist. He has too much to do."[16]

SIP was not exactly a company town, but it was more or less in the direct line of descent. Many companies were involved, relying on their common interest to sustain a system that kept a large pool of quasi-dependent employees in place. The SPF was the social cement that bound the system together as a kind of benevolent society. Yet some obvious problems had arisen in the transition of the provident fund concept from its origins in Singapore's bounded island-state. For one thing, the system was not at all popular among unskilled or low-paid operators who simply could not afford to buy a home in SIP. They could utilize only 20 percent of their personal account for rent, and, in any case, were the most likely to move on. HR managers were hard put to explain the SPF's benefits to workers who had little stake in the future of the park. These employees—many of them migrants—had learned not to trust the government, or any other authority for that matter. What was the SPF to them? They needed cash in their hands and were generally too young to think about their long-term security.

As a model for social security reform, the SPF had obvious appeal to Beijing, especially since it seemed to promote social and demographic stability—one of the Communist Party's highest priorities. But with the recent dissolution of so many state guarantees of housing and job security, the condition of stable employment was now enjoyed by a dwindling minority of China's population. With its high unemployment rates, its huge floating population of migrant workers, and the preference of the growing private sector for flexible workforces, China's economy was unlikely to be able to boast very much security of any kind in the decades to come. A welfare model, like the SPF, that depended on mutual trust between a highly pressured workforce and a cluster of footloose multinational corporations did not seem to be the most promising or viable way forward.

In the case of SIP, any such trust depended on the willingness of employers to stay put. On that score there was already some doubt in the air. The job-hopping among experienced talent, and even among semi-skilled operators, had almost reached a critical point. Every technician or engineer with at least a year's experience was savvy enough to realize that a better situation awaited them in the plant being built across the road. New companies moving into the park needed skilled employees to ramp up, and it was easy to lure them away with higher salaries. Compared with onshore wages, the savings were still colossal, and so greenhorn managers thought little of poaching from the established plants. Their job was simply to get operations up and running. Yet each new hike fueled the salary spiral, and threatened the common interest of existing employers in keeping down labor costs. The park's expansion brought in firms that might add to their supply or sales chain, and thereby benefit their business. But if the newcomers did not play by gentlemen's rules, the outcome would jeopardize the primary reason for coming to China in the first place—to get workers on the cheap.

As some HR managers pointed out to me, the self-contained welfare system contributed to this conundrum. Under the SPF's provisions, employees had an extra incentive to stay in the park, and so their familiarity with the labor market in SIP motivated them to move from one company to another. Inadvertently the fund put them in a good bargaining position within SIP itself. So, while the park was able to retain employees rather well, individual managers were tearing their hair out over the high turnover rates that marred their monthly performance figures. If the problem could not be resolved, then the Yangtze Delta's premier investment attraction would lose its appeal fast. As a Texan manager put it to me, with a touch of native nonchalance, "We'll move on, just like the Old West. In China there will always be a better deal waiting in the next town."

Working on the Value Chain Gang

With its rich lode of job opportunities, Suzhou had become a magnet for those seeking employment in the East, and they had come from far and wide. The city had at least three talent exchange centers where job fairs were held daily to serve different employee groups. Job fairs were traditionally the preserve of agricultural and blue-collar workers, but they had also become popular, in recent years, among college students and white-collar employees who needed a supplement to popular HR websites like zhaopin.com and Job51. One of the job exchanges was in SIP, where, on five mornings of every week, the park's HR agency played host to employers and their potential recruits. On Wednesdays, clusters of giggling country girls showed up at the fair for unskilled operators. Some of them had made the short trip from company dormitories in the park where they sleep eight to ten in a room. This live-in work situation had been pioneered in the South China model, and was associated with Guangdong's infamous sweatshop economy. It was more common in the nearby township of Kunshan, entirely made over by Taiwanese investors, who had the worst reputation in the region for extreme wage pressure and labor discipline.

In SIP, where higher labor and safety standards helped to ensure that the brands of its multinational investors were not subject to sweatshop exposés, unskilled workers were paid a little better. In fact, most earned a wage that was generally higher than the city's minimum wage of 560 RMB ($68). Some operators who had a few years experience, or training in one of the city's many vocational institutes, could earn as much as 1,000 RMB ($121) a month. However, they would likely have worked twelve-hour shifts (with no guarantee of overtime pay) to get this kind of wage packet. SIP's HR guidelines suggested that employers adopt a three-shift pattern (6:30 a.m.–2:30 p.m., 2:30–10:30 p.m., and 10:30 p.m.–6:30 a.m.) or a two-shift pattern (6:30 a.m.–3:00 p.m. and 3:00–11:30 p.m.), but two twelve-hour shifts were customary at most of the large twenty-four-hour manufacturing plants that I visited. For workers, this translated into three twelve-hour daytime shifts, followed by two rest days, and then three twelve-hour night shifts. By commonly instituting this pattern, employers in the park ensured that their operators would not be able to jump ship for better shifts elsewhere. Managers, at Asian-owned companies in particular, generally expected large stretches of overtime from workers, usually far above the national legal limit of thirty-six hours a month. An official from SIP's Labor Bureau explained that, in his job, he had great difficulty keeping companies from different countries in line with China's labor law: "Foreign managers bring their own culture and their own internal labor policies, they all have different ideas about how they should treat workers." Excessive overtime, he reported, was a "huge problem," and occasionally he prosecuted companies that failed to pay workers for two months or more. Though he was charged with enforcing the labor laws, he was working for an authority that bent over backward to please its foreign investors. As a colleague of his in the HR department carefully phrased it for me, "We are neither too strict nor too loose in our enforcement of regulations."

Initially the park's employers were required to hire locally, but rapid growth, constant churning in the labor market, and the emerging clout of employers had forced authorities to allow recruiters to hire at all levels from the provinces in the west, and even from as far away as Inner Mongolia. As a result, migrants drifted daily toward the region, clogging the railway station day and night (it was the only place where most of them could rest or sleep) and lingering around the job exchange centers. If they could find jobs and hold on for three years, even the unskilled could apply for a coveted residence registration in Suzhou. For the skilled talent, the residence card (*hukou*) was virtually automatic once they had found employment. On the face of it, job prospects and opportunities appeared to be plentiful. Every month a new employer opened a plant in SIP or in one of several other industrial parks that ringed Suzhou. Managers knew that with a minimum of training, they could ramp up a workforce of operators fairly quickly. It was quite another story for more skilled positions,

For engineers who were fortunate enough to have the day off or who could drop by for a few hours, the job fair was on Saturday mornings, but on Thursdays an occasional fair was organized for industry clusters, like the electronics group. This was where I met and talked to Xing Xingyao, a mechanical engineer from Subei, the northern part of Jiangsu province. A graduate of Nanjing University of Science and Technology, he had signed on with a Japanese electronics manufacturer only ten months before. Currently he earned about 2,000 RMB ($242) per month, which was about the Suzhou market average for mechanical engineers—electrical engineers got 500 RMB more. Why was he looking around for another job? "I'm not sure if I should move," he explained. "There are many factors I have to consider. But I am really not comfortable in my current job. We are supposed to learn for ourselves, but I can't find any time to do this. We always have to be at the production line, doing support or improving the process." During the week, he reported that he was rarely back in his apartment before 9:00 p.m., and he often had to come into the plant on both weekend days. If he had queries or suggestions, his manager, he said, was "always too busy to listen. He just wants to see the yield go up, there is nothing else for him to say. I think I can learn more in a European or American company, the environment is more open there, and maybe I can do overseas training." His parents, who had worked for the same dry-goods company all their lives, had advised him to leave. "Their generation did not have to make these kind of choices, but they recognize that I will have to."

Prospective recruits waiting in line at the job fair,
Suzhou Industrial Park

Next in line to Xing at the job fair was Yang Wei Feng, a technician from rural Anhui, who said he was trapped inside the Little Taiwan of Kunshan's industrial zone: "I want to escape from Kunshan," he wailed, somewhat melodramatically. "Taiwanese know us Chinese too well, they only want us to work like a horse or dog, and they don't care anything about our welfare." Yang spent all his free time learning English; it was his passport to the job of his dreams in a European or American company. Even so, he was not optimistic. "My English is too poor, and there are too many Chinese just like me," he brooded. "I think I will always be a prisoner of the Taiwanese companies."

With his education, Xing should have been in a position to avoid his neighbor's lot, but he knew he was not in the best position to test the market. By his own admission, he had not been exposed to much training in his current job, so a potential employer might not consider him worth the salary raise he would want as part of the move. So, too, he had heard that American and European managers were reluctant to hire employees from Taiwanese or Japanese companies, believing they had been trained simply to obey the boss and follow process-oriented rules. Xing was especially worried that he would not be able to compete with the new class of spring graduates. He was one of several employees I met who had read a recent article in the *Suzhou Daily*, forecasting a substantial decline in entry-level salaries. Li Xiaoming, also attending the fair, was about to graduate from Nanjing University. His professors in the electrical engineering department had told him to expect a monthly salary of about 2,500 RMB ($302), or almost half what his peers would have been earning three years before. Xing knew that managers would almost certainly choose to take advantage of recruits like Li from this year's cheaper graduate talent pool. Besides, job-hopping was becoming a dirty word in Suzhou. Those who indulged too often were likely to be labeled as high-risk recruits.

Xing was leaning toward a move, but he recognized that he might have to take a pay cut to do so: "If you are young, the money is less important than developing a career." If he stayed put for a while, he might be caught in a downward spiral over the next few years, when the current shortage of talent was expected to turn into an oversupply. His calculation of his place in the labor market, now and in the future, had to be as clear-sighted as that of his potential employers. Xing's dilemma was by no means a quandary of his own making. It reflected a precise moment in China's next round of industrialization, almost as precise as the manufacturing process that he had been hired to supervise.

Because they worked in manufacturing plants, the engineers I interviewed inside SIP firms were more matter-of-fact than the Shanghai IT employees I had met. Unlike the latter, who were learning the indefinite art of spinning business solutions, the Suzhou engineers had a machine-cut understanding of their position. Like Xing, they knew exactly what their skills were worth in the labor market, and they understood the calculus used by their employers to transfer higher-value operations to their workplaces. The cumulative impact of their own decisions to stay or move on would be registered in the price investors would have to pay. Winter Chen, a process engineer for a German firm, put it this way: "The company waited for the market to move, and as soon as the talent pool was good enough, they brought the R&D unit over here like this," he said, snapping his fingers. For Chen, the upgrade came at just the right time. "It made a big difference to my staying or leaving. Now, when I need to adjust the production line for a customer, I just walk over to the R&D guys and I can get high-level feedback and support in the next building. That used to take more than a week. I can also learn much more while I am at work."

Every so often, I found employees whose loyalty was based on "soft" factors like company culture—one of the more strenuous products of industrial psychology. Among the firms I visited in SIP, the Nokia plant (which produced base stations for mobile-phone networks) was one where employees acknowledged they could earn more elsewhere, but were anxious not to lose what they referred to as the "respectful, people-centered culture" fostered by the company. Such comments were quite rare, and even though they were couched in official-sounding rhetoric, I was not inclined to disregard them as HR propaganda. More interesting yet, the social personality of Nokia's Finnish managers was described as "easy for Chinese to adapt to." British and Americans were generally regarded as overly "direct" in their manner of communication. By contrast, the Finns—"silent, nice, and not too straightforward"—were perceived by Chinese employees as more like kindred spirits.

But, in the fully measured environment in which the SIP engineers operated, the impact of "company culture" was too intangible to compute. In multinational firms, every task was subject to a cost-benefit analysis, weighed against its equivalent in several other locations around the world. If employees like Winter Chen were well placed to bargain their labor power, it was not because of the quality of their work; they just happened to be in the right place at the right time. Chen's parents had also been engineers, in a factory that had produced the first tractors in China, making way for the mechanization of the rural communes. But, for all the local fame attached to the company's name, their own salaries and skills had no significance beyond the boundaries of their Henan township. By contrast, their son's pay packet and his work ethic were key links in a global industrial chain.

Given how closely they followed, and identified with, their employers' methods of pricing skills and locations, it was no surprise that Chen and others were already dreaming of starting their own companies. In a few years' time, they imagined themselves and their friends pooling resources and heading to the western provinces, earmarked by the government as the next frontier of opportunity. Who knows, they might even get there before their current employers. "We would like to do something for ourselves," he said, shrugging. "In Suzhou, all the big decisions have already been made, by people far away."

The same opportunistic mind-set often applied to their political or philosophical leanings. A goodly number of my SIP interviewees turned out to be members of the Communist Party. One estimated there were more than 2,000 members among the SIP companies. Initially timid about addressing their affiliations, they usually warmed to the topic and almost always displayed some pride in their membership. The pride was never attached to political passion, however. In college, where science students were often excused from mandatory courses in Marxism, it was considered prestigious to be selected for membership. The party still only wanted the best and brightest, and to be chosen was like graduating summa cum laude. In the private sector, especially among foreign companies, there was virtually no advantage to be mined from a party membership, but no one I met in such companies had given up their affiliation (despite the fact that membership fees claimed as much as 4 percent of their pay). Membership was considered a potentially valuable asset that could be turned to self-advancement at some later point in a career. For the time being, membership meetings in SIP were regarded as social networking opportunities.

The thoughts of Chairman Mao were approached in much the same pragmatic manner. Some employees who had taken on junior managerial positions swore that they used Mao to sharpen their management skills. If this was true, it was in sync with the entrepreneurial leanings of ruling cadres in the party. As one of its projects to commemorate the 110th anniversary (in December 2003) of the Great Helmsman's birth, the party's Central History Publishing Office issued a four-volume set of business management tips based on Mao's teachings. The books drew on Mao's writings about philosophy, politics, and military strategy to offer advice on managing projects, making deals, motivating employees, and incubating start-ups. Some of my interviewees went further and claimed that Mao's more philosophical orientation was of direct use in the workplace. One semiconductor engineer cited Mao's concise statement of dialectical materialism— "One Divides into Two"—as an example of what he often experienced in solving a technical problem: "What looks like different kinds of malfunctions," he mused, "are really two sides of the same problem." I asked him what Mao would think of a place like SIP. "Mao would say, 'Look! This is all my work,' " he answered, with a very wide grin.

Did this pragmatism extend to their private lives? Like the Shanghai employees, most of my Suzhou interviewees defiantly described themselves as traditional, even conservative, in the lives they led outside of their Westernized workplaces. "There is absolutely no innovation in my life" was how one of them proudly described his devotion to this ideal. Bars, clubs, the latest fashions, and even high-tech gadgetry were spurned, almost as a matter of principle. This division between the modern workplace and the traditional home was so commonly cited it was more like a prescription than an inclination.

There were, of course, exceptions who confounded the profile, both in and out of the workplace. One was June Zhao, a Suzhou native, with a degree from Nanjing Normal University, who was employed at one of the larger Taiwanese companies in SIP. Her work hours were punishing—eleven hours on weekdays, most of Saturdays, and often Sunday mornings, too. "My parents are shocked," she said, smiling, "that I work so hard, especially on weekends." In less than a year, Zhao had been promoted to assistant manager of quality control. In her company the women engineers rose quickly, and she could have been on a fast track through the managerial ranks. Yet she had recently requested to be transferred to the position of project engineer, and was promptly approved for the job. "I had no prior technical training," she confessed (she was an English major), "and I wanted to see if I could start at the ground floor and become a real engineer for myself." It wasn't often that I met employees who asked to take a step down the ladder—there would even be a pay cut for her. But Zhao seemed to take pleasure in going against the grain. "All of my friends are teachers or journalists," she reported. "I'm the only one who will get her hands dirty at work."

She was about to enter what she called her "golden period." "For Chinese women," she explained, "it's from twenty-five to thirty years—women are most powerful in their twenties, before they have a family—and for men, it's from twenty-eight to thirty-five." But Zhao did not intend to parlay her industry experience into career capital. "I might have a family, but in any case, in a few years, I will definitely choose another kind of career, go back to college probably, and start over again." Even though she was in a sweet spot, in a business climate that would reward her well for her acquired skills and employment record, she had already decided to go her own way. She tried to explain this decision by appealing to gender: "Men have much more pressure, they have to take advantage of these opportunities when they can. Women don't feel this so much and so they actually have more choices today." She was the only female engineer I met in China who told me that gender had any real bearing on her ambitions, or her ability to realize them. Most denied emphatically that it was a factor.

When Zhao mentioned that she liked to read ancient philosophy, I expected her to sound off on the value of traditions. Citing their taste for folk music or historical literature was usually a way for my interviewees to record their attachment to Chinese culture. Lao Tzu was her favorite philosopher, but her take on the master of Tao was hardly an orthodox one: "He teaches me that our lives are worth nothing." It was not a throwaway comment, and it was not delivered without some hint of mischief. The core Taoist principle of not-doing (*wu-wei*)—customarily translated as "going with the flow"—describes the condition of being so closely attuned to the natural affairs of the universe as to expend the minimum of energy in following their course. Zhao's interpretation was somewhat more nihilist. She assured me it was not a misunderstanding, and was her own Taoist innovation. "If you accept that what you do will have no real impact on the world," she explained, "then it makes you free to think and act."

Her tinkering with Lao Tzu was a reminder that "innovation" was not the sole preserve of her tech industry workplace, but that it also described how Chinese like herself approach traditional knowledge and values. The case for categorizing the new Chinese middle class between modernity and tradition fell apart entirely when it tried to include someone like Zhao, who was so much her own person.

The Managers' Club

The pragmatism displayed by SIP engineers was mirrored in the obsessions of their managers, and never so intently as when they met, as they did regularly, to discuss issues of common interest. They may have been in the same room as their competitors, but they had overriding reasons to share information, and keeping labor costs down was primary among them. PC Loh, a Malaysian manager at Spansion (an AMD subsidiary, manufacturing flash memory cards), was head of the electronics group, which was by far the biggest (60 percent of the total number of firms) and most powerful of SIP's industry clusters. Lamenting the predatory behavior of "start-ups who come and, without much consideration, jack up the prices by taking away our experienced employees," he observed that "paying high salaries in response is not a good policy of retention," and prided his own firm on its responsible approach to stifling wage inflation. He confirmed that in the "general managers' club," as it was known, "the number-one topic is always self-control in hiring talent." To illustrate the point, he pulled out the minutes from the most recent meeting, at which one of the managers present had reported, "My company is doing feasibility studies with a view to departing from this location. Our employee turnover is 3 or 4 percent every month (36 to 48 percent annually), and we cannot stay here unless talent retention improves. We are actively thinking about moving out."

Sentiment within the group had been heading in that direction for some time. "Two years ago," Loh explained, "the salary gap with Shanghai was 50 percent, but now it is more like 75 percent, so there is more incentive for engineers who don't like the city to come here. But it also means there is much more job-hopping within SIP." "That's the scary part of it," commented KG Ching, a Singaporean manager at Philips. "Compared to 1997–1998, the wages are already three times, four times higher. We came here because of the low costs, but this is a little scary. Turnover is well above 20 percent in some SIP companies, and sometimes you have to double the pay to keep employees, just to save the training time spent on them. And for key people you need to pay them a Shanghai salary. For a good manager, the cost is about the same as Singapore, or even Taiwan." The skill sets of engineers and operators in Ching's own company were difficult to duplicate, and so turnover was relatively low. Productivity was another matter. When measured against Philips's multinational "standard hour," a worker in the Netherlands performed at 95 percent, while a Singaporean registered 85 to 90 percent. In China, his factory's productivity rate was only 60 to 70 percent.

Both Loh and Ching agreed with the consensus that hiring fresh graduates was relatively easy. Unlike Ching, who hired 80 percent from Suzhou, Loh's policy was to "hire from outside the province" to keep costs down, to ensure diversity with "people from a variety of backgrounds," and to get workers who were most focused on the job. Local people, he observed, were more distracted: "Their energy usually gets drained away by other issues—their family, parents, buying an apartment, etcetera." In this way he was able to squeeze the most out of fresh talent. But the benefits did little in the long run to offset the bigger headache of the "two-year rotation," as the job-hopping pattern was generally termed among East China's foreign managers. Nor could the situation be controlled if other managers were unwilling to play along.

Foreign managers were always quick to denigrate the lower labor standards of their Taiwanese counterparts. But there was one area where the Taiwanese won a grudging respect. They were very efficient at banding together to control labor costs. All over South and East China, in concentrated pockets like Kunshan, the informal Taiwanese business associations, usually organized around a golfing clique, kept a tight lid on wage packets. Foreign firms seemed incapable of such collective discipline, though it was not for want of trying.

John Bartlett, an Old China Hand who had been doing business in Shanghai since the late 1980s, described how the region's early American manufacturers had made the effort to control costs:

> We wouldn't have gotten together, except we were chasing our tails. First of all, we had to figure out the domestic wage package that would be paid by foreign joint ventures. I think we started with sixteen or seventeen benchmarked positions, then it expanded to hundreds. We'd look around the table and say, "What are you paying, and how do we describe this position?" In those days there weren't many people who spoke English, so it was all pioneering. The basic agreement was to avoid poaching, and outrageous prices. There were no punitive measures, since we were small enough, and we knew that we would see each other often enough to develop a bond of trust. The numbers were so limited we would visit each other's factories.

When joint ventures became the norm, he and other managers discovered that each Chinese organization with whom they were partnered had a different approach: "They would make up the rules as they went along, because joint ventures were as new to the Chinese as they are to Americans. They didn't know which standards to employ. All they knew was that foreigners were willing to pay more for their workers."

Since Bartlett had seen the business landscape mutate over a sustained period, he knew exactly which advantages had been lost along with the concessions won by foreign enterprises to operate on their own. Although managers had been obliged, during the joint-venture era, to absorb more workers than they felt necessary, they were relieved of many onerous responsibilities: "Labor discipline, showing up to work on time, reporting when you are sick, taking care of the pregnant and childbirth, all of those things were out of my hands. I didn't have to worry about it, the Chinese system and the party took care of it. The labor union handled compassion and family issues." But when the state cleared the way for wholly owned foreign enterprises, it transferred these concerns to the companies themselves, along with the fiscal burden of social security, health and pension costs, benefits, and all of the hidden fees and costs that are generally not mentioned during the courting of investors. "I guess one of our disappointments," he concluded wistfully, "has been around the expectation that China would prove a cheap place for us to be."

In general, workers in the Yangtze Delta had access to higher wages than in other regions of China because there was more legal oversight of their labor contracts. That was one of the reasons why migrant workers were deserting Guangdong and flocking to the region. Indeed, there was evidence that the skilled-labor shortage in the south was worse than in the more accommodating Greater Shanghai region. Even in Shenzhen, the highest-paying urban center in Guangdong, the municipal government reported, in the spring of 2005, that there were only 53,000 applicants for its 105,000 vacancies advertised for skilled workers and technicians, and that the city economy was in dire need of more than 2 million skilled workers.[17]

In the fall of 2003, Suzhou's employees got an additional legal boost from the People's Congress of Jiangsu province, which passed legislation giving extra teeth to existing laws on labor contracts. Employees could no longer be penalized for breaking contracts, as long as they gave thirty days' notice of quitting. Employers now had to offer longer-term contracts, they had to pay more during the probationary periods, and they were forbidden from terminating employees without sound reasons.

In conversations and meetings I attended, I heard widely differing interpretations of this new law. Partly this was due to its perceived ambiguity, not uncommon in Chinese law. The director of SIP's Labor Bureau reported, "Every day I have to read the wording very closely. There are many relevant things we look for that are simply not there." For the most part, however, the confusion was simply a result of managers feeling out how rigorously the law would be enforced in SIP. "Our position," explained Molly Shen, SIP's deputy head of HR, "is to maintain the middle ground between workers and management. Actually, we have no choice, because we have to protect the investors as well as the employees." Employees with grievances came to her agency, which would try to settle the disputes before passing them on to arbitration. She acknowledged that there had been a noticeable rise in employee grievances and turnover since the new law was passed.

Perceiving that both the provincial legislature and the labor market were turning against them, company managers in SIP opted for group action in responding. By March 2004, political pressure from the managers' club produced a result. SIP's government authorities cobbled together a compact that would prohibit companies from poaching from one another. Since there were no penalties attached, it was entirely a gentlemen's agreement. Some managers lost no time in scheming how to circumvent the probationary period required of employees before they joined another firm. One SIP official described it bluntly as a "goodwill gesture from the government," another termed it a "paper tiger." Nonetheless, fifty-five companies quickly signed on, and officials worked on the others one by one. For newcomers that still had to hire a workforce, it was a different story. They had no incentive to sign. To encourage them to play along, the park's own HR agency promised to help them bring in new recruits from the north and the west. The agency established a new division for Middle Level Talent, and recruiting relationships were established with universities and technical colleges in select cities in these cheaper regions.

Everyone whom I questioned in the SIP's managers' community insisted that these measures were not examples of government intervening in a "free labor market." But it was difficult to conclude otherwise. SIP's services—in common with every other development zone that offered tax holidays and free infrastructural services—were a government giveaway to foreign investors. The park's roster of tax incentives ranged from huge reductions and exemptions on corporate and local taxes to rebates and exemptions on VAT and other import/export duties. Special preferential policies applied to the semiconductor and software industries. There were even rebates available for the use of utilities. Raw materials and products could be transferred tax-free within the zone and between other export processing zones in China. As for logistics, the park boasted a highly efficient green lane. Through a one-stop service, an independent customs office offered clearance around the clock, even on public holidays. Local government was building public dormitories to make it easier for employers to house their operators. A wealth of other infrastructural services were available gratis. SIP had its own generator, guaranteeing that no investor would suffer from the chronic energy cuts that plagued the rest of the region's industry during the summer months. Factory plants were able to discharge their dirtiest waste and water into a central treatment pipe that delivered to the park's own treatment facility. "If you want to do dirty business," as one official put it to me, "then this is a good place to be. We will take care of it all."

In the face of all of these concessions and subsidies, it was absurd to talk of a free labor market. When all was said and done, China, like other nations in the offshore market, was in the business of buying jobs. Once the investors were there, they expected governments to fill the jobs with the right people, at the right price. The livelihoods of SIP officials depended on pleasing their foreign guests. They were hardly likely to disregard the combined voice of their multinational investors, especially when the threat to pick up and leave was presented as a collective one. Social instability from layoffs was the number-one concern for local government all across the country. The impact from state-owned-enterprise layoffs could be mitigated for a while, since the government had the power to pay a subsistence stipend. But the private sector had become the primary GDP engine, and foreign corporate interests had to be met.

Managers' threats to leave SIP because of wage inflation were intended to intimidate, but they were far from imaginary. In the course of 2004, more than twenty companies moved out of the SIP core, and as many as forty-five moved out of the larger SIP administrative area. "Absolutely nothing will stop jobs leaving Suzhou," affirmed Andrew's Mike Barbalas, languidly gesturing around him. "All these plants and all this land could turn into brownfields." Managers like him assumed that jobs (and not only labor-intensive ones) would inevitably move westward. It was almost as natural as the jetstream blowing eastward. Several SIP managers were looking at land north of the river, in Subei, the poorer and relatively undeveloped part of Jiangsu province, or farther west and upriver. "Most of us wait until an industry leader makes the move," explained the director of a German chemical company, "and then a herd mentality kicks in. It takes longer for the supply chain to move, but in China such things happen quicker than they used to." There were other factors that would make a difference. "If the yuan gets revalued by more than 10 percent," observed Philips's KG Ching, "it means that East China is no longer competitive. We'd have to move to Vietnam or maybe to other places in the west of China that are low in cost."

Although employers were in a position to move west and better their profit margins, their employees were not in a position to do so. If anything, workers in China were accustomed to moving eastward. But whatever mobility they enjoyed gave them leverage. They had no functional representation to promote their interests, even though there were official trade unions in as many as 300 SIP companies. (Many of the foreign firms established a "staff club" or "welfare committee" that provided the social services typically offered by a traditional union, without having to pay the mandatory cost—2 percent of monthly payroll—for an official union.) As a result, workers without skills had no collective means to improve their conditions on site. Like the migrants who failed en masse to report for work in South China after the 2004 Spring Festival, their only form of leverage was to stay at home. But if they had skills and experience, their ability to job-hop became a powerful bargaining tool.

Gao Fenzhen was a machine tool operator, without a university degree, who had trained at Suzhou's Institute of Vocational Technology. Promoted to technical lead after only eighteen months at an American electronics company, he had a clear sense of that power. "I know I can get a better offer by signing with National Semiconductor [currently hiring down the road], and I am almost sure my boss will offer me more to keep me here." His confidence was magnified in Daniel Chou, a college-trained engineer in the same company, who had put in his two years and wanted to work with higher technology: "My career comes first, and I can tell my manager this. The response is up to him, but I don't think I will lose. Chinese like me have to put ourselves first. We don't have the advantage of time." Chou acknowledged that his hard-nosed attitude was shaped, in large part, by the faithless conduct of employers. "Foreigners will leave when they find a cheaper environment," he observed matter-of-factly. "Right now, we are where Singapore was ten years ago, and they will leave as soon as we get to be too expensive, so we must take advantage of them while we can." Job-hoppers like them told me it was almost impossible to understand how American, European, or Japanese employees could work for the same company for thirty years.

While the bargaining power of employees like Gao and Chou was always exercised individually, it was felt collectively as wage inflation by the HR managers of SIP companies. For some firms it had become a factor in whether they would stay for very long. For most of the others it affected the decision about when they would move higher-end operations to the park. This put employees like Chou at the center of an industry-wide dilemma. His desire for a more challenging job, working with higher technology, could only be met by a company that was transferring advanced operations from a more expensive location. Yet corporate executives would only transfer these units when Chinese skills were mature enough to meet the challenges, and when the price of those skills could be contained.

Upgrading the Plant

The bulk of the companies in SIP started out doing assembly and testing, and many had taken on basic product engineering. It was a bigger step from there, however—especially for the park's critical mass of precision manufacturers—to move in more advanced operations, like original concept development. Most of the engineers in the park were supporting or troubleshooting for production lines, and their ingenuity was only called upon in boosting the yield. The bulk of product design was still being done in the home countries, but that would change as soon as the conditions were ripe. In addition to concerns about salary inflation, fear of intellectual-property theft was an issue for many employers. With such high turnover, some employees were likely to walk off with drawings and blueprints. Indeed, companies were regularly asked to buy technology plans from ex-employees of their competitors. So, too, firms transferring design and R&D units would have to deal with the political fallout from laying off high-end employees at home.

Even so, multinational R&D had already begun to stream into the region. GE had built one of its three global R&D centers in Pudong's Zhangjiang Park, to be joined by IBM, Microsoft, Intel, Ericsson, HP, and a host of others. In SIP, as many as fifty companies had R&D units, some of them tucked away in the corners of vast manufacturing plants, some of them based in regional universities. Others were in freestanding facilities in SIP's own Science Park, a cluster of innovation units that included an integrated circuit design incubator and a stack of software firms, many of them outsourcing for American and Japanese clients. Pressure from the customers of multinationals was drawing more and more R&D. Several managers reported that their clients in China (both domestic and foreign) were insisting that they develop the capacity to build and optimize original concepts to fit local demand. A general manager at an American semiconductor facility acknowledged that "to compete in the domestic market here, we will need full transfer of global technology as soon as we can. Otherwise we can kiss China good-bye."

At Philips, KG Ching explained that his company was accustomed to transferring advanced operations from the Netherlands to Singapore before moving them, when mature, to China. Increasingly, however, their customers wanted everything to come directly to China in order to cut costs. "If you are going to Singapore and then to China later on, you take a long learning curve, and the cost reduction is not sufficient for the customer. Conservative companies," he added, "hold back on transferring technology in order to protect domestic workers. But if you are driving very aggressively, it can happen quickly. As far as we can be in China, we try to transfer as much as possible."

Internally, the process of moving a production line offshore had become a finely tuned art. The fact that American measures and standards were not metric was sometimes a problem, but once the support platforms were ready, entire "plug and go" units could be transferred in a matter of weeks, sometimes days. In global companies, documentation was strict, and the same management culture was often shared across all divisions and locations, so the process (often called Copy-Exact) was generally quite smooth. All over SIP, vast rooms in plants and vacant fields outside lay in wait for the transfers. The business of transferring skilled knowledge was more complex. Chinese employees often had to go onshore for training (fomenting protests among onshore employees whose jobs they would be taking over), and lines of communication across language barriers had to be clarified constantly. Above all, the knowledge being transferred had to fit within the limits of what was considered rational (i.e., profit-seeking) corporate conduct. This profile involved the nurturing of intangible qualities like self-initiative, and the suppression of Chinese cultural characteristics such as "face" and the working of interpersonal relationships known as *guanxi*.

The localization of what they called "initiative" was as much a concern for foreign managers in manufacturing as it was in IT services. "On the one hand," explained Spansion's PC Loh, "our Chinese employees like to be in a Western culture type of management environment, but on the other hand they are not totally out of the influence of the old traditional management culture of Chinese people. You don't see lots of young people here who ask questions in a meeting or in a public discussion. And you also can see that they are very supervisor-focused. They expect the boss to direct them to do what he needs to do. Maybe they behave that way unknowingly," he recognized, but they do "carry that kind of cultural burden" into the workplace. Managerial efforts were aimed at taking employees out of their familiar culture. A local custom like "face," for example, was considered an obstacle to efficiency in the manufacturing workplace. In managers' minds, Chinese employees too often held their tongues, or practiced indirection, in order to save the face of a superior. On occasion, however, this local cultural trait could be turned to managerial advantage. Loh acknowledged that he challenged employees to achieve tasks by appealing to their pride, or to the pride of their department. The prospect of losing face, he had found, proved to be a powerful motivation. I was not able to verify the result among the Spansion employees whom I interviewed, but in that firm and elsewhere in SIP, I found a related mentality that had as much to do with nationalistic as with personal face.

For example, one of Jacky Wu's primary tasks, as a process engineer, was to ensure that production lines were transferred smoothly from his company's plants in Penang and Bangkok. His job entailed visits to those sites, and close working relationships with engineers whose knowledge was also being transferred. "It's not very high technology," he explained, "but we still have to prove that Chinese engineers are as good as Thai or Malaysian or Singaporean ones. If China wants to go further and actually create technology, our engineers have to be better, and maybe one day we can be as good as the Americans and Japanese. Then I can work with the really high-tech stuff." If you took his reasoning at face value, then Wu's motivation on the job was driven in part by national pride. He knew, of course, that the jobs of the Thai and Malaysian engineers would be lost as a result. "I think they will have some problems," he noted soberly, "but China has also many people without jobs."

Wu's attitude was common among engineers who worked close to assembly and testing operations. They tended to measure themselves against their counterparts in Asian countries that had hosted the first offshore sites for technology companies ten or twenty years before. For product engineers, the comparison was with higher-level locations— Japan, Europe, and the United States—and it was more complicated by far. "Right now, it looks as if we are still twenty years behind," estimated Li Xiaolin, who oversaw a design division at an American electronics firm, "but Chinese learn very fast, and if we have good access to American knowledge, maybe my country can do it much more quickly. Right now, in my company, I think that Corporate would give us more control over design, but they are worried . . . not about China, but about whether we can retain our talent."

When engineers like Li made comments like this, it was not always clear whether they were identifying with the interests of their employer or those of their nation. Company loyalty was very thin on the ground, but since most wanted to work with higher technology, they were motivated to help their companies move to China as much as was technically possible. To that degree, their personal ambition coincided with the company's goals of further offshoring. In fact, their morale would probably drop if the company failed to do so. Ultimately, however, they tended to view the greatest benefit as falling to China itself. As one engineer memorably put it, "China is always there, somewhere in my mind."

"China," in this equation, was not some atavistic notion of the motherland before which they had been coached to bow. They had been trained as technicians and engineers, after all, and their mind-set was pragmatic, not romantic.[18] When they spoke of the benefit to China, it had more to do with the diet of national development on which they had been weaned from an early age. Indeed, ever since the 1989 repression in Tiananmen Square, the state's propaganda efforts had switched from pushing explicitly Marxist doctrine to patriotic education campaigns about building a strong, modern China.[19] Under this creed, national weakness was the condition that had allowed foreigners to dominate China for over a century, and the cornerstone of the new education was built around the vow to ensure that it would never happen again. Any visit to a patriotic education site of historical importance would illustrate this precept.

Arguably the best example I visited was Nanjing's Memorial

Museum to the Japanese Massacre. As many as 300,000 citizens were slaughtered when the Japanese army invaded the city in 1938. Nanjing is dotted with massacre sites, and the museum is built on top of one, partly exhumed for the purpose of display. The museum does not rank high on the tourist circuit, but on any day of the week it is packed solid with Chinese schoolchildren, for whom a visit is almost as obligatory as a trip to the nation's capital. Signage at the site overflows with heavy-handed lessons about the past and the future. A memorial stone to those who were killed en masse at Zhongshan Wharf reads: "The nation was weak. How could we have been safe? In order to avoid being bullied by foreign nations, a country must rely solely on its own strength." The conclusion to the exhibit warns visitors: "Slowly developing and backward countries can easily come under attack and be humiliated. Therefore we must do our best to build China into a stable, united, prosperous, and powerful socialist country."

Twenty years after the Nanjing Massacre, Mao Zedong tried to hasten the Great Leap Forward by encouraging China's peasantry to build and operate homemade steel furnaces in their own backyards. It proved to be a futile and somewhat disastrous program that diverted farmers from growing at a critical time. The result may even have aggravated grain scarcity to famine levels. But for Mao, the object was not simply to boost industrial productivity to the levels of advanced nations. One of the chief aims in this campaign, as in so many others, was to involve the masses in the forefront of nation-building, and not to leave technical development solely in the hands of specialized experts.[20] There was no equivalent in contemporary China. The specialized division of labor was accepted as a matter of fact, as was the idea that learning from foreign expertise was the best way to strengthen China and guarantee its future independence from foreign mastery. Technology and knowledge transfer, if it was done right, was the key to this future, and the loyalty of engineers was the lock.

In the short term, foreign investors could profit from the patriotic sentiments of their Chinese employees. After all, the zeal of engineers for China to acquire technical knowledge coincided with the corporate need for a workforce that was enthusiastic about moving up the industrial value chain. If, in the minds of employees, their ultimate aim was to grow China out of its technological dependence on foreign expertise, the immediate result was in complete harmony with the foreigners' short-term goal of harvesting offshore profits. Deng Xiaoping's famous dictum—"It makes no difference whether the cat is black or white, as long as it catches the mouse"—worked just as well for the foreign capitalist as for the new kind of communist patriot.

Many of my interviewees noted the irony, but saw no contradiction. "I am in favor of this direction," commented Li Xiaolin, "and our government is doing the right things to keep us on this path. Things may change in ten years, but so far it is win-win for both China and the West." In fact, it was almost always described as a win-win situation. But surely there must be some losers? "In some other countries, yes, I have heard things are not so good, they are losing their industries, and they sometimes blame China," he added, "but China has had so many troubles, all of our families have suffered so much, and we have too many of our own people to take care of."

Pressed on this issue, Li acknowledged that he had personally witnessed some of the international friction generated by offshore transfers. At his company, where operations were about to be transferred from Singapore and the United States, some of his colleagues had noted that their counterparts in those overseas sites had stopped responding to their queries about technical applications. "Maybe they are not happy about losing their jobs," one of them mused diplomatically, "and they don't want to help us anymore. I can understand this behavior, maybe I will feel the same way," she added, in anticipation of what she assumed was a likely occurrence. A Singaporean manager at an American disk drive company, who was responsible for transferring production lines from Singapore, told me that his engineer colleagues over there had pleaded with him to go slowly so that they could hold on to their jobs for a little longer. The "system," he explained to them, would not permit it. Those who had been assigned to come over to teach mainland engineers how to do their jobs were not at all happy. "But they are professionals," he observed, "and they know how to be responsible in their positions."

Earlier that day, I had interviewed a Chinese engineer at Lilly, whose previous job at Trane had required him to be sent to La Crosse, Wisconsin, to learn the ropes as part of a planned production shift to China. "The American workers were very angry," he recalled, "and demanded that the managers send all the Chinese home. I would probably have felt the same way." But there was no personal animus, he added. "Outside of the workplace, in the bars, they were very friendly to us. We had to go instead to the Denver plant for our training, and then, for one reason or another, the production line was not moved to China." The difference in response between the militant American workers who resisted the plant transfer and the Singaporean engineers who aided the transfer because of their "professionalism" wasn't just a difference of class. Regional location was a big factor. Singaporeans had come to accept their lot as a way station in the global production chain. Twenty years ago they had seen the jobs come, and so they were more stoical about seeing them go. By contrast, the workers in Wisconsin had not yet gotten the message—resistance is futile—that employers wanted to send.

But their resistance would not amount to much in the long run, if they could not communicate effectively and meaningfully with their counterparts in Singapore and Suzhou. Acting together on the combined knowledge might help to establish some control over their mutually shared livelihoods. It might even prove more useful to them than shoring up the job know-how that their employers were trying to shift from one workforce to another. In the period of national industrialization, workers in many countries had been able to forge this kind of common solidarity. As a result, they were able to push for strong labor unions, progressive taxation, and a sheltering raft of employee benefits that are the prerequisite for a relatively equal and humane society. Workers in the new corporate free-trade economy—where employers are able to operate runaway shops on a global scale—are having to start all over again, building up the international connections and mutual trust that are needed to bring justice for all.

Go West

As a proven magnet for multinational money, Suzhou had become a regular pit stop on the business lobbyists' circuit. It was no surprise, then, when Bob Kapp, director of the powerful U.S.-China Business Council, dropped by, in March 2004, on a mission to mobilize the faithful. "On the day I meet you here, we are back in another emergency," he began his speech to a lunchtime audience in the Suzhou Sheraton, a monumental edifice that mimicked the architecture of Old China. Other than jet lag, what was keeping him awake? The AFL-CIO, he reported, had just filed a legal petition with the Bush administration charging China with unfair labor practices. By suppressing a broad range of labor rights, the freshly filed petition argued that Beijing had artificially depressed workers' wages (by 47 to 86 percent), resulting in the loss of up to 727,000 U.S. manufacturing jobs. Estimating that these policies had forced a drastic reduction of export prices, the administration was asked to respond by introducing punitive tariffs of up to 77 percent on Chinese imports.[1]

It was the first time that Section 301 of the 1974 Trade Act had been used for an unfair labor practices charge, and it had taken U.S.-China traders quite by surprise. Kapp's job was to rally his member corporations into a lobbying frenzy spearheaded by his own organization. The strategy had worked before, in the 2000 battle in Congress over establishing Permanent Normal Trade Relations (PNTR) with Beijing. At that time the free-trade lobby overcame strong opposition from a coalition composed of the AFL-CIO, environmental and human rights groups, several protectionist U.S. business organizations, and an assortment of right-wing America First groups.[2] "We will have to fight back," Kapp declared, "so we will be calling on all of our companies to help. We have to hear from you quickly with written stuff about local knowledge . . . we have a lot of work to do."

Who knows exactly what role the corporate lobbying played, but within weeks the Bush administration had summarily rejected the petition, which had been carefully crafted and timed to embarrass and damage Republicans in constituencies where job loss was a potent electoral factor. Dismissing the suit as a recipe for "economic isolation," Bush's Cabinet appointees Don Evans, secretary of commerce, Elaine Chao, secretary of labor, and trade czar Robert Zoellick announced that they would put their own diplomatic pressure on Beijing to recognize international labor standards to which the United States itself is barely committed.[3] The Bush administration had developed a keen appetite for flaying China for its violations of international legal standards, but usually only on issues that affected corporate profit, such as intellectual property and the alleged "dumping" of cheap goods on U.S. markets. Outrage over Beijing's loose implementation of the nation's labor laws and concern for the plight of China's workers were not sentiments that Bush officials (or U.S.-China Business Council presidents) normally lost sleep over.

But neither were the petition's prescriptions likely to improve the lot of workers, either in the United States or in China. Blaming Beijing, rather than corporate-friendly trade policies, for American job loss was a misguided choice, with a tragic history behind it. To some eyes, the petition was only the latest in a long record of manipulating anti-Chinese sentiment on the part of organized labor in the United States, beginning with support for the Chinese Exclusion Act of 1882.[4] The anti-Chinese tenor of the petition was pronounced in a way that AFL-CIO protests over labor repression in other countries had not been, and the persistent use of China as a whipping boy for the woes of American union members seemed to be a sorry vestige of the organization's Cold War mind-set.[5] In contrast to trade unions all across the industrialized world, the AFL-CIO had no official contact with China's ACFTU, and American trade unionists who met independently with ACFTU officials were liable to be criticized as communist dupes.[6]

After his Suzhou speech, Kapp acknowledged to me that China's labor record was "lousy," but agreed that high tariffs were probably not the best way to help Chinese workers. On the other hand, his audience had been made up of foreign managers who believed their Chinese employees' wages were already too high. Most were members of Suzhou's newly formed American Chamber of Commerce branch, and they were primarily interested in hearing about business opportunities that could cut their operating costs even further. Never mind the charge that Chinese wages had been artificially suppressed. Where could they go to find a friendly business environment that offered even cheaper labor? Sure enough, the first question after Kapp's speech was not about the AFL-CIO petition but about the business climate 1,500 kilometers upriver in Chongqing, where Kapp had just paid a visit. "It's the place where we see the next great business opportunity," he reported, sounding a dutifully upbeat tone. "But," he added, "if Shanghai is the head of the dragon, you should know that Chongqing is definitely the tail." Referring to its mountainous location, he described it as "ragged and quite poor, more like Appalachia in West Virginia." In contrast, he concluded, "The advantages are so much greater down here in Suzhou."

It was more or less what his audience wanted to hear. For most of them, the time to move west was not quite here, though it might come soon enough, and they should prepare. Some industry leaders had already made the move, and the herd mentality ensured that others would follow. Intel had committed to building a plant in Sichuan, and Ford, as Kapp noted, was already cranking out Fiestas and Mondeos in Chongqing, to be shipped all the way downriver to Shanghai. Chongqing's remote location and near-perpetual fog had helped to confound not a few Japanese bombers when it served as the nation's besieged wartime capital. Now these and other natural disadvantages would pose a logistical challenge to investors looking to mine the low cost of its human resources. Offsetting the obstacles was the vast domestic market offered by Chongqing's 31 million inhabitants, and 90 million more in the neighboring province of Sichuan. Dismayed at the rising cost of doing business in the Lower Yangtze, investors were looking upriver at the prospect of lower cost production and ready access to this kind of mass consumption.

China's Frontier?

Prospective foreign investors would be going upriver with the full backing of the Chinese government. In fact, they would be playing a key role in the realization of a new policy, announced in the last months of the twentieth century, for bringing some of the benefits of the nation's growth to neglected western provinces like Gansu, Guizhou, Qinghai, Shaanxi, Sichuan, and Yunnan, and to the special autonomous regions of Ningxia, Tibet, Inner Mongolia, and Xinjiang. It was called the Great Western Development Strategy, or Go West (*xijin*), and it involved colossal expenditures on infrastructure—for highways, railways, airports, gas pipelines, water diversion, electricity transmission projects, and communication networks.[7] In addition, extensive reforestation efforts were planned both to restore ecological balance and offset fears about the environmental impact of the expected growth. Government officials courted foreign funders to favor the region. To make the policy appear in retrospect as if it had been planned all along, someone in Beijing cooked up a slogan: "Develop the East, Then Shift to the West."

For an older generation, "shifting to the west" had a familiar ring. Indeed, for most of the Maoist period, planners of the national economy had pursued an "interior first" development policy, as a way to compensate for the unequal benefits enjoyed by the treaty-port cities. Beginning with the first Five-Year Plan of 1953–57, and then again with the Third Front policy of defense industrialization, from 1964 to the early 1970s, the command economy diverted the bulk of state investment to inland provinces. However, as market reforms picked up pace after 1979, the scramble for foreign investment in the coastal provinces resulted in the disregard and effective abandonment of these politically inspired efforts. The new Go West policy was unveiled as a long-overdue revival of attention to those in the interior who were being left behind. In reality, it was a crusade of convenience that met several pressing needs.

The primary one, certainly, was to alleviate poverty in the region, where 28 percent of China's population inhabited 72 percent of the national land area, many of them with a household revenue only one-tenth of the Shanghai average. Over twenty-five years, China had achieved the most rapid poverty reduction in human history, delivering 300 million out of poverty, but hundreds of millions of Chinese still lived on less than a dollar a day. Aside from easing the income gap between the coast and the interior, an increase in their disposable spending power would allow westerners to buy goods that were already overproduced in the east, where consumer markets were increasingly saturated. So, too, residents of the most far-flung provinces were sitting on vast reserves of mineral and energy resources that could be mined to fuel the nation's engines of industry. China had nowhere near enough natural resources to feed its growth, and most of what it had was in these remote regions.[8]

But many of the factors driving the policy were political in nature. For one thing, these provinces hosted the largest range of China's national minorities, and some of them, like the Tibetans and Xinjiang's Uighurs, were openly opposed to the incursion of Han (China's ethnic majority) into their homelands. Regional development might help to appease those who saw Beijing's policies as a colonial land grab. Projects like the herculean construction of the Qinghai-Tibet Railway, or the implementation of citywide broadband access in Xinjiang's capital, Urumqi, were touted as highly visible counters to the charge that the central government was bent only on territorial conquest and extraction of resources.

In the far west, the rhetoric of national unity had always sounded feeble. Party officials hoped that large-scale development would go a long way toward bolstering the kind of social and political stability in rural areas that was a paranoid concern for the Communist Party. In addition, Go West promised to fortify China's most vulnerable border areas. Beijing's Cold War fears of encirclement by the United States had been revived and reinforced in the course of the war in Afghanistan, when the Pentagon established new military bases in the Central Asian republics of Kyrgyzstan, Uzbekistan, Tajikistan, and Afghanistan, and added to its access rights in Singapore, Thailand, Brunei, Indonesia, Malaysia, South Korea, and the Philippines, not to mention Taiwan, where arms sales had increased dramatically. The presence of foreign investment in border regions was arguably the best civilian insurance against this perceived threat. Last but not least, Beijing had to explore new ways of easing the nation's chronic unemployment problems. Job creation in the west would relieve some of the demographic pressure on coastal cities from the region's migrant workers, and it would attract back some of the local talent—"peacocks flying to the east"—who had been part of the region's traditional brain drain.

Commentators were quick to compare the policy with American frontier expansionism of the nineteenth century—a notable prior example of inland development on a continental scale. A few of the same apparent factors were present. China's west was a landlocked empire of territory, a promised bonanza for speculators and investors looking to escape regulation, and a potential "safety valve" for resolving imbalances of labor and wealth. In an echo of the Indian Wars, it was also a site of ethnic resistance on the part of the region's minority peoples. The dissimilarities were much more obvious, however, not least that some of the provinces already boasted populations between fifty and a hundred million, cities with advanced urban infrastructures, and a rich legacy of complex settlement on the part of historically powerful dynasties. Yet the analogy with the United States was so seductive that it surfaced in many a news report about the policy.[9] It complemented a tendency (ruinous to so many investors, in the era of joint ventures) to see China's post-reform development as somehow always conforming to American models.

On China's new "frontier," the hand of the state would be all too evident, as indeed it had been on the American frontier, when millions of acres of public land were given away to the railroad companies and homesteaders, or else sold off at rock-bottom prices to speculators. Aside from the hefty public disbursement plan of $35 billion promised for each of the first ten years, foreign investors were encouraged to expect a great deal of state assistance in moving into the western regions. Beyond the basic concession of a 15 percent discount in the corporate tax rate, and further tax exemptions in selected industries, all sorts of sweet deals could be made. For the biggest investors, with a global name to back their capital, virtually everything was negotiable. To cap it all, Go West's massive state investments were exempt from the macro-controls introduced in 2004 to cool down an overheated economy.[10]

A Beijing policy move with such epic dimensions had to show results quickly. Official statistics showed that 2003 and 2004 growth in the western regions was up by 11 percent and 12 percent respectively, and a construction binge generated a spike in employment levels. More notably, a much-hyped national volunteer campaign to recruit up to 6,000 college graduates to help with western development was closed after it attracted 43,763 applicants in just two weeks of advertising. The volunteers chosen worked for a meager 600 RMB ($72) a month, and after a year or two of service, the government helped them find permanent jobs in the region or elsewhere.[11] In a bid to jump-start foreign investment, overseas Chinese from Taiwan and Hong Kong were courted first, just as in the initial phases of coastal development. Some multinationals, especially those currying favor with the central government, began to make commitments. But the first wave of foreign investors made heavy weather of an economic environment that was much less liberalized than the coastal regions, and by 2001 the growth rate of FDI was in the red.[12] In 2003, for example, only 2 percent of all China's FDI went to Sichuan province, which accounted for the ninth-largest gross product in the nation, while the western region as a whole secured only 4 percent.[13] Subsequently, such sectors as mineral exploration, tourism, and agricultural development, which had been off-limits, were opened up to foreign investors.[14] The 2004 figures were better, showing an influx of $3 billion to the region, a 70 percent increase in FDI over the year before.[15]

Despite the hoopla, and the massive construction on the ground, the policy was still more of a concept than a reality for most residents of the region. In the business world, it would take sustained FDI growth for it to register as a success. If this influx materialized, the policy would open up yet another round of low-cost opportunities to take advantage of China's underemployed and underpaid. For investors already established on the east or south coast, going inland would be like going "offshore" without leaving the country.

Going Upriver

Two months after Kapp's speech, I made my own way upriver to visit the Chongqing Economic and Technological Development Zone, which was the first national-level zone in the west, and already boasted multinational names like BP, Honda, Visteon, Ford, Ericsson, B&S, and Suzuki, most of them operating in joint ventures. The southern park (at 9.6 square kilometers) was already full, and the new northern park was an 83.7-square-kilometer construction zone, where an armada of bulldozers was leveling the hilly terrain on a heroic scale reminiscent of some Socialist Realist poster from the Cultural Revolution era. Earth-moving had long been an art form in the "Mountain City" of Chongqing, and the experience of mammoth construction feats had helped build the confidence for mounting the Three Gorges Dam project farther downriver. As we entered the industrial park, breaks in the fog everywhere revealed an epic landscape of torn-open red earth and boulders spilling onto the graded base of fledgling highways.

When foreign investors came prospecting here, what did they want to know? I asked the zone's investment promotion manager. "The number-one question," he replied with admirable deadpan, was "Where will I be able to play golf?" Indeed, on the very day I visited, ground was being broken on the zone's golf course. En route to that spot, we passed the apartment building blocks where many of the site's 180,000 peasant farmers were being relocated, in readiness for their role as ready-made employees in the zone's factories. Would the peasants be able to use the golf course? He assured me that the course would be open to all who wanted to play, though he doubted if many of the farmers would care to do so. Aside from the merit of a passable eighteen holes, the zone, which was promoting itself as an "investment paradise," offered the usual raft of preferential policies for would-be investors. The lavish concessions were further beefed up by tax breaks offered as part of the Go West policy. No local income tax was levied. Corporate tax was waived for the first two years, and then levied at a 50 percent discounted rate for two years after the first profitable year. Firms that met the requirements of encouraged industries, especially in high tech, could enjoy further tax concessions. Other VAT, export, and credit breaks were available, and reinvestment of profits, of course, was further rewarded.[16]

There seemed very little that the zone authorities would not do to attract global brands. Beijing had already jump-started this process by ordaining some key joint ventures; Ford and Honda were assigned to partner, respectively, with Changan and Jialing, both state-owned enterprises with national profiles in the automobile and motorcycle markets. In fact, the zone was being groomed as the automobile production center for all of central and western China. To facilitate shipments, authorities were building the largest container port and railway terminal on the Yangtze. Go West funds were being used to upgrade the east-west expressways and also those that crisscrossed the region. The city center would soon be accessible from any metropolitan location within twenty minutes, and within eight hours from rural spots that, until quite recently, took up to three days to reach.

Ever since the Nationalist government moved here in 1937 to withstand the Japanese advance, the city had been synonymous with the defense of the nation. Chongqing had acquired a sizable portion of China's military production when Third Front military-industrial facilities were transferred to Sichuan, Gansu, Shaanxi, and Guizhou in the late 1960s to distance them from potential Soviet attacks. More than 450 factories from Shanghai alone were transferred to the west during the 1964–71 period, along with battalions of key technicians and engineers. By the late 1960s the region was receiving a full two-thirds of the total national investment in fixed assets.[17] Armaments became a huge regional mainstay (supporting companies like Changan and Jialing), and were joined by other industries—iron, steel, chemicals, textiles—considered key to national production and security in the age of heavy lifting. The continued link was well illustrated just before my visit, when 150,000 residents were evacuated after deadly chlorine gas leaked from a chemical plant explosion. In a dramatic denouement, People's Liberation Army tanks were brought in to bombard the gas tanks with armor-piercing shells in order to neutralize the danger. Once again the citizenry had been saved by its stouthearted soldiers.

Even so, the military factories had not been able to escape the massive layoffs in the state sector. Some had been able to switch to motor-cycle and auto production. All were thirsting for infusions of foreign capital, and so it was convenient that among the city's cultural offerings was a friendship museum dedicated to the role the United States had played in aiding the Chinese wartime resistance against Japanese aggression. Perched on a cliff above the Yangtze, the museum was housed in the refurbished domicile of Joseph Stilwell, the U.S. military attaché who served as Chiang Kai-shek's querulous wartime chief of staff. The sanitized exhibit paid tribute to the Sino-American alliance in the period when the Burma Road was built, and when the much-lionized, though militarily inefficient, mercenary group known as the Flying Tigers flew "over the hump" of the eastern Himalayas to protect convoys carrying supplies to the besieged citizenry of Chongqing and the southwest. American visitors to the city were especially encouraged to visit the site to savor the legacy of Stilwell and Claire Chennault, commander of the Flying Tigers. Though if they ventured farther into the western suburbs, they could visit another museum, the U.S.–Chiang Kai-shek Criminal Acts Exhibition Hall, which told a different story. Set within a former prison used by the Kuomintang to detain and torture Communists during the civil war that followed the defeat of Japanese forces, the exhibit illustrated the connection between the atrocities committed there and the Sino-American Cooperative Organization, which channeled American funding to the Nationalists. The dilapidated state of the museum suggested it was an embarrassing reminder at a time when the American dollar was being courted.

Now that the city's development was once again the object of top-level attention from Beijing, would its heritage of frontline nationalistic struggle help to transform Chongqing into an "investment paradise"? Would the city's workers rise to the occasion by reviving the spirit of sacrifice that had graced its prior moments in the sun? During a visit to a British-invested auto parts factory, an HR manager assured me that his workforce was able to draw on the city's heroic tradition of engineering expertise in the national defense industries. But when I quizzed him further he confirmed that, in practice, he was not likely to be hiring anyone over the age of thirty, least of all any workers laid off from the state-owned enterprises that had actually specialized in these industries. Regardless of their exposure to the ethos of patriotic service, he considered such workers to be damaged goods, tainted by an unproductive work mentality that was out of sync with the requirements of the new market civilization.

As for the savings in wages, the zone's investment promotion manager insisted that high local unemployment, combined with a general lack of savvy about the labor market, would guarantee investors lower rates of turnover and less wage inflation than they had encountered in the Delta region. Within a few weeks, some fresh graduates of Chongqing's universities would try to stymie his prediction when they launched a campaign over the Internet to establish a "salary alliance" among students willing to refuse any starting monthly salary offer below 2,500 RMB ($302).[18] The campaign had a tough time taking hold in the face of anticipated high rates of unemployment among the region's new class of graduates. By the end of the summer it became evident that those who had found employment faced a salary drop of one-quarter to nearly one-third from the previous year.

Chongqing workers were also facing downward wage pressure from the fierce inter-city competition for investment among western cities and regions. Every local and provincial government was busy producing puffed-up claims about the superiority of its investment climate and the relative cheapness of its labor costs. For skilled employees, the hottest competition came from Chengdu and Xian, the region's most highly developed centers of higher education. Native talent from these cities was already a huge presence in the workforce of technology companies on the coast, and both cities were trying to steal a march on Chongqing's extensive high-tech plans—which included an optical-electronic industry park, a digital port, bases for semiconductor R&D and medical engineering, and a national software park.[19]

Storehouse of Heaven

My next visit was to Sichuan's capital, Chengdu, which had been heralded as China's next IT mecca. As a meteorology enthusiast, I consulted the Weather Channel website prior to making the trip. "Smoke" was forecast for the days before my arrival. It was not a designation I had previously encountered. That, along with stories about the dire environmental impact of unregulated growth in Sichuan, had prepared me for a respiratory ordeal. My first impression was that the air quality did not seem appreciably worse than in any other large Chinese city, but I soon learned that flights at the airport had recently been diverted because of poor visibility from drifting smoke.

An official from the American consulate (the only consulate in Chengdu, though the Koreans and Germans were on their way) explained that farmers were accustomed to grow winter wheat and summer rice, and had little option but to burn the excess hay ever since mechanization had brought an end to their use of farm animals. The city was ringed by mountains, and so the drifting smoke accentuated the inversion layer that produced air stagnation in the Chengdu basin. Steps taken by the Environmental Protection Bureau to ban agricultural burning were highly unpopular with farmers, adding to their long list of grievances with the provincial and central governments. Indeed, widespread peasant protests helped to maintain Sichuan's official position in the forefront of provinces with high levels of protest activity.[20] In October 2004, for example, the entire city of Hanyuan was shut down and blacked out by the government after hundreds of thousands of farmers staged fierce protests over their eviction without adequate compensation from land appropriated for the large-scale Pubuguo Dam project.[21]

Reforms in the agricultural sector and traditionally high rural taxation accounted for Sichuan's vast contribution to the floating population of migrant workers in the coastal cities.[22] In many counties, half the workforce was employed in the south or the east of China. In 2002, Sichuan's 15 million migrant workers sent back 55 percent more money than the total fiscal revenue actually collected within the province.[23] Those who stayed and who farmed near the cities were perpetually at risk of having their land seized (at a piddling compensation fee) for export-zone development. Indeed, farmers had complained that the funds allocated through the Go West policy were being spent entirely on urban infrastructure and corporate tax credit. This pattern would only exacerbate the gap between rural and urban income, which was already greater in the western provinces than in the developed coastal regions.[24] If Sichuan had been a democracy, its government might have been suffering the same fate as Andhra Pradesh, where, in the 2004 Indian elections, voters threw out officials whose policies had pandered to high-tech development at the cost of ignoring the state's impoverished farmers.

Instead, local officials were obliged to earn their keep by attracting foreign investment and growing GDP, and, for a variety of reasons, Chengdu's burgeoning IT industry was the preferred vehicle. Its inland location made the city an unlikely site for high-volume export-processing, and so the decision to focus on high technology and especially software was a natural choice. Chengdu was already a major producer of information electronics for the domestic market, and its residents had become sophisticated consumers of these products. The city's IT infrastructure was extensive, with a high percentage of residential access to broadband, and nationally it ranked second and third, respectively, in private possession of mobile phones and cars. Above all else, Chengdu boasted several nationally ranked universities, renowned for their graduates in engineering and technology. Indeed, for IT firms in Greater Shanghai and Beijing, Chengdu's twenty-two universities and more than 2,000 research centers were prime recruitment sites, with the reputation of offering top-quality, hardworking talent at a discount.[25] Experienced engineers were regularly raided by coastal companies from the growing roster of local software firms—more than 400 in all, including several with a national profile.

Unlike Chongqing, Chengdu had not been a treaty-port city, and authorities were relative neophytes at dealing with foreign trade. Until it sank in a vast sea of executive iniquity, Enron had been the biggest foreign investor in the province, charged with deregulating the electric power system. By 2004, however, Chengdu had attracted as many as 3,000 foreign-invested enterprises—many with Taiwanese or Korean backing—and the city boasted almost eighty Fortune 500 companies, including technology giants like Microsoft, HP, Motorola, Intel, Sun, Oracle, Epson, IBM, Samsung, and Cisco. Its Ministry of Information Industry was a dogged promoter of the city's competitive advantage in offering low-cost human resources, utilities, air shipment, taxation, and other duties.

Although I made my business as an author quite clear to all the local officials with whom I met, I was uniformly treated as a potential investor and was tirelessly lobbied as such. Wages in coastal cities, I was informed, were rising almost twice as fast (15 percent annually) as in Chengdu (8 percent). "We can find a way for you to make a very quick profit," proposed one government official. "I don't make money," I replied, "I only study people who do." But this revelation did not deter him. "You should know," he continued, "that turnover is only 5 percent here, compared to 20 to 30 percent in Shanghai." For the record, I was also told that the city had two good golf courses.

Despite the keen lobbying, there was no attempt to sell me an image of a high-tech gold rush. The preferred perception of Chengdu's IT industry was that of being built for the ages. For a local analogy, officials had chosen the Dujiangyan Irrigation Project, an astonishing feat of river engineering, built 2,000 years earlier, which had transformed the Chengdu Plain into a famously abundant "Storehouse of Heaven." Over the long run, the city's IT infrastructure was supposed to do for information what Dujiangyan had done for agriculture. Consequently, many of the local software firms had a record of specializing in informatization—the business of transforming information and operations into databanks and integrated systems that would be digitally accessible on a permanent basis.

One of the bigger firms I visited, Yinhai Software, was the recipient of several government contracts to informatize the national labor and social security sectors, along with telecom, electric power, and finance. In addition, the company had been awarded numerous grants, subsidies, and forgivable loans from ministries and bureaus for a variety of projects, including employee and English language training. Funds from Go West had helped the firm to purchase land for a new facility in the city's high-tech zone. Additional funding and encouragement was available from the Ministry of Science and Technology to help companies like Yinhai get into the software outsourcing boom.[26] It was difficult to imagine a private firm benefiting any more comprehensively from government assistance.

In its own efforts to prime the IT pump, the local Council for the Promotion of International Trade had sponsored the country's premier software trade convention, ChinaSoft, in March 2004. Following a similar meeting the year before, the event attracted an impressive list of participants, including all the major Indian firms in the software outsourcing business, along with representatives from every Indian state with a stake in the IT service industry. Some of this participation was the fruit of recent visits to India, and especially to Bangalore, on the part of Chengdu delegations promoting the city as an offshore IT alternative to Shanghai and Dalian. Dong Yuehua, a young programmer for a state-owned enterprise in the city's West Software Park, had attended both events: "This year, all the big companies came, and so I feel good about my prospects. Very soon they will be hiring here, and I won't have to leave my family to go to work in Shanghai." Like everyone else with whom I talked, Dong, who hailed from a city in the north of the province, was enthusiastic about the quality of life in his adopted city; the climate, the culture of its famous teahouses, the lack of stress, and the inexpensive living. Summing up the virtues of this part of Sichuan, he declared with typical culinary pride, "It's difficult to find bad food here." Few visitors were likely to disagree, though the penetration of Western fast food along with rising incomes was taking its toll on the girth of the citizenry. On one city block I saw a gleaming new clinic specializing in fat reduction.

Dong's local loyalty was a reminder that Chengdu could deliver what was available in no east coast city—a stable workforce with relatively low expectations. Yet, for all the enthusiasm evident at the China-Soft convention, there was still an acute shortage of overseas clients, especially in the nascent business of software outsourcing. Although Chengdu was one of the ten designated national software industry bases, it had not been named as one of the national outsourcing centers. City officials were lobbying hard to be added to the current list that included Dalian, Nanjing, Shanghai, Beijing, Shenzhen, and Xian. Yinhai's managers, for example, had spun off their own outsourcing company, working mostly for Japanese clients, but they felt that the national designation would help secure the more sought-after American business. Yet local firms like Yinhai had little hope of attracting attention directly in such a competitive field. One mark of their desperation was that they regarded people like me as a potential link to U.S. clients.

Chengdu's technology initiative had all the appearance of a lavishly prepared party to which the invitees were not showing up (or, to use a phrase often applied to China's west, it was like "a person going hungry while holding a golden bowl"). Yet many locals felt that the wind had shifted decisively in the wake of Intel's 2003 decision to build a test and assembly plant in the city's high-tech zone. The news produced a flood of new inquiries from potential investors, especially to the American consulate, and some marquee names followed up with announcements of new investments in the city. Intel's recruitment fair in a downtown hotel drew thousands of applicants from all over Sichuan. Despite the excitement, skeptics concluded that Intel's need to maintain good government patronage had heavily influenced the decision. Local industry boosters insisted that the company had made the decision entirely on the basis of analysis of the regional cost structure.

Either way, a visit to the new Motorola software facility in Chengdu's own high-tech zone showed how well the authorities were willing to treat U.S. multinationals. The company was paying a peppercorn rent on a plush office building that had been built for Motorola entirely at government expense. "We provided the specs," explained a manager, "and they built the whole thing for us. Whatever we need, they give us. It's a special deal for having been the first to invest in Sichuan." Motorola had come to China as early as 1986, and had completed the industrial pattern of moving up from assembly operations to pure research, currently done in its Beijing and Shanghai labs. Product engineering (in the form of customizing programs for specific products or markets) was the focus of the Chengdu facility, the only software unit in all of China to boast Level 5 CMM, the industry's highest form of accreditation. Engineers from Canada had done the employee training as part of the transfer of their own onshore unit, which now no longer existed. The manager I interviewed had little trouble recruiting to the Motorola brand name, but he expected competition for talent to explode now as a result of the Intel factor, combined with the strenuous government efforts to establish every last link in the software industry chain.

Several businesspeople back in Shanghai had dismissed Motorola's and Intel's presence in Chengdu as examples of government manipulation. "The free market," declared one IT consultant, "would not have located them there." But there was no free market anywhere in China. Government policies and incentives everywhere shaped the climate

Facility custom-built for Motorola by the Chinese government, Chengdu Hi-Tech Zone

and the environment for investment. In Chengdu, it was impossible not to come across evidence of the state's hand in the fostering of high-tech industry. Aside from the offer of special tax breaks, government agencies were fully involved in developing software with intellectual property rights, incubating new enterprises, establishing a product market, promoting technical standards, fostering links between firms and universities, instituting training programs for personnel, sending students abroad and attracting returnees, and championing local resources in the bid for international investment. It was not simply the prospect of cheap labor that was drawing foreign companies into the region; they were being made an offer they could not refuse.

Jacky Yang, the high-tech zone's foreign investment promotion manager, offered an additional explanation: "If investors want to expand and grow beyond their initial investment on the coast, they usually have no alternative but to add their second or third unit out here." The zone already boasted the names of firms that had followed this pattern: Toyota, Sony, Parker, Ericsson, Siemens, Alcatel, Mitsui, Corning, Sumitomo, Fuji, Itochu, and Acer, in addition to Motorola and Intel. Its southern section was full, and the western part was filling up rapidly. Though Chengdu's moment seemed to have come, he was already thinking ahead. "We are the next frontier," he mused, "but we may not be the last one in China." For labor-intensive operations, especially in garments and electronic assembly, there were many such frontiers left in China. Wage inflation, operating costs, and increased surveillance of factory conditions were pushing low-end producers farther inland from their initial strongholds in the Pearl River Delta to rural provinces like Jiangsi, just to the north. The western provinces lay in wait.[27] Twenty years hence, Yang predicted, "we will lose much of this business to Thailand and Vietnam." For higher-end operations it would take longer, though no one, these days, could underestimate the speeds at which knowledge transfer was capable of being accomplished.

For the time being, however, profits were flowing to foreign companies in the zone. Bernard Yao, a Taiwanese-American owner of an aerospace supplier, was a case in point. From 1987 onward, he had invested in a series of joint ventures, "all of them miserable failures." The Chi-

Administration building of the Chengdu Hi-Tech Zone
(under construction)

nese partners, he recalled, "always promised me independence, but they could never follow through, and they could never deliver on time." With his new (wholly foreign-owned) firm, which supplied parts to Boeing, Parker, GE, and Rolls-Royce, it was a different story. "Initially, we had to offer a 30 percent discount for the 'Made in China' label," he reported. "Customers expected 'China junk,' but then they saw that we were delivering high-quality parts. Now we are getting the same dollar prices as American manufacturers for a fraction of the costs." The only difference was that Chinese officials expected bribes— "they expect shark's fin soup for lunch"—though, he cautioned, "American companies can't and shouldn't do that sort of thing."

Leaving aside the question of whether he was obliged to grease palms, he bragged that his was the only such firm in the aerospace supply business that operated outside of "government interference or connections." Clearly his definition of government ties overlooked the fact that he was operating out of a development zone created specifically to limit costs incurred by foreign firms. Yao's perception of operating in a market environment free of state interference was entirely typical of how foreign investors viewed their privileged situation in China as a whole. Permitted to forget about federal and local taxes, freed from any obligation to bargain with unions formed out of free association, offered virtually free land and a raft of preferential instruments to ease their exports—investors regarded all of these as entitlements rightly due for assuming risks, rather than special concessions granted to artificially boost their profits. When Beijing floated plans in 2005 to increase foreign firms' nominal income tax rate of 15 percent to the level imposed on domestic companies (30 percent), there was a firestorm of protest from multinationals.[28]

In his pursuit of cheap skilled labor, Yao said that he shunned college graduates—"their salary expectations are too high"—and recruited directly from vocational technology institutes. That may have been good enough for his precision manufacturing business, but the technology firms moving into the region could not afford to compromise on their need for high-skill employees. Intel's decision to build was followed rapidly by Philips Semiconductor, which transferred an assembly and testing facility from the Philippines to PSi Technologies Chengdu. In July of 2004, SMIC, Shanghai's integrated circuit (IC) star, announced its own plans to build a testing and assembly plant in the zone, and six months later came the news that Intel would add another assembly facility. Among the firms being incubated by local authorities were several IC design companies, and IC suppliers were emerging to supply the needs of the region's new high-tech concentration. With more than a little help from the government, Chengdu had joined Shanghai in acquiring its very own IC sector.

Silicon Buddha

The talent required in the semiconductor industry was quite specialized, and if it was scarce in Shanghai, there was no reason to find it more plentiful 2,500 kilometers inland. Yet one of China's earliest IC facilities, Leshan-Phoenix Semiconductor (LPS), was located just 130 kilometers south of Chengdu. It began life in 1995 as Motorola's first

China joint venture with the twenty-five-year-old Leshan Radio Company. Subsequently its ownership was rearranged, with the majority of shares now held by Silicon Valley's ON Semiconductor. LPS had been producing surface-mount chips used mainly in such wireless communication products as pagers, digital cameras, and mobile phones, but it was now aiming at total integration and was therefore building its own facility, the first in western China, to produce six-inch wafers. Billed as one of the few truly successful joint ventures in the country, it was a favored tour stop for Beijing officials on visits to Sichuan, and had the official goal of becoming "the largest-volume and lowest-cost discrete semiconductor manufacturer in the world."

The new three-lane highway from Chengdu had cut the travel time by almost a quarter, and had brought Leshan (where an international call had, until recently, required the use of a hand-cranked phone) into the world of modern business logistics. The road passed through the fertile Chengdu basin, where not an inch of farmland had been neglected, either on flat lowlands or on the irrigated terraced hillsides. In contrast to the Yangtze Delta, no litter was visible en route. Indeed, there was no trace of modern consumer packaging anywhere. Most of the farms were as self-sufficient as possible, and so a tight profusion of crops—corn, millet, sweet potatoes, sorghum, soybeans, peanuts, sugar cane, and oranges—complemented the rice and wheat cash staples. Leshan itself boasts the world's tallest Buddha, cut out of a rock face, and has the corresponding serenity of a relatively prosperous Chinese city. I did not find a fat-reduction clinic, but on one side street an emporium of fitness machines spilled its treadmill and punching-bag contents onto the sidewalk, in readiness, presumably, for domestic use.

The old entrance to the LPS semiconductor plant wound its way through a dense, open-air vegetable market. In one of the gestures of government largesse toward the firm, a special shortcut to the highway, named ON Semi Road, had been constructed to avoid the indignity of trucking microchips out through the clutter of onion vendors and hot-pot shacks. But the market route was the one that offered a view of the company's full evolution. It snaked through the old state-owned enterprise compound of Leshan Radio Company—where people bustled around open kitchens, apartment blocks, and grocery stores—before crossing a crop-filled gully to reach the ordered, corporate anonymity of the new LPS factory complex. There a sleek high-tech factory was a lone cathedral of productivity, sited next to an empty plot reserved for expansion. Although it had some shared ties through the holding company, this shipshape semiconductor facility shunned the clustered Chinese companies on the other side of the bridge. As CK Lee, LPS's general manager, put it, "Over here, the system is king; over there, the boss is king." Although, by mutual agreement, neither side poached employees from the other, "there is nothing we can learn from them anyway," declared Lee. "We tried to teach them our production system [inherited from Motorola], but the boss only implemented what he wanted. Only one person sings the song, that's the Chinese way," he concluded.

A Malaysian, Lee had been brought over, like many of his peers in global firms, to transfer a production line from his native country. Once the transfer was complete, he was guaranteed a job back home, but it was more likely he would join his compatriots in managing other operations in China. With their Chinese and English skills, and exposure to international business culture, they were very much in demand. Did he see the transfers as a grievous loss to his own country? "Malaysians have become complacent," he explained, "and the Chinese are hungry, they want to work hard." To prove his point, he reported that "productivity is much higher here than among the Malaysians who had operated the same line," and "labor costs are much lower." As for product quality, the Leshan factory had the lowest field failure rate of all of ON's plants worldwide. Even so, Lee expressed impatience with the lack of loyalty on the part of his sixteen hundred Chinese employees. "They want to get rich fast, and so they expect too much too early."

As fast as he recruited college graduates to work as technicians, the Shanghai recruiters lured them away as engineers. Like so many other foreign managers I had interviewed, Lee had a cultural explanation for this: "The Chinese love titles, because they have high 'face' value." Rather than accept that high employee turnover was a feature of a labor market that employers could not readily control (or that they had created because of an unwillingness to hire older employees laid off from state enterprises), he preferred to interpret his employees' disloyalty as a perverse disposition that the mainland Chinese retained, but would someday slough off. Even with the loss of some of their talent, the firm's turnover rates were still lower than in the Shanghai area, averaging about 11 percent annually (while direct labor turnover was higher, at 16 percent). In Sichuan, LPS was still a big fish in a small pond, and as a high-tech employer the firm had had little regional competition until recently. "Now there are some new firms in Chengdu that I would consider," offered Zhang Xiaolin, a production engineer with three years of experience behind him, "but I'm hoping to upgrade my skills by getting a good job in our own wafer fab when it opens next year."

Finding enough experienced recruits for the new microchip factory (or "fab") would be a big challenge. HR manager Johnson Mei reported that his strategy was to lure back Sichuanites from Shanghai and Shenzhen. "They are homesick, they miss their families and the land, and, most of all, they miss the food. It's also much cheaper here and less stressful." While the monthly starting salary for Leshan engineers was about 1,400 RMB ($169), half the east coast rate, those with experience in the east would command much higher paychecks, especially with Intel and other IC plants moving into the neighborhood.

Like the employees I had interviewed in Shanghai and Suzhou, Zhang was all too aware of his own position in a global industrial chain. He compared his competitive advantage with direct counterparts in Shanghai, Taiwan, Singapore, Malaysia, and Korea. "Right now, we don't feel too much pressure. LPS is not producing the most advanced technology," he noted, "so we do not have be in the lead position. But our productivity has to stay ahead, or we will lose everything." Until Intel came along, he had little reason to make the same calculations across the local or regional labor market. Now, with the prospect of a chunk of the IC industry moving into the Chengdu basin, things would change. Zhang's keen appreciation of the global migration of industry sectors would have to take into account the Sichuan factor. Cutting through all of these comparisons, however, was the national interest. Zhang had little trouble in naming or defining what he called "China's challenge." "We have to make sure we can contain our labor costs," he declared, "or what has happened to America will eventually happen here."

Was Zhang speaking as a would-be manager, conjuring up the threat of job loss to dampen the expectations of employees, or as a patriot might do, with the future security of the Chinese people genuinely in mind? Or was he simply judging his own prospects? For the time being, at least, none of these were at odds with one another, least of all in a region that had been officially designated as China's next big thing. In his industry, however, the workers most immediately hit by mainland competition were in Taiwan, not the United States. The rise of China's semiconductor sector was pulling Taiwan's most capital-intensive industry and its most highly skilled workforce across the strait, tangling up the politics and the economies of the two countries as never before. To complete the regional picture I had been putting together, I decided that Taiwan would have to be my next, and last, port of call.

Cross-Strait Flights

"Yes, I am very worried about losing my job. We've become used to being world leaders, our tech industry is a global pioneer, and no one works harder in any other country. But all this means nothing if my employer decides that Chinese can do the same job as me, for a sixth of the cost." The speaker was not American, and we were not on some carefully landscaped corporate campus in Silicon Valley. He and I were on a bus chugging down the highway from his native Taipei to Hsinchu, the epicenter of Taiwan's high-tech industry. Returning after a family lunch in honor of the Dragon Boat Festival holiday, Wu Xiaolin was musing about his job as a production engineer with the mighty Taiwan Semiconductor Manufacturing Company (TSMC), and about the threat posed by the inexorable rise of China's microchip sector. "Our technology," he lamented, "will go along with the jobs."

Though his concerns were focused on high-tech traffic across the Taiwan Strait, Wu was fully aware of how his quandary might affect the United States itself. "If this continues," he pointed out, "your government will not be able to slow down China." He was referring to Washington's efforts, for the past half century, to contain China through actively fostering Taiwan's industrialization. The Taiwan Strait had been one of the most enduring of the Cold War barriers, effectively "blocking" trade and other kinds of relations with the People's Republic of China (PRC). But it had lately become the most porous, as high-skill jobs, technology, and investor capital flowed from the island to the mainland, all but foiling the geopolitical plans of those who would keep Beijing from advancing to the topmost rungs of the industrial ladder.

The recent actions of Wu's employer, TSMC, clearly demonstrated how and where the wind was blowing. This was the firm that, in 1987, had pioneered the concept of the microchip foundry when it began custom-producing for smaller clients who could not afford the multibillion-dollar prices coughed up by industry titans like Intel to build and operate a captive fab. In so doing, TSMC had effectively introduced the practice of IC outsourcing from the United States and other high-cost countries. As we spoke, the company was sitting atop a domestic sector that produced more than 70 percent of the world's microchips, and it was harvesting record profits from an industry boom. Its foundries were at 100 percent capacity, producing twenty-four hours a day, whereas three years before they had been almost 60 percent idle, still reeling from the post-tech-boom recession and the aftereffects of the Asian financial crisis of 1997–98.[1] "We are supposed to perform annual maintenance work on the fabs," reported Wu, "but this year there's no time to spare, it's all 'go for gold while it lasts.' "

Despite the good times, TSMC's boss, Morris Chang, had recently forecast another IC recession, to begin in 2005, owing to a likely glut generated by all of China's new chip factories.[2] Estimates showed that the new mainland fabs would soon be producing 20 percent of the world's chips and undercutting TSMC's prices by as much as 40 to 50 percent.[3] Chang, who was an industrial hero in Taiwan, had initially scored points in Taiwanese nationalist circles for decrying the expansion of the new mainland producers as reckless. But the criticism was hardly an effective way of dealing with his competitors in the PRC. After vowing that TSMC would not cross the strait, Chang changed his tune and in 2003 applied to the government for permission to build a mainland plant—an eight-inch-wafer fab in Shanghai. Chang's turnaround became one of the more controversial topics discussed in the run-up to the 2004 presidential campaign, which resulted in the disputed reelection of the independence-oriented Chen Shui-bian.

In a bid to retain Taiwan's leading industries (and under some pressure from Washington), the government had imposed controls on high-tech companies transferring their more sophisticated operations to the mainland. A government commission was set up to adjudicate applications that fell below a technological threshold. Amid growing unemployment, fears about the hollowing out of domestic industry had intensified as the flight of operations to the mainland moved higher up the value chain. Chen made campaign pledges to further stem the flow in order to appease nativist advocates of protectionism. As the preeminent firm with a Taiwanese nationalist profile, TSMC attracted heated public debate before the election on account of its application. Yet it took only two weeks after the ballots were counted for the firm's investment plan to be fully, and quietly, approved by the Ministry for Economic Affairs.[4] The wafer plant, with more than 1,000 employees, went up in Shanghai's Songjiang Science Park, and was in trial production by the end of 2004.

TSMC had at least sought an officially approved route for moving its operations to the mainland. UMC, its chief rival, had been redirecting orders to Hejian Technology, a Chinese contract chipmaker (registered in the Cayman Islands) that had set up shop in Suzhou Industrial Park in 2003. Operating in a rather gray legal area, Hejian was run by a team of former senior UMC executives and engineers, and it was widely regarded as a back-door UMC operation. Indeed, the company's CEO was eventually fined by the Taiwanese government in March 2005 for illegally transferring capital and technology to Hejian in a case that Taiwanese nationalists used to push for more punitive responses to this kind of practice.[5]

"The government has never been able to stop investors going to the PRC," commented Wu. "They always found a way of doing it. I don't see my industry as any different. It will go the same way. In fact, I hear it every day from my manager, and he knows that telling me this makes me work harder." Hsieh Hsiang-chuan, former director of the Hsinchu Science-Based Park where Wu worked, had recently voiced this warning: "If we don't improve, some people say we will have to work hard just to find a job in Shanghai."[6] That would be a difficult prospect to stomach, given that Taiwanese engineers already occupied many of the staff positions—more than 50 percent, according to some estimates—in China's IC firms. With the mainland expected to account for 24 percent of global chip demand by 2008 (a $61.9 billion market share), it looked as if there should be a surfeit of opportunities for Taiwanese willing to cross the strait, but competition with China's own rapidly swelling pool of engineering graduates would soon be very tight.

Wu himself had no desire to go to Shanghai. Unlike the golden generation of Tawainese engineers who took college degrees in the United States in the 1970s and 1980s and returned to start up companies, he had enrolled at Tsinghua University, which enjoyed a back-door relationship (literally) with the Hsinchu Park. In fact, when they graduated, he and his peers simply moved their belongings half a mile up the hill from their college dorms to the company dorms, though, with their punishing work schedules, they hardly spent any time in the latter. Hailing from a Taiwan-born Minnan family, he leaned toward the Democratic Progressive Party position that Taiwan was a sovereign nation in all but name, and that the Taiwanese people probably ought to try to formalize this fact. "Of course, that will never happen," he acknowledged. Ever since the 2004 election, Beijing had taken great pains to stridently reinforce its "One China" policy—a nonnegotiable one—that Taiwan would always be regarded as a province of the PRC.

Concerns about job loss on the island were markedly different from the public outcry over outsourcing in the United States. For one thing, the political standoff between Taiwan and the PRC was all-pervasive, and left nothing untouched. In addition, the United States was itself a huge factor in all Taiwanese affairs. The island's high-tech sectors served primarily as "original equipment manufacturers" for U.S. technology firms, having found their niche in the global production chains that were driven from the top by American companies. In addition, American interests in the region were primarily responsible for the historic split between Taiwan and China, and pressure from Washington continued to perpetuate it. Unlike most of his friends, who resented the wasteful size of the island's military budget (one of the world's heaviest per capita defense burdens), spent entirely on American weaponry, Wu believed it was essential to protect Taiwan at all costs.[7]

He wished, however, that the defense expenditure brought some jobs to the island.

Did he feel the same way about domestic job loss as many Americans did? "We don't call it outsourcing. It's more complicated than that . . . everything is more complicated here in Taiwan because of the political situation. Because of our laws, most of the companies that moved their factories were acting illegally, so they didn't outsource, they just ran away, or sneaked away." The first wave were small-time players who invested through Hong Kong or through offshore tax bases like the Virgin Islands, the Cayman Islands, and Western Samoa, and accounted for much of the development of export-processing in Guangdong and Fujian from the early 1980s. Many of them moved overnight, leaving their domestic workers' wages unpaid. Some of the factories they left behind were occupied by their former workers, often for years at a time, demanding back pay before the plant or the land could be sold. In the meantime their new factories in South China, mostly export-processing in garments, toys, and electronics, earned the Taiwanese notoriety for the cruelty of their paternalistic management practices.[8] Though he had heard some of the atrocity stories about the South China sweatshops, Wu, like many islanders with whom I spoke, was genuinely surprised to learn that the fear of Taiwanese employers on the part of mainland employees was so widespread.

In contrast to the patterns of U.S., European, and Japanese investment, which generally started with the largest firms and brought smaller ones in their wake, it was the tail of the Taiwanese supply chain that moved first. These small entrepreneurs were discreetly courted by Beijing as part of China's Coastal Development Strategy, and they came initially in direct violation of Taipei's laws against investing on the mainland. These laws were increasingly relaxed, initially to permit medium-sized investment in a limited list of 3,000 products, and then more expansively after 1995, when capital began to arrive in the form of larger, publicly listed Taiwanese firms. These more recent investors tended to locate in the Yangtze River provinces of Jiangsu and Zhejiang, and put their money into more capital- and technology-intensive operations geared as much toward the local market as for export.[9]

By the turn of the century, the de facto integration of Greater China—the PRC, Hong Kong, and Taiwan—was occurring rapidly, in the absence of any significant multilateral agreements and often in spite of existing government controls and sanctions. Taiwan was one of the PRC's biggest trading partners, and the biggest overseas investor (next to Hong Kong). Forty-eight percent of Taiwan's overseas investment from 1991 to 2004 went to the mainland, surging to 70 percent in the course of 2004.[10] Economic integration had long been a policy actively encouraged by Beijing, and when OECD countries imposed sanctions after the Tiananmen Square crackdown, authorities offered especially generous terms for Taiwanese investors (tax holidays for the first two years, while the next three were taxed at the half rate of 7.5 percent). Officials hoped that these individuals and firms would lobby Taipei on more formal steps toward reunification. In turn, the investors, playing both sides of the game, leveraged their presumed lobbying power into efforts to bargain even more from mainland authorities.[11] By the time Taiwan's rules on most forms of direct investment in the mainland were abolished in 2002, there were as many as 300,000 Taiwanese living in Greater Shanghai. In the years that followed, the numbers swelled (in 2004, the PRC estimated that as many as a million islanders lived on the mainland) as increased anxiety about Chen Shuibian's bid for Taiwanese sovereignty drove more and more across the strait. Taiwanese fear about hollowing-out redoubled now that the cream of the island's human resources was being sucked away.

Taiwan's manufacturing labor force peaked in 1987, with 42.8 percent of the national total, after more than twenty years as a labor-intensive assembly platform.[12] The subsequent loss of jobs to the mainland (and to Malaysia and Thailand) was partly offset by the national effort to restructure the economy into high-value sectors and services. The island's computer manufacturers steadily moved their downstream plants offshore (keyboards and power supply units went first, followed by monitors and motherboards, and then notebooks and laptops). As early as 1996 an estimated 32 percent of low-end production was offshore, with some sectors as high as 86 percent.[13] By 2003, Taiwanese investors in the PRC were responsible for 63.3 percent of the island's hardware production in IT and electronics—about $56.7 billion worth of goods.[14] In the case of other East Asian tigers like Singapore, the government had actively encouraged the low-end transfers, as part of a deliberate strategic policy to upgrade the economy. In Taiwan, for example, a 1992 regulation required firms that moved low-value operations to commit themselves to new, upgraded projects at home.[15]

The most acute panic was felt within the technology industries that had pushed Taiwan so firmly up the development chain, where it trailed only Japan and the United States in the number of patents granted annually. Indeed, no other country was so dependent on electronics production and exports. Now that the microchip foundry giants (along with key players in optoelectronics—the island's most recent boom) were moving across the strait, public worries about hollowing-out graduated to a new level. "We Taiwanese live and breathe electronics," Wu reminded me. "Being an engineer is a way of life here. Even the betel-nut girls are worried, they hear it from their customers," he joked, as our bus pulled onto the lively strip of Hsinchu's Guangfu Road, famous for its barely clad beauties in brightly lit storefronts, who were employed to advertise and administer the mild stimulant.

It had taken the Taiwanese economy forty years to scale the technology heap. The accepted wisdom in the business world was that China might take less than a decade of opening up to foreign capital to leapfrog to the same height. Yet a closer look at the record showed that the PRC was hardly a latecomer to the task of high-tech development. Knowing about its postwar experience in technology innovation (or emulation) was crucial to understanding the nationalistic lens through which China's leaders viewed their efforts to compete with other, more advanced countries.

When the Chips Are Up

In common with its East Asian peers, Taiwan's domestic industries were jump-started by technology transfers from multinational firms that came to the island to exploit its cheap labor pool in the late 1960s. By contrast, the PRC already had more than twenty years of high-level

Bringing up baby—sculpture projecting China's
high-tech future

technological innovation under its belt when its economy began to grow out of the central plan in the late 1970s. In the 1950s, the new communist state established a science and technology R&D network, modeled after the Soviet system, and its electronics arm went on to produce several generations of computers, in many cases with little or no gap behind the capitalist powers. China's first computer was developed in 1958, only one year after Japan's, and its first integrated circuit was produced in 1964, only five years behind the first U.S. patent. A microcomputer was developed by 1977 (even before IBM unveiled its PC), a microprocessor by 1980, and a supercomputer, along with an IBM-compatible PC, by 1983.[16] As in the U.S. and European cases, advanced technology was developed initially with the military end-user in mind, and a large cadre of sophisticated engineers staffed the thousands of research institutes and labs (many of them in the west of China) that fed initiatives like the atomic and hydrogen bomb projects, along with a succession of satellite technologies.[17] After the Soviet pullout in 1960, the goal of self-reliance in technological achievement became a matter of vast national pride.[18] Government engineers were, and still are, lionized for their efforts, as witnessed by the nationalistic orgy spawned by the first manned flight to be achieved by China's space program in 2003.

In the United States, federal funding accounted for between 40 and 45 percent of high-tech R&D from 1958 through the early 1970s. By the late 1970s, the private sector's pace of development and funding commitment for commercial R&D had outstripped that of the defense systems.[19] By contrast, China had virtually no civilian or commercial demand, and so the government's research elites, often isolated from one another in their labs, had no incentive to pass on the innovations to would-be industrial exploiters. Even so, when the state reformed its system in 1985 to create cooperative links between industry and the institutes and universities, the results were quite striking. Four new electronics enterprises—Stone, Legend (now Lenovo), Great Wall, and Founder—made rapid advances, and quickly rose to dominance in the emerging domestic computer market, establishing leadership in several areas of export. Relying on joint ventures or alliances with U.S. and Japanese giants for technology transfer, each took advantage of local Chinese features (especially the need to engineer products for Chinese language capability) to enter into product design at a much earlier stage than had been achieved by industries in other East Asian nations. Arguably, this prodigious pace of technology learning was possible because of the firms' roots in the state's strong tradition of technological research and innovation.[20] Lenovo's December 2004 acquisition of IBM's PC unit, making it the world's third largest PC maker behind Dell and HP, was a landmark step in the global expansion of China's high-tech capital.

A less spectacular story applied to the IC sector, even though it was considered the ultimate key to China's high-tech development. Despite a well-funded campaign (in the Five Year Plan of 1991–95) to produce national champions like Taiwan's TSMC or UMC, the domestic industry fell far short of expectations. Successful IC manufacturing was dependent on international expertise, and the cost of building fabs and upgrading machinery was astronomical. Eventually, China's policymakers looked to foreign talent and investment to establish a fully competitive industry. Joint ventures with NEC, Motorola, and Philips led the way, before the Taiwanese were encouraged to enter the field, supplying engineers and capital for many of the wafer fabs that sprang up in the first few years of the new century.

The national campaign to establish a semiconductor industry had begun in 1986 when a policy for revitalizing the electronics industry set the goal of mass production targets within ten years.[21] The Ministry of Electronics set up Project 907 to develop five-inch-wafer production. In 1987, No. 58 Microelectronics Institute was relocated from Sichuan to the Lower Yangtze city of Wuxi to help jump-start domestic chip-making through the creation of a company called Wuxi Huajing Microelectronics. While production was successfully established, the company lost money and failed to achieve mass-volume output. Nonetheless, Huajing would become the Fairchild of the Chinese semiconductor industry, feeding its trained engineers into other firms as they developed. In one of the first of many unofficial trips to Taiwan to recruit talent for the industry, government officials lured Peter Chen, the founder of Hsinchu Park's Mosel Vitelic to take over and upgrade Huajing's fabs. A joint venture (Wuxi CSMC–Huajing) with Hong Kong investors was formed in 1999, and after only fifteen months the firm broke even by producing low-end chips for the domestic market. CSMC became the first open foundry (making custom chips for fabless clients) in China, and it thrived at a time when the semiconductor business in the rest of the world was in a heavy recession.

Located at the western end of East China's technology corridor, Wuxi abuts two bodies of water, the Grand Canal and the gargantuan Tai Lake, both of which were seriously polluted by the city's hectic industrial development in the 1990s. Rapid downtown retail growth attracted the same oversized shiny boxes that had smuggled shopping malls into the heart of every large Chinese city. The city's name, which, literally, means "without tin," recalled a much earlier history of industrial ruination. Originally called You Xi ("has tin"), the name changed during the Han dynasty when the valuable mineral deposits were exhausted. The CSMC plant bordered a new version of the Grand

Canal, where grain-laden barges still plied the city's stretch of the ancient 1,700-kilometer waterway. Behind it rose the hilly mound where the tin mining had once been concentrated. It would be hard to find a more evocative location for the mother ship of the country's newest and most volatile industry.

CSMC's facilities shared a sprawling factory compound with several other firms and institutes that had evolved in similar ways from the original state-run research complex. A hospital, a power plant, and several canteens dotted the compound. All of the plants had a shopworn, institutional feel that contrasted sharply with the futuristic fabs of TSMC, Hejian, SMIC, and other international IC highfliers farther downriver, in Suzhou and Shanghai. The company staff was also a hybrid affair, where fresh-faced "children of Deng" worked alongside hundreds of employees left over from the state-owned Huajing years. Zhang Maiyou, one of these old-timers with a nonchalant view of the culture clash between the two groups of employees, recalled that microelectronics did not carry much of an aura of excitement for his generation (class of 1987). "I worked on Project 907," he explained. "It was just another government project, though we felt it was a special kind of workplace. Maybe you could say there was a sense of national destiny, but we did not feel any pressure to perform in a particular way. Now, in this company, all the pressure comes from the business side. It feels very different." Maiyou and his peers (10 percent of the original Huajing workforce) knew that they were unlikely survivors in an industry where the appetite for fast profit captivates younger recruits. "We're doing better now" was all the enthusiasm he would proffer for the entrepreneurial vim that was propelling the firm's marketing profile.

The whiz kids responsible for that profile had no reason, or inclination, to dwell on the firm's past, except to dismiss it as the by-product of an era that did not understand the modern business world. Indeed, they dated their own attachment from the much more recent date, 2003, when CSMC became a wholly foreign-owned company, funded by overseas investors and run by a fully international management team. The old guard were viewed as a drag on the firm's ongoing effort to overhaul its image, and their failure to make a success of the initial company was viewed with some derision. As one of the new Taiwanese managers sniffily put it to me, "It was like asking street vendors to manage a McDonald's franchise." The younger engineers on staff steered clear of the internal friction. For most of them, the company was merely a vehicle for their personal advancement. Some spoke, typically, of aspirations to start their own company as quickly as possible; others reckoned they would very soon move to one of the gleaming new Shanghai fabs. CSMC's efforts at an IPO had been postponed again and again (its subsequent listing, in August 2004, was a disappointment), and declining morale among the stock-option-bearing workforce was making retention doubly hard.

For these ambitious young recruits, CSMC was more of a training ground than an environment where they could test their mettle. For one thing, its success had been built on supplying mature technology: low-end chips for consumer electronics that still made up 70 percent of the domestic market. As Japanese, Taiwanese, and American producers phased out their six-inch fabs in pursuit of the more sophisticated eight-inch and twelve-inch facilities, CSMC was assured of a long-term supplier position in a country that had become the world's biggest producer of electronic appliances. The firm had largely achieved that position by buying up used production lines—from Agere, in New Jersey, and Chartered, in Singapore—in regions that were getting out of the low-end chip business.

Yet this discount buying spree only reinforced younger engineers' impression that they were not on the cutting edge. The company's plans to build an eight-inch plant in the sprawling Wuxi New District Zone would energize some of them, but when mass hiring started in the Shanghai fabs, turnover in Wuxi would increase. In addition, other, more challenging alternatives were emerging locally. In the New District, Memsic, a Massachusetts start-up, had built a "semi-fabless" plant for specialized production of its sensor chips, while retaining its design unit in the United States. This onshore-offshore model was representative of what venture capitalists increasingly demanded, though it was only a matter of time before the design was wholly offshore. Many of

Huajing's former employees were in Memsic's engineering group, and their fraternal bonds were an important part of the company's esprit de corps. One engineer who had been employed, after leaving Huajing, by Japanese and Korean chipmakers, acknowledged that it was a rare opportunity these days to be able to reconnect with familiar colleagues: "Engineers are like migrant workers," he observed wryly. "They move almost as often. Here, we are more like brothers."

In addition, Memsic's product, an accelerometer chip, was a new technology, and so its development was more interesting to him and his mates than the typical consumer IC. As a result of these factors, the firm's turnover was low, especially for a city that had not been spared the skilled-labor shortage plaguing the Yangtze Delta. Indeed, the Ministry of Labor and Social Security reported that in the second quarter of 2004, several Wuxi enterprises had failed to find a single qualified technician despite posting hundreds of vacancies.[22]

Rules of Trade and War

In the mid-1980s, when governments around the world were all trying to create clones of Silicon Valley, China's national managers had four potential locations under consideration: Shanghai, Beijing, Shenzhen, and Wuxi. The Ministry of Electronics actually favored Wuxi at the time, but eventually all four cities were considered worthy of high-tech development. Zhongguancun Science Park, close to home in Beijing, turned into a regional technology powerhouse in the mid-1990s by attracting a cluster of prominent foreign firms, but it was Shanghai that eventually emerged with the top prizes.

As early as 1980, several of the city's research centers, like the Institute of Metallurgy and Fudan University's Institute of Microelectronics, were given the green light to develop high-tech projects at Shanghai Radio factories Number 14 and Number 19, along with Components Factory Number 5. In 1988, Caohejing Park, in a southwestern suburb of the city, was designated as a high-tech zone for development and technology transfer from multinationals like Philips and ITT.[23] It was not until 1993, however, when approval to open up and develop

Pudong included plans for the state-of-the-art Zhangjiang Hi-Tech Park, that the momentum to achieve advanced technology manufacture picked up. Jiang Zemin and Zhu Rongji, kingpins of the Shanghai Clique and both engineers by training, were in power in Beijing, guaranteeing a steady funding stream to back the city's bid to become the economic hub for all of East Asia. With its cluster of top universities and critical mass of high investment in top-end ventures, Shanghai proved a natural host for the capital-intensive industry of microchip production. By the end of the decade, Beijing announced that the state would no longer invest directly in the IC industry, but instead would make it irresistible for overseas investors to do so.[24] As part of the new policy, the government lowered the VAT paid on ICs from 17 percent to 6 percent for Chinese producers. A further concession (that would come close to fomenting a minor trade war with the United States) awarded an additional 3 percent rebate for domestically designed devices.

While Shanghai's high-tech development enjoyed strong backing from the central government, its distance from the political hothouse of Beijing was a direct boon to the microchip business. No industry (not even steel in the heyday of Mao's Great Leap Forward) was more closely tied to national security, and therefore more likely to trigger geopolitical tensions. Advanced IC technologies were considered dual-use (a resource for developing weaponry), and so the fraught political triangulation between Beijing, Taipei, and Washington threatened to take precedence over the increasingly powerful economic ties that bound the three countries together.

Though it did not hinge directly on military friction, Washington had already lived through one semiconductor trade war with Japan in the 1980s. From the mid-1970s onward, the huge technological advantage enjoyed by the U.S. semiconductor industry was sharply reduced by Japanese competition. By the mid-1980s, Japanese IC manufacturers had taken the lead in an industry governed by breakneck innovation and susceptible to rapid diffusion across national borders. Even in the absence of any national security links, Washington's will to protect a leading-edge industrial base, coupled with its desire to retain control over the rules of international trade, would have impelled it to action. As Kenneth Flamm has argued, "The chip industry wraps up in a single package virtually every industrial attribute likely to spawn changes to rules for international trade and investment based on textbook premises about competitive markets."[25]

Allegations of dumping in the United States and blocked access to Japanese markets prompted a series of legal actions that resulted in the 1986 U.S.-Japan Semiconductor Trade Arrangement. This bilateral agreement set a template for "managed trade" between the two IC powers that melted away over the next decade and a half as the industry took on a truly transnational scope. U.S. firms reinvented their production by building an international network of industrial "partners" in Korea, Taiwan, Malaysia, and Singapore, each of which hosted low-cost manufacturing, or boutique production centers, while Americans retained the design and architecture of the products, and determined the standards and platforms that everyone else had to use. As had been the case in the United States and Japan, the industry enjoyed massive levels of national government subsidy and protection in each of these countries. By the time China entered the picture, the myth of an open global market where semiconductor companies competed freely should long since have dissolved except in the addled minds of free-market fundamentalists.

It was the industry's ties to advanced weapon systems, however, that drew special attention. Washington had long used its superior technology assets as a geopolitical tool to limit the military development of potential enemies. Indeed, one of Beijing's primary responses to American criticisms of the U.S.-China trade "imbalance" was that Washington barred the transfer of advanced U.S. technologies on the grounds that they could be put to military use. The background to this complaint was a complicated one, revealing hypocrisy on both sides.

Under the rules of the Coordinating Committee for Multilateral Export Controls (COCOM), established in 1949 by the United States and its Cold War allies, the PRC became a proscribed country for exports of Western goods considered dual-use. The definition of "hostile military uses" observed by the COCOM controls was quite expansive in scope and was actively used to retard the industrial development of countries in the communist bloc. But, beginning in the early 1980s, the rules for China were gradually relaxed under the Reagan administration as part of the strategy to counterweight the PRC against the Soviet Union.[26] The official technology transfer category for China was switched, in 1980, from "Y" to "P," allowing sale of selected dual-use technology, and, in 1983, from "P" to "V" ("friendly state"), which meant that the majority of Chinese license requests fell into the green zone of automatic approval. After the Tiananmen Square repression of 1989, arms transfers were frozen and high-level military-to-military meetings were halted, but the momentum picked up again over the next decade, much to the chagrin of anticommunist hardliners. With the ending of the Cold War, COCOM was replaced in 1996 with the more informal Wassenaar Arrangement, whose thirty-three member countries enjoyed considerably more individual discretion to control sensitive exports. This much looser agreement, combined with the loss of the U.S. commercial high-tech monopoly, meant that Washington could no longer effectively control technology denial to countries on its enemy list.

In the meantime, the commercial trade in licensed exports to China shot up, and by 2003 the export of general-purpose microprocessors was entirely decontrolled. Hardliners continued to insist that China should be kept two generations behind in its access to advanced technology. On the other side, the powerful business wings of both political parties were acutely aware that China was already using its access to international technology and knowledge transfers to jump-start its own high-tech industries, and that U.S. firms would lose vital opportunities if the more stringent controls were not relaxed.

For the most part, the hardliners fought a losing game. In September 2002, for example, a group of hawkish Republican senators, led by Jesse Helms, charged that China was using its joint ventures and foreign investments "to develop advanced systems with a goal of attaining military capabilities equal to or exceeding those of the United States," and that Beijing was continuing "to transfer dual-use technology to states that support international terror networks," in particular to Iraq.[27]

Feeding this political pressure was a steady stream of neoconservative opinion. The Heritage Foundation pushed several buttons labeled "national paranoia" by arguing that "in order to gain access to advanced technology for its military, China is now pressuring foreign firms to allow increasing levels of Chinese government oversight of domestic semiconductor operations. In some cases, the Chinese government has apparently set up 'false foreign devil' wafer fabs—ostensibly under Taiwanese direction but owned by the Chinese government—and is outfitting them with state-of-the-art imported chip-making machinery," to build an industry for which "there is no economic need."[28]

These kinds of wild-eyed warnings about Chinese duplicity were reinforced by a long legacy of race-based suspicion that linked Chinese-Americans working in U.S. government and military labs with espionage activities. The cases of Qian Xuesen in the 1950s and Wen Ho Lee in the 1990s, both charged (without any evidence) with spying, were only the highest-profile examples.[29] Nor were Taiwanese in the United States free of suspicion; many were mistrusted for their assumed allegiance to the motherland. In 2005, American regulators on the Committee on Foreign Investments in the United States considered blocking Lenovo's takeover of IBM's PC unit on the grounds that Lenovo employees might be used to conduct industrial espionage in the United States.[30] If Chinese-American scientists and engineers working under tight security surveillance in the United States were habitually suspected without cause, there was little chance that Chinese operating on their own soil would be trusted.[31]

So, too, neoconservative outrage over Beijing's nation-building tactics consistently glossed over the similar methods employed by other East Asian nations on their development path. Japan used every protectionist measure in the book to jump-start its technology industries. South Korea employed import tariffs and insisted on technology transfers from foreign firms. As in these other countries, Taiwan industrialists often took reverse engineering well beyond its legal limits. Because they were directly in Washington's Cold War camp, their errant ways were excused.

Most U.S. firms, and foreign investors in general, have come to accept that technology transfer, even the illegal appropriation of their own intellectual property, is part of the price of doing business in China. Indeed, the offer of technology transfer is a routine dealmaker for U.S. firms seeking better investment terms or market access. Most recently, the cost of access has been the establishment of a joint training or R&D center with a Chinese university or research institute. By dangling the promise of its vast domestic market, China has been able to attract the kind of technology and resources that it needs to upgrade its economy.

When SMIC (presumably one of the "false foreign devil" firms fingered by the Heritage Foundation) began eight-inch-wafer production in Shanghai in 2001, and subsequently announced plans to build a top-of-the-line twelve-inch fab in Beijing, the American debate about "containing" China's march up the technology ladder became moot. By 2004, IC manufacturing boasted more than thirty-five foundry fabs and 180 assembly and testing plants, with some, like Intel's Shanghai plant, assembling the most advanced chip products.[32] More than 400 IC design houses nationwide were being incubated or had already set up shop, auguring the rapid emergence of a key high-tech sector with its own system-level intellectual property.[33] Some domestic giants like Haier had also succeeded in making their own chips, and the Ministry of Information Industry was pushing on all fronts to boost patent applications, and develop national standards in areas like wireless encryption, 3G mobile phone technology, and Enhanced Versatile Discs (EVD) in a bid to establish ownership over emerging technologies.[34] In response, U.S. officials conceded that there was no effective way of keeping advanced semiconductor machinery out of China, and so Washington's strategic policy efforts shifted onto purely economic grounds, aimed at promoting competitive advantages for U.S. firms. In March 2004, the Bush administration mounted its first formal WTO case against China by challenging the preferential 14 percent VAT rebate offered to domestically designed and produced chips.[35] Responding to a barrage of heated rhetoric about a coming trade war, Beijing agreed to scrap the policy in July, but vowed to introduce new WTO-compliant policies for supporting semiconductor R&D at levels that were in line with those of other advanced producer nations.[36]

By the end of 2004, Washington had bowed to the clamor from U.S. firms by softening its controls. An agreement on "end-use visits" was negotiated, and controls on the export of advanced semiconductor manufacturing equipment were eased.[37] While the chip producers and equipment makers celebrated, the decision only added to Taiwanese anxieties. The U.S. dual-use controls had helped to keep the island's chip industry one step ahead, and it was widely feared that U.S. firms would abandon their hard-won loyalty to the Taiwanese contract producers in the face of greater savings or profits on the mainland. The island's domestic producers would have little choice but to move more and more of their operations across the strait.

Taking Care of Business

U.S. firms had "abandoned" Taiwan before. The first wave of foreign investors, in the late 1960s, were the American electronics manufacturers RCA, Philco, and Zenith, persuaded by their supplier, General Instruments, to set up assembly plants to take advantage of Taiwan's cheap labor and loose regulatory environment. RCA, once labeled a model investor by the Taipei government, transferred to Singapore in 1992 partly to avoid paying employee pensions that were mandatory after twenty-five years under Taiwanese law. The firm also left a highly poisonous legacy. In 1998, Taiwan's EPA designated RCA's former Taoyuan plant as a site of "permanent contamination," after uncovering evidence that the company illegally dug wells to dump toxic wastes and organic solvents such as trichloroethylene and tetrachloroethylene. In the interim, more than 200 former employees had suffered cancer-related deaths, and as many as 800 more workers and residents in the area affected by contaminated drinking water were diagnosed with cancer. As one former employee put it, "No wonder those foreign managers all drank bottled mineral water! Only we foolish laborers drank toxic water every day! We lived in the plant, ate in the plant, and even showered in toxic water!"[38]

Of course, RCA was hardly alone in an industry that has left a toxic trail leading from all the way from some of the original semiconductor facilities in Silicon Valley.[39] Employees in the plants themselves worked in an industry where workers suffer industrial illnesses at three to four times the average rates for manufacturing jobs in chemical-intensive industries like petroleum, paper, coal, steel, plastics, and rubber. "Fenceline" communities that border high-tech parks in places in Hsinchu lived with the almost certain prospect that leakage of highly dangerous chemicals was ruining their health.[40] In a major incident in 2000, Sheng-li, a licensed firm that handled toxic waste for 80 percent of Hsinchu's IC companies, was found to have dumped solvent waste in the Kaoping River, seriously contaminating two major water systems in southern Taiwan.

In local working-class communities, the RCA case was remembered with great bitterness. According to the investment manager of Hsinchu Park, it had left a bad impression of U.S. companies. Even the director of Taipei's American Chamber of Commerce acknowledged to me that the case had created an image problem for American business. In high-tech business circles, however, the name RCA was still held in high esteem. For one thing, it had been a licensed technology transfer from the American company (7-micron IC technology) that made possible the spin-off of UMC, the first of the country's chip giants, in 1982. The Taiwanese went on to perfect the art of reengineering licensed mature technologies from U.S. and Japanese multinationals to launch their own domestic competitors.[41]

For each of these profitable births, the midwife was the Industrial Technology Research Institute (ITRI), a government R&D organization founded in 1973 to disseminate directly to industry the results of its research. A citadel of labs and research centers in dozens of technology subfields, ITRI, located just minutes from the Hsinchu Park, employed more than 6,000 engineers. Modeled to some degree on its Japanese and Korean counterparts, it has played a vital role as a catalyst and incubator for entire sectors of Taiwan's technology industry. Scouring the world for products to absorb, upgrade, and pass on to domestic firms, ITRI's record of leveraging and diffusing technology is unmatched in any other country. Leaving aside the many other channels through which public policy helped to shape Taiwan's high-tech empire—grants, subsidized credit, tax exemptions, and direct government investment—the role of ITRI alone is a case study in how government agencies can deliver the technological competence required to win a high-end position in the global production system.[42]

Such evidence of sustained government involvement undermines the persistent claims of industry analysts and neoclassical economists that the East Asian Miracle, as the World Bank called it in a famous 1993 report, was primarily a result of entrepreneurial competition and free-market activity, "guided" through very light and "selective interventions" on the part of the state.[43] In addition, the outcome of this intensive state activity complicates an enduring left-wing assumption that the development even of relatively advanced nations remains captive to the interests of Western multinationals. As multinationals shifted more and more of their operations offshore, Korea, Singapore, Hong Kong, and Taiwan all developed as new regional cores. Each developed their own low-wage manufacturing peripheries in China, Malaysia, Indonesia, and Thailand, and each succeeded in shaping their own position in the global production chain.[44]

Unlike in Japan and Korea, where the state concentrated development in a small number of major (*zaibatsu* and *chaebol*) firms enjoying a virtual market monopoly, Taiwan encouraged a relatively open field of new entrants. This was particularly important at a time when the internationalization of the semiconductor industry was generating new and specialized divisions: chip design, fabrication, masking, bonding, testing, assembly, and packaging. Every few years these divisions broke down further, to open up new horizontal segments that were quickly exploited by Taiwan's myriad small independent firms looking for their production niche. In addition, Taiwanese industry benefited from a very close association with Silicon Valley. A large pool of Taiwanese engineers working in Californian companies created a bridge between Silicon Valley and Hsinchu Park that kept the island's industry abreast of cutting-edge development. Over time, the brain drain to the United States was reversed as Taiwanese policymakers actively recruited returnees to transfer knowledge and start up companies at home.[45]

The implicit support and backing of the United States kept the boom afloat until the early 2000s. Major U.S. computer firms like Dell, HP, Compaq, Gateway, and IBM came to regard the island as a primary base for original equipment manufacturing, and alliances between the leading technology companies in both countries could not have been tighter. The cozy relationship between Taipei and Washington even extended to dual-use exports. Controlled U.S.-origin technology that had been exported to Taiwan under generous license exceptions could only be moved to the mainland with approval from the U.S. Commerce Department. The rule even applied to foreign-made equipment with as little as 25 percent U.S. content. Yet, as Taiwanese companies rushed to invest in China and transfer what they needed to harvest short-term profits, the already blurred line between civilian and dual-use technologies eroded further.

As the transfers increased, ITRI's position began to mutate. The officials I met there described how their jobs increasingly turned to business models and managerial strategy, competencies that lay outside of their traditional areas of expertise. Their task of funneling new technologies to domestic industries had gotten more complicated now that the eyes of investors were fixed on the mainland. In fact, ITRI was already sitting on a pile of technologies and patents it could not exploit short of auctioning them off. In the past, ITRI staff had had a fairly straightforward mission of serving as a "technology bridge." Now they were moving into the more intangible realm of "total asset management," where the business arts of market positioning, intellectual-property protection, and brand manipulation helped firms to leverage whatever edge they could to retain an advantage. This was a sure sign that the future of Taiwan's comparative advantage lay less in front-end manufacturing than in the services that depended on creating a market niche for products. It was also an acute reminder that the island's high-tech cluster faced marginalization unless it could move up even further. At the other end of the seesaw, the China State Technology Transfer Center was being established in Shanghai. Composed of research bodies like the Shanghai Institute of Silicate, the Shanghai Institute of Technical Physics, the Shanghai Institute of Optics and Fine Mechanics, the Shanghai Observatory, and the Shanghai Institute of Organic Chemistry, it would be performing the same kind of role for China's tech industries that ITRI had for Taiwan's.[46]

In Hsinchu Park itself, founded in 1980 on cheap land adjacent to Tsinghua and Jiaotong universities, and near the ITRI labs, there was also a cautious air. Investors were still lining up, and expansions were opening in satellite parks nearby and in the southern city of Tainan, so Hsinchu officials could hardly be despondent. Nonetheless, an investment promotion manager acknowledged to me that "the skilled worker is now at risk, and we can definitely feel their fear." To stay on the island, she reported, "investors now expect the Taiwanese government to deliver the same perks as Beijing is doing. They also expect the same efficiency treatment, which is difficult in a democracy." So, too, the physical impact of the last two decades of overwork had left its harrowing legacy. "Businesspeople who are barely over forty," she observed, "look like they are sixty years old. Their hair is already white and their skin is sagging." In looking to the future, the park was setting its sights on becoming a global R&D and digital design center for multinational and Taiwanese companies, with manufacturing in China, financing in Hong Kong, and sales in the United States and the European Union. It was a plan that dovetailed with the government's recently unveiled vision of Taiwan as a "global logistics center." Under this rubric, Taiwan would exploit its strategic location at the geographic center of all the leading Asia-Pacific ports to replace Singapore as the regional hub for everything from shipments to product R&D.

Both of these plans could come undone by the rise of Shanghai alone. By the end of 2004, Shanghai's existing port had outstripped Rotterdam as the world's busiest, and the biggest deep-sea port in Asia was being built twenty miles out into the Yellow Sea. Nor had it been slow in acquiring global R&D centers of its own, several from leading multinationals. Like every other economy in the region, Taiwan's new economic policies were being driven by China's effort to compete for skilled jobs and capital-intensive production.

The UN of Chipmakers

En route to its fateful decision to go offshore, TSMC had sued SMIC, Shanghai's rising microchip star, on charges of trade-secret espionage and patent infringement. In its rush to ramp up, SMIC had allegedly hired more than a hundred key TSMC employees who took, or appropriated, information vital to the Taiwanese firm's latest chipmaking processes. Affidavits from SMIC's TSMC recruits affirmed that the Shanghai company had copied up to 90 percent of the sequence of steps used to make the microchips. The case, initially filed in a San Francisco court in December 2003, was finally resolved in an out-of-court settlement in January 2005, by which time TSMC's Shanghai plant had started production, and the two firms were going head-to-head in the same town. In the interim, SMIC had risen to become the world's third-biggest foundry—after TSMC, UMC, and Chartered—by global revenue.[47]

The TSMC-SMIC espionage suit highlighted the consequences of knowledge transfer when an operational move across borders takes place outside the bounds of intra-firm outsourcing. When a company transfers the jobs and knowledge of its employees to some cheaper location, it is legally sanctioned labor arbitrage. When the employees themselves move to better their situation, they fall under the suspicion of acting as common thieves, especially when they cross borders that are politically and militarily "hot." In the semiconductor field, this syndrome is especially rife, because competition is directly tied to the breakneck rate of innovation. Employers will impose the strictest measures on hoarding the technical knowledge of their personnel rather than accept that they might benefit from knowledge acquired through the recruitment of employees from their rivals.

To build its knowledge base in preparation for starting pilot production at the end of 2001, SMIC hired almost a thousand engineers from the world's top semiconductor firms: Intel, IBM, Texas Instruments, TSMC, UMC, Chartered, and WSMC, the original company of SMIC's founder, Richard Chang. A dozen flags flapped outside SMIC's facility in Zhangjiang Park, broadcasting its reputation as a corporate UN. Its funders (including Goldman Sachs, Toshiba, and

Motorola) were equally international, and it exploited the tax shelters offered by registration in the Cayman Islands, but it was nominally a Chinese company. For all intents and purposes, Beijing promoted the firm as the national flagship of its microchip initiative, though it would be more accurate to regard it as a new beginning after so many failures. Several recent chipmaking joint ventures, including the showcase Huahong-NEC (heavily subsidized by the Ministry of Electronics and the Municipality of Shanghai to the tune of $1.2 billion during the Ninth Five-Year Planning Period of 1996 to 2000), had performed dismally. SMIC's launch was a by-product of the shift in government IC policy toward less direct forms of state support. Shanghai Grace Semiconductor, SMIC's neighbor and great rival in Zhangjiang Park, was another example of this shift in policy. Founded by Winston Wong, son of Taiwan's Formosa Plastics tycoon Wang Yung-ching, it had private backing from Jiang Mianheng, son of Jiang Zemin. By 2004, several other major semiconductor projects, conceived and funded by Taiwan veterans, had been announced.[48]

China's semiconductor star—SMIC and its UN of flags,
at Zhangjiang Hi-Tech Park

Perhaps the most visible symbol of Beijing's new flexibility on foreign investment could be found on a construction site near the SMIC facility. SMIC's founder, Richard Chang, a devout Christian, had obtained permission to build a church for his employees, many of whom, it was widely alleged, had come to China with the mission of being pioneers for Christ. Though the existence of the church was hardly trumpeted around, corporate executives did not go out of their way to conceal their pride. On one of my facility visits, I was taken to view the construction site and was assured that the company intended to abide by the principles of the Three Selfs Declaration (self-administration, self-support, and self-propagation), to which Christians in the New China of 1950 had pledged themselves in order to protect their faith from government incursions.

Chang, an American-educated Taiwanese from a family of Kuomintang refugees, had been more open with the international religious press in describing how the firm enjoyed the backing of God as much as that of the Chinese government: "We come here as engineers to help build this industry in China," he declared, "and the Chinese government supported us to have Sunday service as we share God's love through our work." Divine guidance, he implied, actually controlled the timing of the company's growth, not to mention its profits.[49] Indeed, shortly after the fab opened in 2001, Chang observed, "our orders for next year are very, very full, thanks to the grace of God."[50]

The association of high technology with religious evangelism was far from new. Indeed, the history of technological utopianism is deeply interwoven with Christian millennarianism.[51] But consider the setting: not only was this China, it was also the nation's leading science park, where the main roads were named for famous scientists and where a sculpture garden hosted busts of Newton, Einstein, Darwin, and an array of Chinese scientists. Foreign investors had become accustomed to a wide range of perks from government officials, but this concession was a little out of the ordinary, and quite surreal in the context of its location.

Virtually everything that SMIC did attracted media notice. Its weak IPO on Hong Kong's Hang Exchange in April 2004 was interpreted as the end of the China stock boom, and when it added a twelve-inch fab

Einstein, Newton, and Curie lend their authority
to construction at Zhangjiang Hi-Tech Park

in Beijing, another eight-inch plant in Tianjin (to supplement its three
in Shanghai), and a testing and assembly factory in Chengdu, the firm
was assumed to be overextended. Nonetheless, the rise in its revenues,
to $1 billion in just four years, made it one of the fastest-growing com-
panies ever, anywhere. Even behind the gates, the firm's maverick reputation was touted to outsiders. "It's a little different from other
companies," explained the public-relations manager who supervised
my visits. "It's more of a community that you really believe in, and that
you want to be part of this unique project." Her own wistful desire to
believe was underpinned by a more formal obsession with security, no

doubt buttressed by all the attention from the press. She insisted on sitting in on all of my interviews, even after I pointed out that her presence probably made the employees quite uncomfortable. Of all the companies I visited in China and Taiwan, SMIC was the only one that decided on such a requirement, and only Hejian, its quasi-UMC rival in Suzhou, was more guarded in how it received me.

SMIC's security culture was pervasive for those on the job, especially where it applied to employees working with sensitive information. None of the engineers was allowed to have a laptop, a floppy drive, or a CD burner, and all their e-mail was logged. As a result, they spent much more time on-site than they might have done, since their work, in practice, could not be taken home. Fortunately, for most of them, home was nearby. The company, which holds thirty-five acres and room for nine fabs, had built an extensive housing complex, comprising dorms for operators, apartments for skilled employees, and villas for senior engineers, managers, and officers. Also within walking distance was the firm's bilingual international school, modeled on the Texas state curriculum, and with ties to Dallas Baptist University.

Even without the secrecy regulations, employees were not likely to see much of their homes. Though it had been three years since production began, the start-up culture of long hours and overwork prevailed. Jiang Yun-wing, an in-line supervisor from Henan, described his typical working day: "I arrive at 7:00 a.m. and go to a series of production meetings to plan out the day's schedule and set production targets. We discuss troubleshooting and how to improve productivity on the line. In the afternoon I have to attend production control meetings, and check in-line reports and delivery schedule. After five-thirty, we break and have dinner." I half-expected to hear him describe what he did for recreation after hours, but his work narrative continued through the late evening: "I usually go home at 11:00 p.m. On Saturdays I only work eight hours, and Sundays are free. My boss tells me to go enjoy myself, but usually Fab 1 plays Fab 2 at soccer." I was left with the impression that he would have worked a seven-day week, if Sunday had not been ordained as a day of Christian rest.

Jiang's manager, he said, regularly compared his work rate to that of foreign counterparts, with the intended effect: "If we work very hard," he insisted, "we will do better than other countries." But overall he did not have a high impression of the chipmaking sector. "It's low value-adding," he sniffed. "Even the U.S. looks down on these kinds of fabs because they are polluting industries." Like so many young Shanghainese engineers, he had his sights on an MBA and a top-flight managerial career.

Despite the political buzz swirling around the company, employees and managers had more to say about internal politics at SMIC. Recruiting the knowledge of engineers from several different companies was a common strategy in the IC business, but the employees also brought along their own company cultures. The resulting friction was not just about culture cliques. Each engineer had been trained to think differently about how to run a fab. Those who had worked previously at an integrated manufacturer (making chips for the company's own use) were used to mass production of high-volume product. Those who had trained at TSMC were accustomed to a unified culture and a generic process flow with a clearly defined system of tasks. Both kinds of employees struggled to assimilate to SMIC's multicultural staff, and to the reality of its highly customized foundry operations, continually adapting to the process flows of its many different customers.

For all its internationalism, and for all the official efforts to claim SMIC as a Chinese success story, its mainland employees (just as at CSMC in Wuxi) still regarded it as a Taiwanese company. As one put it, "You can tell it's Taiwanese because everyone complains about the salary and benefits." At the factory gate, a supplier offered the supplementary evidence to support the stereotype. "They want too much for too little money," he reported. "They are the worst among our clients, and their payments are often late." He resented that Taiwanese, as he put it, "had been given such a huge loan from our government to fund the company." In Wuxi, CSMC employees also spoke of the "stinginess" of their employer, which they associated with Taiwanese management. "Taiwanese don't put any focus on training," observed one recent recruit. "It's all self-training here. I guess it's their culture, they want to spend less, and make you contribute earlier. Taiwan is part of China," he added, reflecting the most common mainlander view, "and we are all Chinese, but, for the time being, they are in a position to take advantage of us. Foreign experts and companies are our teachers. For the sake of national unity, we must learn from them to get stronger." According to his stream of thought, Taiwanese were more foreign than they were Chinese, and so they could not be included in the "national unity" equation.

It might have been different if the Taiwanese in his company had been lower-level employees, as opposed to managers. Mainlanders typically only encountered Taiwanese as people with superior resources at their disposal (unquestionably, this perception helped Taiwanese managers establish their authority over workers). Taiwanese farmers who visited the mainland as tourists, or in search of a wife, might have been considered behavioral "bumpkins" in the eyes of most Chinese, but they were still regarded as enjoying a better standing in the world. If there was an exception to this rule, it would be among the famously self-regarding Shanghainese—descendants of migrants themselves—for whom all outsiders were somehow lacking.

By the turn of the century, many islanders felt they had little choice but to go to the boomtown, either to save their small businesses or to seek job opportunities that were dwindling at home. The coming of the microchip factories (up to 70 percent Taiwan-funded) was the icing on the cake, drawing, or draining, personnel who had been among the island's heroes during its boom years from the 1970s through the 1990s. By 2004, "Shanghai Fever" had lured a sizable population of *taishang,* as they were called back in Taiwan, where the Taiwanese nationalist press ritually lambasted them as traitors. This partially submerged expatriate group numbered as many as half a million, and counted among its ranks highly educated and cultured professionals, entrepreneurs, and retirees, where earlier waves had mostly been composed of small-time investors in shoes, toys, or karaoke.[52] The resources or salaries of these "stateless" newcomers could purchase a relatively extravagant lifestyle that included upscale houses or apartments, along with maids to service them. After the 2004 Taiwan election, there was a noticeable spike in Shanghai housing sales, suggesting that Taiwan's independent path was forcing the *taishang* to consider permanent residency in a country with which their own was still officially at war.

The Spring Festival of 2005 saw the temporary lifting of a fifty-six-year ban on direct flights across the strait. The opening of the air link between Shanghai and Taipei was not only official recognition of the voluminous traffic between the two cities, but also a highly visible step toward normalization of relations and, ultimately, the possible reintegration of the two countries. For the best part of twenty years, the informal, often underground, networks among businesspeople had sustained the links. Now economic necessity was driving them above ground.

The Last Interviews

In the course of the workplace interviews I did for this book, I had only one opportunity to talk to employees who were doing more or less the same job in China as employees based in another country. Although I had not set out with the goal of making a direct comparison like this, it seemed to be the final piece of the story I had been putting together. My chance came when the manager of a factory in Suzhou Industrial Park (SIP) agreed to give me access to a similar company plant in Taiwan. The comparison would allow me to test some of my observations about how employees in different countries, or labor markets, are played off against each other.

For instance, I had found, even in my interviews, that mainlanders and Taiwanese often indulged in stereotypes of each other. Usually these were a convenient way for mainland employees to describe hard treatment by Taiwanese managers or, alternately, for those managers to describe how their PRC employees failed to stack up. At other times, however, the cultural differences between the two populations could be manipulated more shrewdly by managers in order to boost productivity and curb employee expectations. As it turned out, my interviews in these two plants of the same firm offered some solid evidence of this latter practice.

The company was AUO, a market leader in the boom sector of optoelectronics, producing LCD (liquid crystal display) technology. Among all the high-tech fields, LCD had seen the biggest growth in recent years. With 15,500 employees, AUO had expanded rapidly since its formation in 2001, and was the world's third-largest TFT-LCD manufacturer, hosting ten fabs in Taiwan alone. Its 320,000-square-meter Chinese factory, built to host more than 7,000 employees, was one of the largest in SIP, and went into pilot production in June 2002.

As was common with the unskilled workforce in SIP's plants, the majority of the operators in the AUO plant were country girls, all of whom "cycle out," I was told, by the age of twenty, either to marry or to "look for better jobs." Almost certainly, however, they were on labor contracts that actively pushed them out. Some women in their late thirties, with their child-rearing years behind them, might be recruited back into the workforce as supervisors, but women in their twenties and early thirties were not considered suitable workers. I was told that their work demanded delicate and flexible hands, and keen eyesight apparently only available in teenage girls. When I asked a manager for a facility tour, he said, "As long as you don't mind the smell." I shrugged my shoulders. "Don't worry, I realize that factories are sometimes a little smelly." "No, you don't understand," he replied. "I meant the smell of the workers."

By contrast, AUO's female engineers in their twenties were valued more highly, and were actually promoted more rapidly than their male peers. The reason offered to me was that they were more loyal and disciplined than the males. Given SIP's turnover rate, this seemed highly plausible. In common with other SIP employers, AUO's mainland managers had trouble retaining skilled workers. Johnny Chang, an operations manager from South Taiwan, preferred to recruit employees from the northeast. "They are hardier," he pointed out, "than the 'soft' South Chinese, and are descended, like the Taiwanese, from pirates." He also sought out engineers from as far away as Mongolia and Xinjiang in order to keep salaries down. But regardless of which region of the mainland they hailed from, their overall productivity, in his opinion, left a lot to be desired:

Even after you have trained them, seventy Chinese engineers cannot contribute as much as thirty Taiwanese engineers. If the

PRC wants to be the next Taiwan, this work mentality will have to change. The right kind of managerial pressure will get you higher productivity from Chinese engineers after a while. At first, however, they refuse to do it, then they learn some problem-solving skills. But there is still a huge gap between performance and potential. Taiwanese engineers are more able to take responsibility. Here they can really only identify the problem, they can't solve it.

Of course, the lower productivity was more than offset by wage savings. Chang did the arithmetic: "Right now, the cost ratio of U.S. to Taiwanese engineers is around 1:5 or 1:6, and the PRC-Taiwan ratio is 1:4, so the Chinese are twenty-four times cheaper than the Americans, but not much cheaper than our people, and in Shanghai the ratio is even less."

Chang also mentioned that, in Taiwan, AUO could get college-educated engineers to do basic maintenance on the factory floor, and in companies like TSMC and UMC with strong stock, employees with graduate degrees were willing to work as operators just to get stock options. "Here, you would never get engineers willing to do these kinds of jobs," he assured me. It was the first but not the last time I heard this said about Taiwanese engineers. Later I was told a similar story by a Taiwanese HR manager at Hejian, the quasi-UMC microchip firm that had set up recently in SIP. To build up Hejian's initial workforce, she had recruited many college graduates for positions as operators, but discovered very quickly that they were unwilling to do the repetitive work. After experiencing massive turnover, the policy was abandoned. In Taiwan, she and her associates had been told that mainlanders would do anything for the right money, but she had found that their Chinese employees "were nowhere near as motivated as we expected." "They talk about the balance between their work and their lives," she reported, as if puzzled by this concern, "whereas Taiwanese work until late at night and know how to respond to pressure. Here, they think they deserve much better pay for the additional pressure." In its efforts to start up and break even, the company found that it had to rely unduly on the 200 Taiwanese engineers—accustomed to crushing pressure—who had been imported to kick off production.

In Taiwan itself, I found that the story about college graduates working as operators was dismissed as delusory. Every engineer I interviewed there declared that it was virtually impossible under any of the standard rules of the labor market. Wu Xiaolin, the TSMC employee I met on the bus from Taipei, said that he had heard this rumor, but had never seen any evidence of it. Most likely, it had germinated at a time when the idea of employee stock options was relatively new, or when the recession was particularly bad, and that it had lived on as a convenient myth that managers could use in recruiting or in extracting more output from employees. In this capacity, the myth had crossed the strait, where it might be even more efficiently employed. Evidently the Taiwanese who came over to start up Hejian believed it could be implemented as HR policy.

The mainland engineers at AUO-Suzhou had also been told the story by their managers. Although they could not verify it, they knew that it was probably intended to impact on their work psychology. "I am supposed to feel lucky about having this kind of job because the Taiwanese are under so much more pressure," acknowledged a Sichuanese production engineer, promoted after only six months, "but I know I can do better and earn more elsewhere, so it does not affect me so much." She and her peers were reminded that whereas they went home, after a twelve-hour shift, along with the operators in the company buses, their counterparts in Taiwan worked much longer hours, knocking off at 10:00 or 11:00 p.m. She was well aware of the implication, but rejected it. "Twelve hours is long enough," she assured me. "The Taiwanese work style is too demanding. They expect too much."

At the company's plant in Taiwan, the longer day was seen as an acceptable part of engineers' work culture on the island. "Engineers in the IC design houses work the longest hours, and we do about the same as the IC manufacturers," explained Marshall Cheng. "I come in at 8:00 a.m. and don't leave until ten minutes to midnight. After taking a shower in my dorm room, I read electronics literature to keep up with my field, and then sleep for five or six hours." To catch up, he said he slept for much of the weekend. "The operators only work for twelve hours," he observed, "but we have more responsibility." Though I had listened to many accounts like this in the course of doing interviews for this book, it was still staggering to hear employees describe these brutally long work days. Engineers' contracts did not usually stipulate working hours, but clearly this kind of semi-voluntary version of overtime abuse was an expectation of the job. Under Taiwan's labor laws, if seasonal production demanded it, and if employees and unions agreed, overtime hours could be extended to a maximum of forty-six hours per month for men and twenty-four hours for women. In China, the nation's labor laws were gender-neutral, mandating a maximum of thirty-six hours per month, but foreign investors knew that, for the right price, local government officials would enforce the laws with an attitude referred to as "opening one eye, with the other closed."[53]

Since punishingly long working days—up to sixteen hours—were regarded as the company norm in Taiwan, the shorter Suzhou day, where AUO engineers only put in twelve hours, was viewed as an anomaly, requiring an explanation. After all, it was a commonly held perception in Taiwan that mainlanders in general were willing to work longer hours. Cheng and his peers in Taiwan had been told that their Suzhou counterparts had to take the company buses out at the earlier hour, or else be stranded at the plant. In addition, managers in both locations reported that it generally took three Suzhou engineers to match the output of one in Taiwan. This assessment was put to use in different ways. On the Suzhou side, the implication was that the mainland employees were not pulling their weight. In Taiwan the imbalance was ascribed to the fact that Suzhou engineers were given routine tasks that required little in the way of problem solving.

Like the Suzhou fab, the Taiwan plant, located in a Longtan technology park half an hour north of Hsinchu, produced modules, and so, strictly speaking, it was sufficiently low-end to fall below the government's technology threshold for export to the mainland. Though this meant it was vulnerable to being moved offshore, some products were pilot-run at the Longtan facility and so, for the time being, it still graded slightly higher than Suzhou. Employees were not only aware of this slim advantage, they were reminded of it constantly. "We must keep our advantage here," observed Cheng. "We must think more or better than them, or we will lose our competitive slot. My manager tells us every day that if we don't work harder, the fab will move to the PRC." Cheng had little faith that Taipei's export controls on higher technology could be maintained for long. After all, the Chinese could easily get higher-generation optolectronic technology from Samsung, the Korean global leader in TFT-LCD, or from one of its Japanese competitors. "Everyone I know is worried sick about losing their jobs," he lamented. A manager in another unit confirmed the general anxiety: "We can feel our engineers' worry, they know that their higher productivity is the only thing that keeps the jobs here."

Cheng and his colleagues knew they were being pitted against their Suzhou peers. They seemed surprised, however, to learn from me that some of the same managerial tactics were used in Suzhou to boost the work tempo of the mainlanders. The two groups of engineers were in regular and sometimes daily contact to discuss technical operations, but they rarely if ever talked about working conditions, pay levels, or workplace pressure. Only those who had been to Suzhou to do knowledge transfer were in a position to do so, and their reports focused on the quality of the food (poorer) and the living environment (lonely). Most of them were pro-independence, and had a low opinion, politically and culturally, of the mainland, but they accepted that one day soon they might have little choice but to follow the flow of jobs there. If it had occurred to them to try to make common cause with their mainland counterparts to resist the managerial squeeze, nothing had been done about it. As Cheng put it, "our communications are not evolved enough to speak so directly." The subtlety with which he chose his words spoke volumes about the gulf between the two groups. The "blockade" maintained for so long across the Taiwan Strait was falling apart rapidly, and investors were reaping the dividends. But the thawing of the trade and investment freeze had thrown up a new kind of barrier: mutual distrust now stood in the way of effective communication between workers on either side.

Epilogue

Taiwan is about the same distance from the coast of China as Cuba is from the United States, and like the Caribbean island state, it is separated by a similar remnant of Cold War history. But the company employees I interviewed in Suzhou, on the mainland, and Longtan, in Taiwan, were more like broken halves of the same coin—sharing a cultural heritage, a language, and a linked economic destiny. That they could not talk with each other about this destiny in any consequential way was a tragedy, yet theirs was a predicament shared by workers all over the global economy. Their mutual employer, who had no such difficulty, was in a position to take advantage of their lack of communication. In fact, the company they worked for benefited directly from any employee insecurity that resulted from differentials between its onshore and offshore workplaces.

Proponents of corporate-driven globalization would like to keep it that way. Foremost among them are global companies that can profit from the exploitation of locational differences among the most vulnerable and disconnected workers. They have learned to play the game of labor arbitrage almost as skillfully as the traders who speculate on cross-border financial transactions on a short-term basis, swapping their investments in a heartbeat when perceptions of risk shift. Of course, investing in factories, offices, and people is still nowhere near as liquid as betting on futures in the global financial casino. But the goal is clearly to move in this direction as quickly and as far as possible. The technical and legal capacity of corporations to transfer their physical and fiscal assets with minimal friction is the key to doing so, and the rules of free trade have been written to facilitate it.

Knowledge transfer, however tricky, is a fairly advanced version of this process; it does not require the migration of people, but only of the ideas and thought processes inside their heads, now often legally defined as the intellectual property of their employer. In this respect, the most recent explosion of skilled outsourcing is neither a business fashion nor a temporary scheme for readjusting to economic globalization. It is rapidly becoming a way of life—a social habit as well as an economic one. Beneficial in the short term to some investors, it is a threat to everyone's interests in the long run, because, if left unregulated, it will strip the right of communities and nations to safeguard living standards, erode any durable sense of loyalty to employers and organizations, and inevitably reduce all employee prospects to the status of a gamble—here today, gone tomorrow. Government officials and state managers who do not recognize this, and who treat the underlying free-trade doctrine as if it were a force of nature, are party to a blunder of epic dimensions.

Opening up China and India to foreign investment has been the single biggest move driving the overseas transfers. The dissolution of trade barriers in these countries has brought into capitalist play the largest and the cheapest workforces, both skilled and unskilled, in the world. Although the arbitrage between those two workforces is in its infancy, the chapter I have devoted to Indo-Chinese IT outsourcing suggests that it is already shaping the global allocation of jobs and work. But it is the rise of China in particular—with its powerful state hand, its vast labor surplus, its developed infrastructure, and the promise of its domestic market—that has tantalized investors in hot pursuit of a capitalist Shangri-la with just the right kind of authoritarian profile.

China's rulers have extended all sorts of freedoms and privileges to businesspeople, but virtually none to employees, beyond an abstract commitment to labor laws that are barely observed by the official trade union federation, let alone by employers. Aside from the customary pitfalls of dealmaking, capital owners experience fewer and fewer obstacles in their efforts to do business within China. Entrepreneurs, including foreigners, can even hold membership and ranking office in the Communist Party. Yet the same cannot be said for advocates of economic and social justice, who face censorship, privation, and prison time. With a few piecemeal exceptions, China is a gaping hole in the global communications network that links the multitude of trade unions, NGOs, and movement activists who are forging cross-border cooperation on labor and environmental standards. International initiatives and actions on the part of these individuals and groups have become a prominent feature of the landscape of globalization. As a result, sustainable alternatives are now on the table. Corporations and the unelected voices of the WTO and IMF are no longer the only players in the game of global reach, and their power to operate at will is no longer unchallenged. But virtually none of this applies to China. From the perspective of the movement for alternative globalization, China is still closed for business.

Even in the absence of links to international justice advocacy, China is hardly a paradise for the average investor without a social conscience. For one thing, profits are still hard to come by, and the domestic market is already beset by overproduction. As my interviews showed, the powerful patriotism and the hunger for self-advancement of mainland Chinese may coincide with the short-term interest of foreign investors, but these qualities also place real limits on the corporate loyalty and conduct of employees. Nor is the labor market as reliable as the investment promoters have reported. Worker protests are widespread, and while they are mostly uncoordinated and liable to swift suppression, they are proof that a restive spirit of militancy is alive and kicking in China's transitional economy. Unexpected labor shortages have appeared, even among unskilled migrant workers. Portions of this book have focused on an even bigger headache for foreign managers: a scarcity of technically skilled workers and professionals with the requisite work mentality and experience. Indeed, I found that wage inflation, high turnover, and rampant self-interest among these employees is impeding the pace of value-added outsourcing. Prone to jump ship with some regularity, their paper-thin loyalty to employers is generating disquiet among investors. Only yesterday, Chinese livelihoods were guaranteed by an iron rice bowl. Today, job-hopping is a national pastime, salutary to some fly-by-night investors, but an affliction to most employers, who want a steady workforce on their own terms.

It is not easy to say whether these tendencies are road bumps on the path to a capitalist Shangri-la, or symptoms of more lasting volatility (if not resistance) generated, in part, by the fickle climate that comes with free trade. But I repeatedly came across evidence of their impact in my research for this book, and I tried to describe the outcome in the daily workplace, especially in the miscommunication and discord that surface in the contact zone between Chinese employees and foreign managers. These conflicts, I conclude, cannot be put down solely to problems of cultural adjustment, to be resolved through the right kind of personnel training. They should also be seen as part of an ongoing conversation about how to negotiate the rules of work. China's dramatic entry into the league of leading economies has hardly been a textbook example of "industrialization by invitation." Far from being a grateful and obsequious invitee, Beijing has been careful to retain its autonomy and its bargaining rights. This unbowed attitude has not been lost on the educated workers who belong to what I have called "the sent-up generation," and who are discovering their own keen appetite for self-direction.

While they are often persuaded that they are making their own way in the world, released from the strictures of Confucian and Maoist doctrine, the engineers and others who feature in this book are not entirely new actors. On the one hand, they have inherited the mantle of early-twentieth-century intellectuals (from the May Fourth movement) who grasped hold of useful Western ideas in order to strengthen the nation. On the other, they already have an allotted role in the global industrial chain, clearly determined by their technical caliber, the price of their labor, and their orientation toward multinational business practices. How they balance the two, while retaining their new sense of self-propulsion, is being closely watched by investors with control over high-tech capital, but it is a matter of no small interest to governments and populations around the world.

For a variety of reasons, these employees are feared outside of China, and at times they are unfairly blamed for taking away skilled jobs. The blame is largely misplaced. In most respects, the real sources of unjust conduct can be found in the offshore environment created by and for global corporations under free-trade auspices and with the ardent participation of China's rulers. In common with many other offshore governments, Beijing has been ruthless in suppressing activities and rights that jeopardize the privileges afforded to investors by this environment. Nor are these exclusively labor-related. As is the case elsewhere—wherever growth has been driven primarily by foreign investment—the fast money has brought extensive ecological damage to the host country. In China's case, pell-mell growth has required an unsustainable rate of consumption of the world's resources. In the large scheme of things, China's growth is indeed a threat, but not for the

Government warning about corruption in the shift
to a market economy

geopolitical reason—fear of military-industrial expansionism—that many of its hawkish critics allege. The danger lies in its jumbo capacity to command the norm for conduct in the global economy as a whole.

In the course of the year I spent in Shanghai and its environs, I found myself in a position to examine the daily reality of the corporate version of free trade, and to test the claims made on its behalf. Given the raft of handouts—tax holidays; discounted land, power, and water; fast-track approvals; soft regulation of labor and environmental obligations—made available to China's foreign investors, it is clearly a misnomer even to speak about free trade. Indeed, it would be more accurate to say that China, like other offshore countries, is in the business of buying short-term jobs from corporations. Foreign direct investment has flowed in response, but this infusion does not create new jobs in a vacuum. Foreign capital enters an economy where, as part of a quid pro quo for the new money, massive quantities of public assets have been sold off and tens of millions of public-sector jobs have been liquidated.

For onshore countries, the balance sheet is no less ominous, though by now it is more familiar. As outsourcing, along with capital flight, marches further up the value chain, sharply reducing the opportunities left available for its casualties, the devotees of free trade have had a harder time portraying it as a win-win scenario. But they have had some success in portraying their critics as narrow-minded protectionists. In principle, there is nothing wrong with protectionism. People surely have the right to secure their livelihoods by any legal means necessary, and there are several policy suggestions circulating that make sense to me and that are appropriate to mention here.

Tighter government control over capital flow in the form of a flight tax seems like a practical beginning. Standardized rewards for companies that stay put is a responsible next step, followed by reforms of corporate tax codes that are indefensibly regressive. The current federal tax code, through its leniency toward foreign tax credits, explicitly encourages offshore ventures. It allows companies to defer taxes on profits earned abroad, and with routine help from creative accounting that hides profits in overseas havens, this arrangement means that many firms can avoid paying any taxes, either at home or abroad. (An estimated $500 billion in overseas untaxed profits has been stockpiled by U.S. corporations.) So, too, the trade-adjustment assistance that is currently available to dislocated workers pales by comparison with the substantial tax handouts enjoyed by employers who have lost business to trade dislocation. Finally, I believe that a more extensive system of social insurance programs (including publicly guaranteed health and pension benefits) should be funded, in part, by increased taxes on offshoring corporations. Such measures fulfill the minimum criteria for a society that values its citizens and residents.

But reform proposals like these are not the only things to have emerged from the row over outsourcing and corporate flight. The furor has also spawned its share of insular chauvinist sentiment, fueled by ugly, reactionary calls to close down borders and restrict trade. Let us remember that nation-based resistance is neither the only way nor the best way to respond to the often cruel changes wrought by globalization. More innovative alternatives to the corporate vision of free trade do exist. They are equally global in scope, and they are based on the principles of fair trade, sustainable economics, and socially conscious investment, rather than on short-term profit and plunder.

For those who favor the alternatives, China is a different and in many ways greater challenge than it has been for multinationals looking to reap easy profits. Beijing, after all, has effectively segregated its suppression of alternative ideas from its zealous efforts to harness the power of the dollar. But, however daunting, there is no ducking this challenge. Without China, any discussion about the future shape of globalization is incomplete, because not only outsourcing but China itself is becoming a way of life for all of us.

Notes

Introduction

1. Melinda Moore, "R&D in the PRC," *AmChat: The Journal of the American Chamber of Commerce in Shanghai,* November 2004, 12–15.

2. Thomas Friedman, *The World Is Flat: A Brief History of the Twenty-First Century* (New York: Farrar, Straus and Giroux, 2005).

3. The Directory of the China-America Council of Commerce and Industry, *A Guide to Nearly 400 Companies Interested in Developing Trade Between China and the U.S.A.* (New York, 1946).

4. According to a Department of Labor summary in 2003, only 26 percent of laid-off manufacturing workers find jobs that pay as well or better than the old jobs. Cited in Sarah Anderson and John Cavanagh with Thea Lee, *Field Guide to the Global Economy* (New York: The New Press, 2005), 43.

5. These consumption levels were achieved in spite of central planned efforts to slow down growth. Yu Bin, "The Fault Lines That Could Shake Asia," *Asia Times,* January 6, 2005.

6. Paul Krugman, "The Chinese Connection," *New York Times,* May 20, 2005.

7. Lou Dobbs, *Exporting America: Why Corporate Greed Is Shipping American Jobs Overseas* (New York: Warner Books, 2004), 22. Also see Ron Hira and Anil Hira, *Outsourcing America: What's Behind Our National Crisis and How We Can Reclaim American Jobs* (New York: AMACOM Books, 2005).

8. Patrick J. Buchanan, *Where the Right Went Wrong: How Neoconservatives Subverted the Reagan Revolution and Hijacked the Bush Presidency* (New York: St. Martin's, 2004); and *The Great Betrayal: How American Sovereignty and Social Justice Are Being Sacrificed to the Gods of the Global Economy* (Boston: Little Brown, 1998).

9. Dana Frank gives the best account of this history in *Buy American: The Untold Story of Economic Nationalism* (Boston: Beacon Press, 1999).

10. One survey, from the Conference Board (in conjunction with the National Bureau of Statistics of China) estimated that between 1995 and 2002, China lost 15

million manufacturing jobs overall, compared with 2 million in the United States. The biggest losses were in textile manufacturing, steel processing, machinery, and nonmetal mineral products. For that same period, China's industrial labor productivity growth exploded at a 17 percent annual rate. The Conference Board, Report R-1352-04-RR, *China's Experience with Productivity and Jobs: Benefits and Costs of Change* (http://www.conference-board.org). After the State-Owned Assets Supervision and Administration Commission announced in 2003 that it would concentrate on retaining and restructuring fewer than 200 of the large state-owned enterprises, plans were set in motion to sell more than 190,000 state companies to private investors. Allen Cheng, "Labor Unrest Is Growing in China," *International Herald Tribune,* October 27, 2004. As for the number of peasants released from farm labor in the last decade, estimates range as high as 150 million. The numbers are likely to be augmented by WTO compliance rules that eliminate crop subsidies and open the domestic market to foreign imports.

11. The firms I visited ranged, in size and scale, from Chinese start-ups to top-brand multinationals. I interviewed employees at global corporations like GM, GE, Lucent, Lilly, IBM, DuPont, Nokia, Philips, Maxtor, Hewitt, Bearing Point, AMD, Cadence, Motorola, Fluor, Kulicke & Soffa, National Semiconductor, and Fairchild, as well as at smaller companies, both local and foreign, in the private sector. The three main sites for my interviews in the Yangtze Delta region were Shanghai Pudong Software Park, where IT and software services firms are clustered; Zhangjiang Hi-Tech Park, where microchip fabs and R&D centers are located; and Suzhou Industrial Park, the biggest magnet for foreign investment in all of China, which hosts a range of high-tech and precision manufacturing plants. In addition, I conducted interviews in industrial parks in Wuxi and, in the west of China, in Chongqing and Sichuan. In Taiwan, my visits were to Hsinchu Science-Based IndustrialPark and its high-tech environs. In central Shanghai, my interviews were conducted among the membership of the American Chamber of Commerce, and at selected service-sector companies, primarily foreign-invested.

12. Dorothy Solinger, "Workers of China Unite in a Paradox for Communism," *Straits Times,* February 14, 2005. Ching Kwan Lee, "Pathways of Labor Insurgency," in Elizabeth Perry and Mark Selden, eds., *Chinese Society: Change, Conflict and Resistance* (New York: Routledge, 2000), 41–61. The Public Security Ministry reported 74,000 mass protests and riots in 2004. Howard French, "Land of 74,000 Protests," *New York Times,* August 24, 2005.

13. Liu Weifeng, "Labour Shortage Puzzles Experts," *China Daily,* August 25, 2004; "Migrant Worker Shortage Affects Enterprises as Well as Society," *Gongren ribao* [Worker's Daily], September 14, 2004; Chua Chin Hon, "Some Chinese Cities Run Short of Migrant Workers," *Straits Times,* August 6, 2004; Yao Yuan, "China, Land of 1.3 Billion, Is Short of Labor," *Asia Times,* August 16, 2004; "China's Factories Face Labour Shortage," *Straits Times,* September 2004; Fan Ren, "Drought of Migrant Labour," *Beijing Review,* August 5, 2004; Tim Johnson, "Chinese Factory Workers Begin Protesting Low Wages, Poor Conditions," *Monterey Herald,* September 7, 2004.

14. Faced with rising protests over the gap between rural and urban incomes, Hu Jintao's government took steps, beginning in 2003, to reduce the burden of rural tax-

ation, and to phase out the agricultural tax by 2006. The State Statistical Bureau reported that farmers' per capita income increased in 2004 by 12 percent to 2,936 RMB ($355), which, adjusted for inflation, showed a 6.8 percent increase. The tax burden on peasants dropped by 44.3 percent. "Farmers' Per Capita Income Stands at 2,936 Yuan," *China Daily*, February 2, 2005.

15. Many municipalities in the region raised their minimum wage levels. Government officials in the Guangdong township of Xiaolan took the opportunity to welcome only those investors willing to pay 600 RMB ($72), well above the minimum wage of 450 RMB ($54). Alexandra Harney, "Guangzhou and Shanghai Slug It Out," *Financial Times*, December 7, 2004, 5.

16. "Migrant Workers Learn to Say 'No' to the Market" *Sina.com,* September 21, 2004. In 2003, as much as 41.7 billion yuan (over $5 billion) in late wages was owed to 8.5 million of the country's 100 million migrant workers. "Rules Mapped Out to Protect Workers' Rights," http://china.org.cn/english/2004/Dec/113778.htm.

17. For analysis of workers' increasing use of legal channels, see Mary Gallagher, " 'Use the Law as Your Weapon!' Institutional Change and Legal Mobilization in China," in Neil Diamant, Stanley Lubman, and Kevin O'Brien, eds., *Engaging the Law in China* (Stanford, Calif.: Stanford University Press, 2005).

18. To alleviate the shortage, the government lifted a decade-long ban on hiring fresh migrant workers in Guangdong after the Lunar New Year Festival. But the numbers were down again in 2005, and railway authorities in Anhui noted a 20 percent decrease in traffic to Guangdong and a 30 percent increase to the Yangtze Delta, where labor conditions were better. Olivia Chung, "Guangdong Labor Lures Not Working," *The Standard,* February 25, 2005; "South China Feels Acute Labor Shortage," Xinhua News Agency, March 3, 2005.

19. Dexter Roberts, "Is China Running Out of Workers?" *BusinessWeek,* October 25, 2004, 60. Jim Yardley and David Barboza, "Help Wanted: China Finds Itself with a Labor Shortage," *New York Times,* April 3, 2005; Thomas Fuller, "China Feels a Labor Pinch," *International Herald Tribune,* April 20, 2005.

20. Dali L. Yang, "China's Looming Labor Shortage," *Far Eastern Economic Review* 168, no. 2 (February 2005): 19–24.

21. Ulrich Beck describes this pattern well in *The Brave New World of Work* (Oxford, England: Polity Press, 2000), arguing that the working life to come will resemble women's experience more than men's—a combination of part-time work and occasional stints at full-time employment.

22. Alan Tonelson, *The Race to the Bottom: Why a Worldwide Worker Surplus and Uncontrolled Free Trade Are Sinking American Living Standards* (Boulder, Colo.: Westview Press, 2000).

23. Ralph Nader et al., *The Case Against "Free Trade": GATT, NAFTA, and the Globalization of Corporate Power* (San Francisco: Earth Island Press, 1993); Andrew Ross, *Low Pay, High Profile: The Global Push for Fair Labor* (New York: The New Press, 2004).

24. For the most recent, widely discussed, example of a flawed prediction about China, see Gordon G. Chang, *The Coming Collapse of China* (New York: Random House, 2001).

The Shanghai Squeeze

1. See Gus Tyler, *Look for the Union Label: A History of the International Ladies' Garment Workers' Union* (Armonk, N.Y.: M. E. Sharpe, 1995).

2. The swelling list of books about the alternative globalization movement includes the following: John Cavanagh et al., *Alternatives to Economic Globalization: A Better World Is Possible* (San Francisco: Berrett-Koehler, 2002); Kevin Danaher and Roger Burbach, eds., *Globalize This! The Battle Against the World Trade Organization and Corporate Rule* (Monroe, Maine: Common Courage Press, 2000); Jeremy Brecher, Tim Costello, and Brendan Smith, *Globalization from Below* (Cambridge, Mass.: South End Press, 2000); Naomi Klein, *Fences and Windows: Dispatches from the Front Lines of the Globalization Debate* (New York: Picador, 2002); Sarah Anderson and John Cavanagh with Thea Lee, *The Field Guide to the Global Economy* (New York: The New Press, 2000); Amory Starr, *Naming the Enemy: Anti-Corporate Movements Confront Globalization* (London: Zed Books, 2000); Richard Falk, *Predatory Globalization: A Critique* (Cambridge, England: Polity Press, 1999); Lori Wallach and Michelle Sforza, *The WTO: Five Years of Reasons to Resist Corporate Globalization* (New York: Seven Stories, 2000); Tom Mertes, ed., *A Movement of Movements: Is Another World Possible?* (New York: Verso, 2004); Notes from Nowhere, *We Are Everywhere: The Irresistible Rise of Global Anti-Capitalism* (New York: Verso, 2003); Alexander Cockburn, Jeffrey St. Clair, and Allan Sekula, *Five Days That Shook the World: The Battle for Seattle and Beyond* (New York: Verso, 2001); Mike Prokosch and Laura Raymond, eds., *The Global Activist's Manual: Local Ways to Change the World* (New York: Thunder's Mouth Press, 2002); Andy Opel and Donnalyn Pompper, eds., *Representing Resistance: Media, Civil Disobedience, and the Global Justice Movement* (Westport, Conn.: Praeger, 2003); B. Gills, ed., *Globalization and the Politics of Resistance* (New York: St. Martin's, 2000); and Walden Bello, *Deglobalization: Ideas for a New World Economy* (London: Zed Books, 2002).

3. The anti-free-trade coalition that opposed PNTR brought together some curious bedfellows: the officialdom of the AFL-CIO, America First right-wing nationalists like Pat Buchanan, and the burgeoning voice of small or medium-sized enterprises, whose owners could not afford to make the highly profitable move to China. A coalition that had cut its teeth on the passage of NAFTA in 1992, it surfaced with some regularity on free-trade issues, and it had its backers in Congress. John MacArthur describes the making of the coalition in *The Selling of "Free Trade": NAFTA, Washington, and the Subversion of American Democracy* (New York: Hill and Wang, 2000).

4. Kate Bronfenbrenner, *Impact of U.S.-China Trade Relations on Workers, Wages, and Employment: A Pilot Study Report* (U.S.-China Economic and Security Review Commission, June 2001), 4.

5. Ibid.

6. Kate Bronfenbrenner and Stephanie Luce, *The Changing Nature of Corporate Global Restructuring: The Impact of Production Shifts on Jobs in the U.S., China, and Around the Globe* (U.S.-China Economic and Security Review Commission, 2004).

7. Robert Scott, *U.S. China Trade, 1989–2003: Impact on Jobs and Industries,*

Nationally and State-by-State (Economic Policy Institute Working Paper no. 270, January 2005), http://www.epinet.org.

8. Vice-Chair Richard D'Amato's remarks at San Diego hearings on "China as an Emerging Regional and Technology Power: Implications for U.S. Economic and Security Interests" (U.S.-China Economic Security and Review Commission, February 12–13, 2004), 3.

9. Economic Policy Institute, *Economic Snapshot,* December 17, 2003 (http://www.epinet.org/content.cfm/webfeatures_snapshots_archive_12172003).

10. Henry Farber, "Job Loss in the United States, 1981–2001," National Bureau of Economic Research, Working Paper no. 471 (Princeton University, May 2003).

11. These "long-tenured displaced workers" (as the Department of Labor calls people who lost jobs they had held for at least three years, for reasons such as a plant closing or the elimination of a position) were more likely to lose their jobs than in any downturn since 1981–82, and those who found new jobs took bigger pay cuts—an average of 18.7 percent—than ever before. Indeed, the hardest hit were workers aged fifty-five to sixty-four. Floyd Norris, "Job Picture Looks Good Now But Recession Left Fears That Endure," *New York Times,* August 6, 2004.

12. On occasion, a prominent economist broke ranks with the consensus, as Paul Samuelson did when he published his broadside against the assumption that outsourcing would benefit the U.S. economy in the long run. "Where Ricardo and Mill Rebut and Confirm Arguments of Mainstream Economists Supporting Globalization," *Journal of Economic Perspectives* 18, no. 3 (Summer 2004): 135–46.

13. Christopher Koch, "Backlash," *CIO Magazine,* September 1, 2003.

14. Ashok Bardham and Cynthia Kroll, "The New Wave of Outsourcing," Report no. 1103 (Berkeley: Fisher Center for Real Estate and Urban Economics, University of California, 2003).

15. Paul McDougall, "Big IT Outsourcing Deals on the Rise," *Information Week,* July 20, 2004.

16. Eduardo Porter, "Outsourcing Is Becoming a Hard Sell in the U.S.," *New York Times,* March 6, 2004.

17. Ariadan Bhattacharya et al., Boston Consulting Group, *Capturing Global Advantage: How Leading Industrial Companies Are Transforming Their Industries by Sourcing and Selling in China, India, and Other Low-Cost Countries* (Boston, April 2004).

18. Kathleen Walsh, *Foreign High-Tech R&D in China: Risks, Rewards, and Implications for U.S.-China Relations* (Washington, D.C.: Henry L. Stimson Center, 2003).

19. Spencer Ante and Robert Hof, "Look Who's Going Offshore," *BusinessWeek,* May 17, 2004.

20. Ralph Gomory and William Baumol, with a contribution by Edward Wolff, *Global Trade and Conflicting National Interests* (Cambridge, Mass.: MIT Press, 2000).

21. The Employment Law Alliance survey ("America at Work") can be found at http://fm.employmentlawalliance.com/ela/FMPro?-DB=ela_articles.fp5&-Format=article.html&-RecID=33239&-Find.

22. Jennifer Bjorhus, "Survey: Most Investors Oppose Outsourcing," *Seattle Times,* April 29, 2004.

23. Steven Greenhouse, "IBM Explores Shift of Some Jobs Overseas," *New York Times,* July 22, 2003.

24. David Beckman, "IBM Plans to Accelerate Offshore Outsourcing," *Wash-Tech News,* July 22, 2003 (http://www.washtech.org/news/industry/display.php?ID_Content=4591).

25. William Bulkeley, "IBM Documents Give Rare Look at Sensitive Plans on 'Offshoring,' " *Wall Street Journal,* January 19, 2004.

26. Quoted in David Beckman, "AT&T Wireless Exporting Tech Jobs to India," *Tech Worker News,* November 19, 2003 (http://www.techsunite.org/news/techind/031119_att.cfm).

27. John Cook, "AT&T Wireless Outsourcing Jobs Overseas" *Seattle Post-Intelligencer,* November 20, 2003.

28. These Bureau of Labor Statistics figures, the highest recorded in more than twenty years, are cited in Steve Lohr and Matt Richtel, "Lingering Job Insecurity of Silicon Valley," *New York Times,* March 9, 2004; see also Steve Lohr, "High-End Technology Work Not Immune to Outsourcing," *New York Times,* June 16, 2004.

29. Economic Policy Institute, "Offshoring Issue Guide" (http://www.epinet.org). A University of Illinois report prepared for the Washington Alliance of Technology Workers (CWA Local 37803) showed that, in the post-recession years, the IT industry still showed a larger impact from outsourcing job loss than other industrial sectors. Snighda Srivastava and Nik Theodore, "America's High-Tech Bust" (Chicago: Center for Urban Economic Development, 2004).

30. The figures are culled from *BusinessWeek*'s annual survey of CEO pay (April 19, 2004) for 2003. See the analysis by United for a Fair Economy at http://www.faireconomy.org/press/2004/CEOPayRatio_pr.html.

31. According to the Center on Budget and Policy Priorities, cited by Paul Krugman, "The Oblivious Right," *New York Times,* April 25, 2005.

32. Andrew Sum, et al., "The Unprecedented Rising Tide of Corporate Profits and the Simultaneous Ebbing of Labor Compensation: Gainers and Losers from the National Economic Recovery of 2002 and 2003" (Boston: Northeastern University Center for Labor Market Studies, 2004).

33. Sarah Anderson, John Cavanagh, Chris Hartman, Scott Klinger, and Stacey Chan, *Executive Excess 2004: Campaign Contributions, Outsourcing, Unexpensed Stock Options and Rising CEO Pay,* 11th Annual CEO Compensation Survey (Washington, D.C.: Institute for Policy Studies; Boston: United for a Fair Economy, 2004).

34. "New Face for the Old Bund," *Shanghai Daily,* March 3, 2003.

35. For analysis of the "blood fraternity" of overseas Chinese investors, see Aihwa Ong, *Flexible Citizenship: The Cultural Logics of Transnationality* (Durham, N.C.: Duke University Press, 1999).

36. Quoted in Joe Studwell, *The China Dream: The Quest for the Last Great Untapped Market on Earth* (New York: Atlantic Monthly Press, 2002), 172.

37. For a range of opinions on the topic, see Andrew Walder, ed., *China's Transitional Economy* (New York: Oxford University Press, 1999). Other relevant economic analyses include Nicholas Lardy, *Foreign Trade and Economic Reform in China, 1978–1990* (Cambridge, England: Cambridge University Press, 1992); *China in the*

World Economy (Washington, D.C.: Institute for International Economics, 1994); and *Integrating China into the Global Economy* (Washington, D.C.: Brookings Institution Press, 2002); Barry Naughton, *Growing out of the Plan: Chinese Economic Reform, 1978–1993* (Cambridge, England: Cambridge University Press, 1995); Susan Shirk, *The Political Logic of Economic Reform in China* (Berkeley: University of California Press, 1993).

38. China's central state-owned enterprises showed rapid profit growth from about 2002. Fueled by the high market demand for energy and power, 189 of the flagship SOEs, concentrated in transportation, metallurgy, petrochemical, and power sectors, recorded $36.2 billion of profits in 2003, and a combined profit of $27.2 billion alone in the first half of 2004, with estimated profits of $45.9 billion for the full year. Sun Min, "Sharp Profit Rise Expected for Central SOEs," *China Daily*, August 14, 2004. By 2004, the average salary in state companies, while a good deal less than the equivalent in foreign-invested firms, was growing more rapidly. According to a survey conducted by Zhaopin, the leading HR website, 2,789 RMB ($337) was the average 2004 monthly salary at state-owned enterprises—a 19 percent increase over 2003—while employees at foreign-invested firms saw a 16 percent increase for an average of 3,820 RMB ($461). The domestic private sector saw a rise from 2,714 RMB to 2,916 RMB ($352), while civil servants only got a 3 percent raise to 2,552 RMB ($308). Rachel Yan, "Wages at State Firms Rise Swiftly," *Shanghai Daily*, December 8, 2004.

39. See Joseph Stiglitz's rosy account in *Globalization and Its Discontents* (New York: W. W. Norton, 2002).

40. Lynn T. White III, *Unstately Power: Local Causes of China's Economic Reforms* (Armonk, N.Y.: M. E. Sharpe, 1998).

41. Lynn White and Cheng Li, "Politics and Government," in Brian Hook, ed., *Shanghai and the Yangtze Delta: A City Reborn* (Hong Kong: Oxford University Press, 1998), 53.

42. Foreign-invested exports accounted for 63.6 percent of the city's exports in 2003, and grew much faster—an increase of 60.8 percent—than the share of domestic companies. Private Chinese companies accounted for only 3.7 percent of exports. "Shanghai Economy Booming, Thanks to Foreign-Invested Companies," *AmChat*, March 2004, 9.

43. Barry Naughton, testimony before the San Diego hearings on "China as an Emerging Regional and Technology Power" (U.S.-China Economic Security and Review Commission, February 12–13, 2004), 23.

44. Michelle Zhang, "More Find Work in Foreign Firms," *Shanghai Daily*, October 18, 2004.

45. For China as a whole, economists had widely differing views. At an AmCham meeting in October 2003, members heard an estimate from Jonathan Andersen, an economist from UBS Investment Research, announce that FDI was responsible for up to 45 percent of China's GDP (Charles Twanmoh, "China: Boom or Bust," *AmChat*, December 2003, 13), while members at an October 2004 meeting heard Jonathan Woetzel, from McKinsey, argue that FDI only accounted for 3 to 4 percent of China's GDP, and that growth was driven primarily by the high national rate of

savings and productivity. According to 2004 statistics from the Ministry of Commerce, there were 250 million urban employees in China, 25 million of whom worked for foreign-funded companies. The jobs of 80 million Chinese were directly related to foreign trade. For a book-length treatment of the topic, see Yasheng Huang, *Selling China: Foreign Direct Investment During the Reform Era* (Cambridge, England: Cambridge University Press, 2003).

46. *2004 Business Guide to Shanghai and the Yangtze River Delta* (Hong Kong: China Briefing, 2004), 148.

47. Jan Kot, "China's Most Wanted," *China International Business* 192 (November 2003): 22–26.

48. Gary Bowerman, "More Opportunity—But Less Money," *AmChat,* January 7, 2005.

49. Nicholas Clifford, *Spoilt Children of Empire: Westerners in Shanghai and the Chinese Revolution of the 1920s* (Hanover, Vt.: Middlebury College Press, 1991).

50. The business bible of the era is Kathy Butler, ed., *The Life and Death of a Joint Venture in China,* 2nd edition (Hong Kong: Asia Law & Practice, 1996). For a more scholarly analysis, see Margaret Pearson, *Joint Ventures in the People's Republic of China: The Control of Foreign Direct Investment Under Socialism* (Princeton, N.J.: Princeton University Press, 1991).

51. The figures are from a global survey of the costs of living for corporate expatriates conducted by the Mercer Human Resource Consulting firm.

52. See Ching Kwan Lee's study of two Hong Kong–owned garment factories, one in Hong Kong and one across the border in Guangdong province. *Gender and the South China Miracle: Two Worlds of Factory Women* (Berkeley: University of California Press, 1998).

53. Quoted in You-tien Hsing, *Making Capitalism in China: The Taiwan Connection* (Oxford, England: Oxford University Press, 1998), 83.

54. Anthony Bianco and Wendy Zellner, "Is Wal-Mart Too Powerful?" *BusinessWeek,* October 6, 2003.

55. Studwell offers an account of this history in *The China Dream.*

56. Quoted in Leon Hellerman and Alan Stein, eds., *China: Readings on the Middle Kingdom* (New York: Simon & Schuster, 1971), 145.

57. According to an influential report to the governor of Hong Kong by an assistant magistrate in Hong Kong by the name of Mitchell, exports had declined by three-quarters of a million pounds sterling in the period from 1844 to 1850. Mitchell concluded that the self-sufficient nature of China's domestic economy would forever thwart the aspirational foreign trader. Frances Wood, *No Dogs and Not Too Many Chinese: Treaty Port Life in China, 1843–1943* (London: John Murray, 1998), 58.

58. John King Fairbank, *The United States and China* (Cambridge, Mass.: Harvard University Press, 1979), 171.

59. Nathan Pelcovits tells the story of this conflict in trade diplomacy between 1839 and 1906 in *Old China Hands and the Foreign Office* (New York: King's Crown Press, 1948).

60. Paul Varg, "The Myth of the China Market: 1890–1914," *American Historical Review* 73, no. 3, (February 1968): 742–58.

61. Carl Crow, *Four Hundred Million Customers* (New York: Harper & Brothers, 1937), 304.

62. Studwell, *The China Dream,* 274.

63. The chambers' member survey showed that 75 percent of U.S. companies operating in China made a profit in 2002, but only 38 percent reported that their profit margin in the country was higher than their global average. In 2003, the figures were almost the same, with slightly more companies (16 percent) reporting a "very profitable" year. *White Paper: American Business in China* (Beijing: American Chamber of Commerce PRC/AmCham Shanghai, 2003 and 2004 editions). The *Shanghai Daily* reported that foreign investors in Shanghai had a much better year in 2004. The 35,000 foreign-invested firms saw their returns grow by 57 percent in the first three quarters, the top sectors being in high-tech and real estate. Chen Liying, "Investment Returns Rise," *Shanghai Daily,* October 27, 2004.

64. Total China earnings for U.S. companies rose from $1.9 billion in 1999 to $4.4 billion by the end of 2003 (plus services and licensing for a total of $8.2 billion), but the revenue was still small compared with countries like Mexico and South Korea. Richard McGregor, "China Not as Profitable an Investment Market as Smaller Ones," *Financial Times,* December 6, 2004, 1; Joe Studwell, "China's Market Is Not So Lucrative," *Financial Times,* December 5, 2004, 3.

65. James Kynge, "Trade in Yangtze Far Outstrips the Pearl," *Financial Times,* May 11, 2004.

66. Among the more popular books that chronicle the life and times of expatriates in Old Shanghai are Harriet Sergeant, *Shanghai: Collision Point of Cultures, 1918–1939* (New York: Crown, 1990); Stella Dong, *Shanghai: The Rise and Fall of a Decadent City, 1842–1949* (New York: Morrow, 2000); Noël Barber, *The Fall of Shanghai* (New York: Coward, McCann & Geoghegan, 1979); Leo Ou-fan Lee, *Shanghai Modern: The Flowering of a New Urban Culture in China, 1930–1945* (Cambridge, Mass.: Harvard University Press, 1999). Wang Jinhai, *The Ugly Old Shanghai* (Shanghai, 2002), is a bilingual publication, originally published by the Shanghai Academy of Social Science, which offers a seamy antidote to the nostalgia. It recounts all the vices and exploitative practices associated with semi-colonial life in the entrepôt port. The more unscrupulous figures in the book include "Manure Overlords," "Dock Tyrants," "Traders in Children," "Number Ones," "Slippery Fellows," "Ground Beetles" (real estate speculators), the Green Gang, and fraudsters and prostitutes of every description.

67. Gang Tian, *Shanghai's Role in the Economic Development of China: Reform of Foreign Trade and Investment* (Westport, Conn.: Praeger, 1996), 32.

68. Ibid., 27. Population control has always been a form of social control in China, and so mass deportation from Shanghai has been used as a way of controlling the city's size and its social stability. See Lynn White in Y. M. Yeung and Sung Yun-wing, eds., *Shanghai: Transformation and Modernization Under China's Open Policy* (Hong Kong: Chinese University Press, 1996).

69. Christopher Howe, ed., *Shanghai: Revolution and Development in an Asian Metropolis* (Cambridge, England: Cambridge University Press, 1981), xii.

70. White, *Unstately Power,* 79.

71. Wong Siu-lin, "The Entrepreneurial Spirit," in Yeung and Sung, eds., *Shanghai: Transformation and Modernization Under China's Open Policy*, 39.

72. Even the official media cited a figure "close to the international alarm level of 0.4." Xin Zhigang, "Dissecting China's 'Middle Class,' " *China Daily*, October 27, 2004.

73. For a perspective that sees Shanghai's "state-owned enterprise mentality" as a major obstruction to its economic development, see Pamela Yatsko *New Shanghai: The Rocky Rebirth of China's Legendary City* (New York: John Wiley, 2001).

74. Dorothy Solinger, *Contesting Citizenship in Urban China: Peasant Migrants, the State, and the Logic of the Market* (Berkeley: University of California Press, 1999); Li Zhang, *Strangers in the City: Reconfigurations of Space, Power, and Social Networks Within China's Floating Population* (Palo Alto, Calif.: Stanford University Press, 2001).

75. For a description and analysis of the *danwei*, the all-encompassing Maoist work unit, see Xiaobo Lü and Elizabeth Perry, eds., *Danwei: The Changing Chinese Workplace in Historical and Comparative Perspective* (Armonk, N.Y.: M. E. Sharpe, 1997); Andrew Walder, *Communist Neo-Traditionalism: Work and Authority in Chinese Industry* (Berkeley: University of California Press, 1986).

76. Michele Chen, "The Jobless: Victims of China's Economic Success," *Asia Times*, March 31, 2004.

77. He Qinglian's *China's Pitfall* (Hong Kong: Mingjing Publishing House, 1998) is the most trenchant account of corruption and graft in the era of the sell-offs.

78. By 2004, as many as 100,000 families were still being evacuated or relocated annually. Shen Yanfei, "Poor May Still Find Door Shut," *Shanghai Daily*, April 12, 2004.

79. The 23 percent estimate comes from research by the Rand Corporation. Charles Wolf, "China's Rising Unemployment Challenge," *Asian Wall Street Journal*, July 7, 2004.

80. The Shanghai Labor and Social Security Bureau reported that there were 160,000 youth unemployed, equal to 62.2 percent of all registered unemployed. "Unemployment Hits Youth in Shanghai," *China Business Infocenter*, March 15, 2004 (http://www.cbiz.cn/news/showarticle.asp?id=2056).

Raising the Bar

1. This latest alliance was hardly a permanent one, of course. NAM eventually aligned itself with the Fair Currency Alliance in pushing for a revaluation of the yuan. The coalition considered presenting a Section 301 petition under the 1974 Trade Act. The AFL-CIO pursued its own course on the specific issue of job loss by presenting its own 301 petition in the spring of 2004 (see "The Suzhou Price" for details). The Bush administration rejected the latter, and stifled the first before it even came to formal process.

2. "Foreign Funded Firms Bigger Winner of China's Trade Surplus," *People's Daily*, April 30, 2005.

3. In 2002, the rate of return for U.S. multinationals in computer and electronic products was estimated at 21.2 percent, while the rate of return for U.S. direct invest-

ment in China generally was 14 percent. K. C. Fung, Lawrence J. Lau, and Joseph S. Lee, *U.S. Direct Investment in China* (Washington, D.C.: AEI Press, 2004).

4. Patrick Cranley, "China and the Six o'Clock News," *AmChat,* August 29, 2003. Indeed, during the 1994 fight to renew China's MFN status, AmCham had appointed a media speciality chair who could do effective fifteen-second sound bites.

5. Quoted in Richard Pearson, "Inside Washington: How US Businesses in China Can Get Their Messages to DC," *AmChat,* April 2004, 12.

6. Arthur Ransome, *The Chinese Puzzle* (London and Boston: Houghton Mifflin, 1927).

7. Nicholas Clifford, *Spoilt Children of Empire: Westerners in Shanghai and the Chinese Revolution of the 1920s* (Hanover, Vt.: Middlebury College Press, 1991), 260–61.

8. William Crane Johnstone, *The Shanghai Problem* (Stanford, Calif.: Stanford University Press; London: H. Milford, Oxford University Press, 1937), 37.

9. Paul Varg, *Missionaries, Chinese, and Diplomats: The American Protestant Missionary Movement in China, 1890–1952* (Princeton, N.J.: Princeton University Press, 1958), 4.

10. Ibid., 303.

11. Noël Barber, *The Fall of Shanghai* (New York: Coward, McCann & Geoghegan, 1979), 164.

12. Jonathan Spence, *To Change China: Western Advisors in China, 1620–1960* (Boston: Little, Brown, 1969).

13. For analysis of the anti-sweatshop movement, see Andrew Ross, *Low Pay, High Profile: The Global Push for Fair Labor* (New York: The New Press, 2004); Liza Featherstone and USAS, *Students Against Sweatshops* (New York: Verso, 2002); Andrew Ross, ed., *No Sweat: Fashion, Free Trade, and the Rights of Garment Workers* (New York: Verso, 1997); Edna Bonacich et al., eds., *Global Production: The Apparel Industry in the Pacific Rim* (Philadelphia: Temple University Press, 1994); Pamela Varley, ed., *The Sweatshop Quandary: Corporate Responsibility on the Global Frontier* (Washington, D.C.: Investor Responsibility Research Center, 1998); Ellen Israel Rosen, *Making Sweatshops: The Globalization of the U.S. Apparel Industry* (Berkeley: University of California Press, 2002); Robert Ross, *Slaves to Fashion: Poverty and Abuse in the New Sweatshops* (Ann Arbor: University of Michigan Press, 2004); Naila Kabeer, *The Power to Choose: Bangladeshi Women and Labour Market Decisions in London and Dhaka* (London: Verso, 2000); Daniel Bender and Richard Greenwald, eds., *Sweatshop USA: The American Sweatshop in Historical and Global Perspective* (New York: Routledge, 2003); Archon Fung, Dara O'Rourke, and Charles Sabel, *Can We Put an End to Sweatshops?* (Boston: Beacon Press, 2001); Daniel Bender, *Sweated Work, Weak Bodies: Anti-Sweatshop Campaigns and Languages of Labor* (New Brunswick, N.J.: Rutgers University Press, 2004); and, in the China context, Anita Chan, *China's Workers Under Assault: The Exploitation of Labor in a Globalizing Economy* (Armonk, N.Y.: M. E. Sharpe, 2001); Pun Ngai, *Made in China: Women Factory Workers in a Global Workplace* (Durham, N.C.: Duke University Press, 2005). The reader might also consult the following reports by the National Labor Committee: *Paying to Lose Our Jobs: Free Trade's Hidden Secrets: Why We Are Losing Our Shirts* (1993); *Haiti After*

the Coup: Sweatshop or Real Development? (1993); *The U.S. in Haiti: How to Get Rich on 11¢ per Hour* (1996); *Wal-Mart's Shirts of Misery: Bangladesh Factory Conditions* (1999); *Behind the Label: Made in China* (1998); *Made in China: The Role of U.S. Companies in Denying Human Rights* (2000); *Propping up the Dictators in Burma* (2001); *"Made in the USA?": American Samoa and Indentured Servitude* (2001); *Bangladesh: The Struggle to End the Race to the Bottom* (2001). See also Asia Monitor Resource Center, *We in the Zone: Women Workers in Asia's Export Processing Zones* (Hong Kong, 1998); Asia Pacific Labour Law Review, *Workers' Rights for the New Century* (Hong Kong, 2003); *Smashing the Iron Pot: Workers and Unions Under China's Market Socialism* (Hong Kong, 1988); Hong Kong Christian Industrial Committee, *How Hasbro, Mattel, McDonald's and Disney Manufacture Their Toys* (Hong Kong, 2001); and with Asia Monitor Resource Center, *Working Conditions in Sports Shoe Factories in China: Making Shoes for Nike and Reebok* (Hong Kong, 1997).

14. Mark Barenberg, a legal expert at the International Labor Organization, testified to Democrat senators that managers of major U.S. multinational corporations in China had told him that 80 percent of their contractors flouted labor laws. The contractors "keep double or triple books" to hide the fact that they're not paying minimum wages or overtime and are breaking China's maximum-hour laws, Barenberg quoted the managers as saying. "In their official statements, however, these same U.S. corporate managers say they're paying minimum wages, and the media and think-tank researchers often take these official statements at face value." "US Companies Accused of Condoning Workers' Rights Abuses in China," *Channel NewsAsia,* March 30, 2004.

15. For some explanation of this history, see Anita Chan, "Chinese Trade Unions and Workplace Relations in State-Owned and Joint-Venture Enterprises," in Malcolm Warner, ed., *Changing Workplace Relations in the Chinese Economy* (New York: St. Martin's, 2000), 34–56.

16. A local trade unionist explained to me how union officials are supposed to interpret their role according to the theory of Jiang Zemin's "Three Represents": "They should promote workers' interests," he observed, "but not stand in the way of company growth," since the state was obliged, under this theory, to represent the interests of entrepreneurs, or "advanced productive forces," in addition to those of workers and peasants.

17. "Some Transnationals Go Seriously Against Trade Union Law," *People's Daily,* October 27, 2004. ACFTU statistics indicate that only one-fifth of China's 400,000 foreign companies had anything resembling a union. "Unions Fight for More Recognition," *China Daily* September 24, 2004 (http://www.en.ce.cn).

18. Wal-Mart was just one of the many U.S. firms whose Chinese suppliers had been accused of fostering abusive labor conditions. For an exposé of the sweatshops contracted by the giant retailer, see Dexter Roberts and Aaron Bernstein, "A Life of Beatings and Fines," *BusinessWeek,* October 2, 2002, 122–25.

19. "Wal-Mart Concedes China Can Make Union," Associated Press, November 23, 2004.

20. "China's Industrial Investment and Exchange Rate Policies: Impact on the United States," Hearings before U.S.-China Economic Security and Review Commission, September 25, 2003, 9. The Schumer-Graham-Bunning Bill (S.1586) was

designed to impose tariffs of 27.5 percent (halfway between the 15 percent and 40 percent estimates of the yuan's undervaluation), if China refused to revalue its currency.

21. Dana Milbank, "Bush Distances Himself from Job-Loss Comment," *Seattle Times,* February 18, 2004.

22. Martin Crutsinger, "Treasury Chief's Remark Refuels Fight over Loss of U.S. Jobs," *Seattle Times,* March 31, 2004.

23. Economic Policy Institute, "Final Grade on the Bush Tax Cuts," *JobWatch,* January 7, 2005 (http://www.jobwatch.org).

24. "Bush Pick Bows Out After Dem Criticism," *Houston Chronicle,* March 12, 2004.

25. "Bush Campaign Ran from Noida Call Centre," *Hindustan Times,* May 16, 2004.

26. Louis Uchitelle, "In Business, Washington Pursues Two China Policies," *International Herald Tribune,* December 11, 2003.

27. Friedman's *New York Times* columns from Bangalore were "Meet the Zippies," February 22, 2004; "30 Little Turtles," February 29, 2004; "What Goes Around . . . ," February 26, 2004; "Globalization 3.0: From Small to Tiny," March 3, 2004. His book is *The World Is Flat: A Brief History of the Twenty-first Century* (New York: Farrar, Straus and Giroux, 2005).

28. Tom Tomorrow weblog, March 9, 2004 (http://www.thismodernworld.com). Tomorrow also referred readers to an article published in the *Times of India* that may have been the source for the engineer Friedman mentioned. The article reported on the widely publicized career of anti-outsourcing crusader Scott Kirwin, who was fired from his software programming job after showing Indian temps the ropes. Information Technology Professionals Association of America, the organization he subsequently started, became one of the best known of the anti-outsourcing websites. The Indian article concluded in a vein not unlike Friedman's: this American has made a lucrative career out of being laid off. Kirwin, alerted to the rumor, reported that he had made exactly sixty dollars from sales of his own T-shirts: "My Job Went to India and All I Got Was This Stupid Pink Slip."

29. "China's Industrial Investment and Exchange Rate Policies: Impact on the United States" (Hearings Before U.S.-China Economic Security and Review Commission, September 25, 2003), 19.

30. Ibid, 174.

31. "U.S.-China Trade and Investment: Impact on Key Manufacturing and Industrial Sectors: Field Hearing in Akron, Ohio" (U.S.-China Economic Security and Review Commission, September 23, 2004), iv.

32. C. Xikang, L. Cheng, K. C. Fung, and L. J. Lau's estimate was thirty cents of each dollar, and in the case of exports to the U.S., only twenty cents, in "The Estimation of GDP and Employment Induced by Exports: An Application to Chinese Exports to the United States" (University of California, Santa Cruz; Stanford University, revised December 2001). Gordon Hanson and Robert Feenstra put the figure at thirty-six cents for every dollar in "Ownership and Control in Outsourcing to China: Estimating the Property Rights Theory of the Firm," National Bureau of Economic Research, Working Paper no. 10198 (Cambridge, Mass., 2003).

33. Vivek Agrawal and Diana Farrell, "Who Wins in Offshoring?" *McKinsey Quarterly,* Special Edition: Global Directions, 2003, 36–41.

34. Cited in Paul Krugman, "Bush's Own Goal," *New York Times,* August 13, 2004.

35. Anderson and Cavanagh, *The Field Guide to the Global Economy,* 56.

36. Robert McIntyre and Coo Nguyen, "Corporate Income Tax in the Bush Years" (Citizens for Tax Justice and Institute on Taxation and Economic Policy, September 2004).

37. For example, Commerce Secretary Evans brandished the White Paper at an AmCham talk in Beijing in October 2003, while thundering, "China's current trade practices are exploiting our open markets and creating an unfair advantage that is undercutting American workers." Chow Chung-yan, "China Will Take More Imports from U.S.," *South China Morning Post,* October 20, 2003.

38. American Chamber of Commerce PRC and AmCham Shanghai, *White Paper: American Business in China* (Beijing and Shanghai, 2003), 6.

39. Beijing officials played along by organizing a lavish shopping expedition to the United States in December 2003. More than a hundred firms and ministries were represented in the purchases of aviation, telecom, and space and chemical technology. "Shopping Spree to Aid Trade," *Shanghai Daily,* October 30, 2003, 1.

40. Barbara Koh, "Brave New World," *AmChat,* July 2004, 10–15.

41. Robert Tanner, "Outsourcing Bans Considered in 35 States," *Myrtle Beach Sun,* April 25, 2004.

42. In addition, rewards began to flow to the currency speculators who had poured billions of dollars of "hot money" into the PRC in anticipation of the revaluation.

The Sent-up Generation

1. Yan Zhen, "Locals Better Paid in Yangtze Delta," *Shanghai Daily,* March 23, 2004.

2. "Graduates' Hopes Dampened by Salary Fall," *China Daily,* June 15, 2004.

3. The figures for multinationals are from the Shanghai office of Hewitt. Shanghai saw more than 100,000 university students graduate in 2004, an increase of 20,000 over the previous year. Because of the glut, many graduates had to look for jobs outside the city. "Graduates Find Work but Many Leave the City," *Shanghai Daily,* June 7, 2004.

4. Peter Marsh, "World's Manufacturers March into China," *Financial Times,* June 22, 2004.

5. HR surveys in Shanghai showed an annual rise of 7 percent in professional salaries for foreign-invested firms in 2003 and 2004, and 11 percent for hot fields like engineering, IT, sales and marketing, business development, and mid-to-upper-level management. Barbara Koh, "China's Labor Shortage," *AmChat,* October 2004, 22–23.

6. For essays that document the change from the traditional work unit, see Malcolm Warner, ed., *Changing Workplace Relations in the Chinese Economy* (London: Macmillan, 2000).

7. In addition, Microsoft, HP, and Ericsson had set up global software R&D cen-

ters in the city. Chen Liying, "City Rises as Hub for Software," *Shanghai Daily,* September 20–21, 2003, 1.

8. A report by the U.S.-based market research house IDC, showed two-thirds of China's outsourcing sales coming from Japanese buyers and 17.8 percent from U.S. buyers, but predicted a growing share from the United States as the market expanded. Liu Baijia, "Firms Keen on Software Outsourcing," *China Daily,* May 12, 2004, 10.

9. See Aihwa Ong, "Re-engineering the 'Chinese Soul' in Shanghai," chapter 14 of *Re-Engineering Citizenship* (Durham, N.C.: Duke University Press, forthcoming). The exact cultural origin of Chinese social customs, such as the all-important *guanxi* (interpersonal connections), is the object of much scholarly debate. See Thomas Gold, Doug Guthrie, and David Wank, eds., *Social Connections in China: Institutions, Culture, and the Changing Nature of Guanxi* (New York: Cambridge University Press, 2002).

10. Laurence Brahm, *When Yes Means No! (or Yes or Maybe): How to Negotiate a Deal in China* (Hong Kong: Tuttle, 2003).

11. Several Shanghai firms (Shanghai HRO Consulting, Professional Way, Xunda Professional Services) were developing HR software or personality tests specifically for the Chinese labor market.

12. Lynn White in Y. M Yeung and Sung Yun-wing, eds., *Shanghai: Transformation and Modernization Under China's Open Policy* (Hong Kong: Chinese University Press, 1996).

13. From a short story by Shen Rong, which imagined that the Chinese Communist Party decreed that everyone from the "sent-down generation" could deduct ten years from their age: "Ten Years Deducted," translated by Gladys Yang, in Ying Bian, ed., *The Time Is Not Ripe: Contemporary China's Best Writers and Their Stories* (Beijing: Foreign Language Press, 1991), 193–216.

14. See Stuart Schram's discussion of "Mao Tse-Tung's Thought from 1949 to 1976," in Merle Goldman and Leo Ou-fan Lee, eds., *An Intellectual History of Modern China* (Cambridge, England: Cambridge University Press, 2002), 395–498.

15. Samuel Ho and Ralph Huenemann analyze the steps in this process in *China's Open Door Policy: The Quest for Foreign Technology and Capital* (Vancouver: University of British Columbia Press, 1984).

16. On Chinese nationalism, see C. X. George Wei and Xiaoyuan Liu, eds., *Exploring Nationalisms of China: Themes and Conflicts* (Westport, Conn.: Greenwood Press, 2002); Peter Hays Gries, *China's New Nationalism: Pride, Politics, and Diplomacy* (Berkeley: University of California Press, 2004); Jonathan Unger, ed., *Chinese Nationalism* (Armonk, N.Y.: M. E. Sharpe, 1996).

17. Dimitri Kessler analyzes the nationalism of Chinese engineers in "Nationalism, Theft and Management Strategies in the Information Industries of Mainland China," in Ching Kwan Lee, ed., *Working in China: Ethnographies of Labor and Workplace Transformation* (London: RoutledgeCurzon, 2006).

18. Later that month, the government announced that migrant workers could now apply for Shanghai's much-sought-after residency cards (affording access to social security programs and public education), previously available only to non-Shanghainese skilled professionals.

19. Cited in Thomas Fuller, "China Feels a Labor Pinch," *International Herald Tribune,* April 20, 2005.

20. "China Badly Needs 'Gray-Collars' for Manufacturing," *China Daily,* March 21, 2004.

21. "Bright Prospects Ahead for Technicians," *China Daily,* April 2, 2004.

22. Shanghai's municipal government went one step further. In April 2004, it announced changes to the one-child rule, the first significant alterations to the national policy. Divorcées with one child would be allowed to have another if they remarried. In addition, the city's general rules against a second child were eased if both parents hailed from a single-child family. Officials cited concerns about the eroding tax base and the graying of the city's population. In addition, it was proposed, the changes would help to balance the rights of urbanites with those of rural parents who were able to take advantage of lax enforcement to build families beyond the regulation size. "Shanghai Reworks One-Child Policy," *People's Daily,* October 10, 2003; Jonathan Watts, "And Baby Makes Two: Shanghai Eases One-Child Policy," *The Guardian,* April 15, 2004.

23. Norman Matloff's work was most influential in debunking the myth of the IT worker shortage. See http://heather.cs.ucdavis.edu/wel.html.

24. The rage to learn had produced its own language evangelist, Li Yang, the progenitor of "Crazy English," who urged his mass following to yell out phrases in public places. Li's mass motivational techniques for learning English are the subject of Zhang Yuan's documentary film *Crazy English* (1999).

25. For typical opinion pieces along these lines, see Xie Kechang, "English Equation Unbalanced," *China Daily,* March 18, 2004; Liu Qing, "Students Shun Native Tongue," *China Daily,* November 11, 2005.

26. "Koreans Spare No Effort in Bid to Grasp English," *Shanghai Daily,* January 3, 2004.

27. James Farrer, *Opening Up: Youth, Sex Culture, and Market Reform in Shanghai* (Chicago: University of Chicago Press, 2002), 42–45, 100–105. To illustrate the iconic status of the Shanghai Girl, Farrer describes a famous statue, since stolen, of a young woman in a midriff blouse and short skirt talking on a cell phone. Capitalizing on its reputation, Ericsson, the phone company, erected a facsimile outside its office on Yongjia Road (see page 125). In 2004, the city's Urban Planning Bureau resolved to replace the two-meter-high statue in its former location on the corner of Huaihai Road and Maoming Road. The original was "widely believed to be stolen by migrant workers for its copper content." Zhang Jun, "Famous Stolen Street Statue to Be Replaced," *Shanghai Daily,* May 1, 2004, 3.

28. "Office Workers Want a Raise," *Shanghai Daily,* December 11–12, 2004.

Mister Tata Comes to Town

1. Balaji Reddy, "India and China Joint Military Exercise Precursor to Strong Asian Defense Alliance," *India Daily,* May 26, 2005.

2. The Gartner estimate proved altogether premature. A January 2005 McKinsey report showed China's revenues from IT services were barely half of India's $12.7 billion a year, and their growth was being driven by domestic demand from small and midsized companies.

3. Raju Chellam, "China Can Become Software Superpower," *Business Times,* April 18, 2003; "China Software Exports to See Robust Growth," *People's Daily,* September 23, 2002.

4. For examples of these comparisons, see G. P. Deshpande and Alka Acharya, eds., *Crossing a Bridge of Dreams: 50 Years of India-China* (Delhi: Tulika, 2001).

5. Marcus Franda, *China and India Online: The Politics of Information Technology in the World's Largest Nations* (New York: Rowan and Littlefield, 2002).

6. Some organs, like the business-oriented *Shanghai Daily,* had a local incentive to promote this factoid. Thus a September 20, 2003, headline story on the software boom ("City Rises as Hub for Software") reported that companies paid $3,000 to $4,000 for an Indian engineer, and only $2,000 to $3,000 for the Chinese counterpart.

7. Among other things, the bilateral declaration signed by Vajpayee was a non-aggression pact, and it included India's first formal recognition of Tibet as an autonomous region of China.

8. F. R. Harris, *Jamsetji Nusserwanji Tata: A Chronicle of His Life* (London: Oxford University Press, 1925), 6.

9. Kejia Yan, "Parsis in the Opium Trade in China," paper, Shanghai Academy of the Social Sciences (http://www.asianscholarship.org/publications/papers/Kejia%20Yan%20%20Parsis%20in%20the%20Opium%20Trade.doc).

10. Harriet Sargent, *Shanghai: Collision Point of Cultures, 1918–1939* (New York: Crown, 1990), 131.

11. Sassoon brought as much as $30 million with him from Bombay to Shanghai. Nicholas Clifford, *Spoilt Children of Empire: Westerners in Shanghai and the Chinese Revolutions of the 1920s* (Hanover, Vt.: Middlebury College Press, 1991), 331, n. 95.

12. Stanley Jackson, *The Sassoons* (New York: E. P. Dutton, 1968), 225.

13. A 1919 survey estimated there were 181,485 factory workers and 116,000 employed in transportation. By 1928, the factory workers numbered 223,680, with more than 120,000 in transportation. S. A. Smith, *Like Cattle and Horses: Nationalism and Labor in Shanghai, 1895–1927* (Durham, N.C.: Duke University Press, 2002), 18.

14. Elizabeth Perry, *Shanghai on Strike: The Politics of Chinese Labor* (Palo Alto, Calif.: Stanford University Press, 1993).

15. N. Sivakumar, *Dude, Did I Steal Your Job?: Debugging Indian Computer Programmers* (Bridgewater, N.J.: Divine Tree, 2004).

16. "IT R&D BPO Market to Touch $9.1 billion," *Economic Times,* April 26, 2004.

17. "India to Ride Knowledge BPO Wave," *Rediff.com,* July 13, 2004. The estimate came from the business research firm Evalueserve.

18. Babu Ramesh, " 'Cyber-Coolies' in BPO: Insecurities and Vulnerabilities in Non-Standard Work," *Economic and Political Weekly* 39, no. 5 (January 31–February 6, 2004): 492–504.

19. Thomas Babington Macaulay, "Minute of 2 February 1835 on Indian Education," in *Macaulay, Prose and Poetry,* selected by G. M. Young (Cambridge, Mass.: Harvard University Press, 1957), 729.

20. Arundhati Roy, *Power Politics* (Boston: South End Press, 2001), 83–85.

21. Arlie Hochschild, *The Managed Heart: Commercialization of Human Feeling* (Berkeley: University of California Press, 1983).

22. Anders Riel Müller and Raj Patel, "Shining India? Economic Liberalization and Rural Poverty in the 1990s" (San Francisco: Food First/Institute for Food and Development Policy, May 2004).

23. N. Vidyasagear, "Feeling Good, But Where Are the Jobs?" *Times of India,* January 18, 2004, 17.

24. See S. S. Gill, *Information Revolution and India—A Critique* (New Delhi: Rupa, 2004).

25. Saritha Rai, "Indian Voters Turn a Cold Shoulder to High Technology," *New York Times,* May 12, 2004.

26. Amy Waldman, "Low-Tech or High, Jobs Are Scarce in India's Boom," *New York Times,* May 6, 2004.

27. Marcus Franda, *China and India Online* (Lanham, Md.: Rowman & Littlefield, 2002) 29–30.

28. The estimates, from the Information Technology Association of America, were cited by Chidanand Rajghatta, "US Makes a Mountain out of a BPO Molehill," *Times of India,* January 18, 2004.

29. "Outsourcing Ban Isn't Fair: Vajpayee," *Times of India,* January 29, 2004.

30. For example, a *China Daily* editorial observed that Washington had long exploited its own definition of China as a "non-market economy" by treating the pricing of certain exports as instances of "dumping." "Double Standards of US Trade Policy Exposed," March 12, 2004.

31. Rashmee Ahmed, "UK Union Chief Mouths Litany of Indian BPO Woes," *Times of India,* January 21, 2004.

32. "More Stealth as Outsourcing Picks Up Speed," Reuters, December 29, 2003.

33. Bhupesh Bhandari and Bipin Chandran, "Anti-BPO Drive Gives Indian Firms $89 Million Free Publicity," *Rediff.com,* June 7, 2004. Increasingly, some IT outsourcing companies sought to respond to the backlash by taking over an entire department of an overseas company, mostly non-core activities like IT or HR functions, in a move described as "entire-process outsourcing." This entailed retaining the client's existing staff, initially at least. Anil Sasi, "Now, IT's Entire Process Outsourcing," *The Hindu,* November 25, 2004.

34. The next closest trend, "failure of corporate governance," drew a paltry 14 percent of the vote. Lisa DiCarlo, "Readers Comment on the Most Significant Trend," *Forbes,* December 23, 2003.

35. "The Great Hollowing-Out Myth," *The Economist,* February 19, 2004; Douglas A. Irwin, " 'Outsourcing' Is Good for America," *Wall Street Journal,* January 28, 2004; Manjeet Kripalani and Pete Engardio with Steve Hamm, "The Rise of India," *BusinessWeek,* December 8, 2003. George Will and other conservative columnists joined the bandwagon: " 'Ideal Economy' Has Its Tradeoffs," *Sacramento Bee,* February 19, 2004.

36. N. Vidyasagar, "Now, Outsourcing of Media, Publishing Work," *Times of India,* August 26, 2004; Randeep Ramesh, "Reuters Is Covering US Corporate Reporting," *The Guardian,* October 7, 2004.

37. Roman Catholic churches in the United States also began outsourcing services, like saying mass for special intentions. Saritha Rai, "U.S. Outsourcing Prayers to India," *New York Times,* June 14, 2004.

38. Bill Magee, "India's Call Centres Losing Attraction," *The Scotsman,* August 17, 2004.

39. Noam Scheiber, "As a Center for Outsourcing, India Could Be Losing Its Edge," *New York Times,* May 9, 2004.

40. John Ribeiro, "India's BPO Market Likely to Lose Market Share," *InfoWorld Media,* August 30, 2004 (http://www.infoworld.com/article/04/08/30/HNindiabpo _1.html).

41. For a comparative study of land use, see Tapati Mukhopadhyay, *Shanghai and Mumbai: Sustainability of Development in a Globalizing World* (Delhi: Samskriti, 2001).

42. Naresh Fernandes, "Reaching for the Sky: Bombay Is in a Shanghai State of Mind," *Oriental Express,* December 19, 2003.

43. Anupama Katakam, "A Blueprint for Mumbai," *Frontline* 20, no. 24 (November 22–December 5, 2003).

44. For various discussions of the World Social Forum, see Jai Sen, Anita Anand, Arturo Escobar, and Peter Waterman, eds., *World Social Forum: Challenging Empires* (New Delhi: Viveka Foundation, 2004); and William F. Fisher and Thomas Ponniah, eds., *Another World Is Possible: Popular Alternatives to Globalization at the World Social Forum* (London: Zed Books, 2003).

45. Joseph Kahn, "China Blocks International Meeting Focusing on Workers' Rights," *New York Times,* December 9, 2004. Two months previously, the All-China Federation of Trade Unions (ACFTU) hosted an international forum to address problems faced by trade unions in an age of economic globalization. The ACFTU seized the occasion to push for a Beijing Consensus that "respected every country's model for the operation of their trade unions and the national development policy based on their national reality." In this way, the event was used to deflect criticism of the ACFTU. Qing Jize, "Trade Unions Launch Beijing Consensus," *China Daily,* October 11, 2004.

46. See, for example, *The Liaoyang Workers' Struggle: Portrait of a Movement* (Hong Kong: China Labour Bulletin, July 2003). Aside from the China Labour Bulletin (http://www.china-labour.org.hk/iso), the other watchdog organizations that cover this labor news are Asian Labour News (http://www.asianlabour.org) and China Labor Watch (http://www.chinalaborwatch.org). Each has a record of archives and publications on labor issues inside China.

47. Yasheng Huang and Tarun Khanna, "Can India Overtake China?" *Foreign Policy,* July–August 2003. First published (in Chinese) in *Economic News,* February 2004.

48. "Will China Be Replaced by India?" *People's Daily,* March 13, 2004.

49. Rebecca Buckman cites this Infosys estimate in "Indian Software Firms Tap China," *Asian Wall Street Journal,* December 23–27, 2004.

50. Danyll Wills, "Japan Embraces China's Skills," *South China Morning Post,* April 13, 2004.

51. For a business consultant's view on the cultural differences encountered in India, see Mark Kobayashi-Hillary, *Outsourcing to India: The Offshore Advantage* (Berlin: Springer Verlag, 2004), 219–29.

52. At an AmCham committee event on "Software Excellence" (April 2002), Frank Mulligan, managing director of Technology Industry Recruitment Solutions, reported that "Westerners tend to take a sequential approach—A to B to C to D—while Chinese people are more synchronic, and more flexible even while focusing on the objective." Evidence is drawn from anecdotal insights like the following: "You can see this in any bank in China. A clerk may be in the middle of serving you and switch to somebody else as they come along. Flexibility is the key in this type of approach." According to Mulligan, nonsynchronic cultures have been the most successful at developing software.

The Suzhou Price

1. "Yangtze River Delta Offers One Third of China's Foreign Trade," *People's Daily,* May 6, 2004.

2. Helen Sun, "Yangtze Delta Boom Queried," *Shanghai Daily,* November 8, 2004.

3. These, and the statistics that follow, are from Liu Tao, "Suzhou's Investment Situation" (Suzhou Bureau of Trade and Economic Cooperation, March 2003).

4. Florence Chan, "Lies, Damn Lies and Chinese Statistics," *Asia Times,* October 23, 2004.

5. It was widely assumed that Beijing was pushing green development, as opposed to unadulterated GDP growth, as an acceptable way to cool down China's overheated economy, which was groaning from overproduction and from overconsumption of the world's petroleum, electricity, aluminum, copper, coal, and steel. "Plan for Green GDP Reflects New Reality," *China Daily,* March 10, 2004; "Linking Prosperity to Environmental Harmony," *China Daily,* March 12, 2004; "Zhejiang Sets Out for Balanced Development," *China Daily,* May 12, 2004; "GDP Worship Declining in Green Growth Drive," *Zhejiang Online,* April 28, 2004 (http://www.zjol.com.cn/gb/node2/node138665/node139012/node139014/userobject15ai2561444.html).

6. Linda Baker, "Through the Smoke: China Embraces Sustainability—One City at a Time," *E Magazine* 15, no. 3 (May–June 2004).

7. The findings of the survey (Work China Employee Survey: The Keys to Commitment in China), by the HR consultancy Watson Wyatt were presented at a meeting organized by AmCham's Human Resources Committee on Employee Recruitment and Retention in Suzhou (September 22, 2004). The figures for China (13.1 percent) were the highest in the Asia-Pacific region. Thailand came second, with 11.8 percent, and Malaysia came last, with a turnover rate of 5.5 percent.

8. Andre Gunder Frank, *ReOrient: Global Economy in the Asian Age* (Berkeley: University of California Press, 1998), 131–64.

9. Figures are from IT research firm iSuppli's newsletter, *Market Watch China,* September 2002.

10. Lee Kuan Yew, *From Third World to First: The Singapore Story, 1965–2000* (New York: HarperCollins, 2000), 650.

11. Ibid., 653.

12. "State Set to Clamp Down on Land Abuses," *People's Daily,* February 20, 2004.

13. Ben Dolven, "The New Frontier," *Far Eastern Economic Review,* December 6, 2001.

14. These figures are from a service breakdown provided by Shanghai Foreign Service Co., Ltd. (SFSC), a company providing HR services to foreign-invested representative offices, joint ventures, SOEs, and privately owned enterprises in China. It was more or less the same breakdown mandated for companies in Pudong's showcase Zhangjiang High-Tech Park.

15. Margaret Crawford, *Building the Workingman's Paradise: The Design of American Company Towns* (New York: Verso, 1995).

16. Quoted in Dolores Hayden, *Redesigning the American Dream: The Future of Housing, Work, and Family Life* (New York: W. W. Norton, 2002), 8.

17. You Nov, "Nation Hungry for Skilled Workers," *China Daily,* May 6, 2005.

18. Dimitri Kessler, "What Are You Doing for China?: The Nationalism of Engineers in the Greater China Area," in Ching Kwan Lee, ed., *Working in China: Ethnographies of Labor and Workplace Transformation* (London: RoutledgeCurzon, 2006).

19. Peter Hays Gries, *China's New Nationalism: Pride, Politics, and Diplomacy* (Berkeley: University of California Press, 2004).

20. For two accounts of this idea, see William Hinton, *China: An Unfinished Battle: Essays on Cultural Revolution and the Further Developments in China* (Kharagpur, India: Cornerstone Publications, 2002); and chapter 12 of Maurice Meisner, *Mao's China and After: A History of the People's Republic* (New York: Free Press, 1999), 204–13.

Go West

1. The full text of the AFL-CIO petition can be found at http://www.aflcio .org/issuespolitics/globaleconomy/upload/china_petition.pdf. For media commentary, see Aaron Bernstein, "Labor's Savvy Charge on China Trade," *BusinessWeek,* March 19, 2004; Steven Greenhouse and Elizabeth Becker, "A.F.L.–C.I.O. to Press Bush for Penalties Against China," *New York Times,* March 16, 2004; Harold Meyerson, "China's Workers," *American Prospect,* March 22, 2004.

2. The case for the AFL-CIO's anti-PNTR campaign is made in Mark Levinson and Thea Lee, "Why Labor Made the Right Decision," and the case against in Kent Wong and Elaine Bernard, "Labor's Mistaken Anti-China Campaign," both in *New Labor Forum* 7 (Fall–Winter 2000): 19–29. For other articles critical of the anti-PNTR coalition, see Walden Bello and Anuradha Mittal, "Dangerous Liaisons: Progressives, the Right, and the Anti-China Trade Campaign," Institute for Food and Development Policy/Food First (May 2000) at www.foodfirst.org; Sze Pang Cheung, "We Have Met the Enemy: Fighting China or the WTO?" *Against the Current,* no. 87, June–July 2000; Anuradha Mittal and Peter Rosset, "The Real Enemy Is the WTO, Not China," *PeaceWorks,* March 1, 2000 (http://www.foodfirst.org/media/ opeds/2000/3-1-china.html); Robin Hahnel, "Once Again, China and the WTO," *Z Magazine,* April 13, 2000.

3. Elizabeth Becker, "Bush Rejects Labor's Call to Punish China," *New York*

Times, April 29, 2004. In June 2004, as part of a China visit by Secretary of Labor Elaine Chao, the two countries signed letters of understanding aimed at improving work safety and protecting workers' rights on the mainland. One of the agreements covered cooperation in the event of emergency responses to mining accidents. Another sought to raise public awareness of wage and working-hour laws. In return for working on these issues, Beijing was promised a review of its trade status as a "non-market economy."

4. Alexander Saxton, *The Indispensable Enemy: Labor and the Anti-Chinese Movement in California* (Berkeley: University of California Press, 1971).

5. Kent Wong, "Blaming It All on China," *New Labor Forum* 13, no. 3 (September 2004): 90–94. For follow-up, see the dialogue between Wong and the AFL-CIO's Barbara Shailor, in *New Labor Forum* 14, no. 1 (Spring 2005): 105–12.

6. See Gregory Mantsios, "Tea for Two: Chinese and U.S. Labor: A Report from China," *New Labor Forum* 11 (Fall–Winter 2002): 61–73. One of its critics' arguments is that China's trade union confederation (the biggest in the world, with more than 100 million members) is too closely associated with the government. Yet that is the case in many other countries, including Malaysia, Singapore, Mexico, South Africa, and Zimbabwe. While Chinese trade unions are not independent from the government, they often fight to ensure that workers' concerns are not ignored by the government, and, in this respect, are the only pro-worker bureaucracy left in the PRC. Along these lines, see Anita Chan's argument for engaging with the ACFTU in "Labor in Waiting: The International Trade Union Movement and China," *New Labor Forum* 11 (Fall–Winter 2002): 54–59.

7. The official website for the Western Development Policy is http://www.chinawest.gov.cn/english.

8. Three volumes that describe and analyze the Go West Policy are Ding Lu and William Neilson, eds., *China's West Region Development: Domestic Strategies and Global Implications* (Singapore: World Scientific, 2004); Y. M. Yeung and Shen Jianfa, eds., *Developing China's West: A Critical Path to Balanced National Development* (Hong Kong: Chinese University Press, 2004); and Hu Angang, ed., *New Strategies for Western Development* (Beijing, 2001).

9. For a typical example, see Robert Marquand, "Go West: China Looks to Transform Its Frontier," *Christian Science Monitor,* September 26, 2003.

10. "Western Areas Get More Funds," *Shanghai Daily,* October 15, 2004.

11. "China's 'Go West' Program Attractive to College Graduates," *People's Daily,* June 26, 2003.

12. Wen Mei, "Marketization Versus Foreign Direct Investment," in Ding and Neilson, *China's West Region Development,* 557.

13. Agence France-Presse, "China's 'Go West' Plan Fails to Close Investment Gap," *Taipei Times,* October 9, 2004, 12.

14. "Foreigners Encouraged to Invest in West," *China Daily,* July 28, 2004.

15. "'Go West' Drive Focuses on Sustainability," *China Daily,* November 19, 2004.

16. Chongqing Economic and Technological Development Zone, *Investment Guide* (2003).

17. Gang Tian, *Shanghai's Role in the Economic Development of China: Reform of Foreign Trade and Investment* (Westport, Conn.: Praeger, 1996), 14.

18. "New Grads Taste Bitter Reality," Xinhua News Agency, June 16, 2004.

19. Chen Yue, Chen Caiti, and Lin Hui, "Chongqing," in Yeung and Shen, *Developing China's West,* 451–55.

20. For a firsthand account, see Jiang Daqing, "A Truthful Account of a 'Peasant Insurrection,' " China Study Group, January 6, 2003 (http://www.chinastudygroup .org/index.php?action=article&type=view&id=3). Also see Lynette Ong's vignette of Sichuan farmers' lives, "Modern Mask Hides Conditions in Rural China," *Asia Times,* September 22, 2003.

21. Li Yongyan, "Anger Rages in Sichuan," *Asia Times,* November 12, 2004.

22. In March 2004, president Hu Jintao announced major tax relief for China's 800 million peasant farmers. "Agricultural Tax to Be Phased Out in Five Years," *China Daily,* September 11, 2004.

23. James Kynge, "Migrant Chinese Workers Transform the Fortunes of Their Home Towns," *Financial Times,* November 10, 2003, 10.

24. Shi Yulong and Du Ping, "On the Urban-Rural Relationship in Western Region Development Program," in Ding and Neilson, *China's West Region Development,* 219–37.

25. Chengdu Municipal Informatization Office, "Analysis of Environment for Chengdu's Software Industry Development" (2003).

26. The Ministry of Science and Technology chose forty-seven Chinese companies to back in software outsourcing. Mure Dickie, "China Eyes Outsourced Software Market," *Financial Times,* April 10, 2004.

27. Reuters, "China's Manufacturers Sing Pearl River Delta Blues," *Taipei Times,* June 16, 2004, 12.

28. Zhu Qiwen, "Unified Tax Offers Level Playing Field, *China Daily,* January 27, 2005. More than fifty multinationals joined forces to lobby the State Council for a transition period of five to ten years. Fons Tuinstra, "Multinationals Join Forces Against New Tax Law," *ChinaBiz,* January 14, 2005 (www.cbiz.cn).

Cross-Strait Flights

1. It was a short-lived recovery for TSMC. After posting record profits in 2004, clients began to cut orders, and the numbers for the first quarter of 2005 were down over 10 percent from the previous year.

2. Of the fifty-seven microchip fabs operating in China by 2004, nine were producing eight-inch wafers. Grace, SMIC, Shanghai Belling, and Huahong NEC were in Shanghai, and Hejian in Suzhou, while new eight-inch fabs were being built by TSMC in Shanghai, the Haier Group in Qingdao, and SIM-BCD in Changzhou.

3. Macabe Keliher, "China Set to Flood the World with Chips," *Asia Times,* February 3, 2004.

4. The first phase of the investment had been approved in February of the previous year. Approval for the second phase was conditional on the company ramping up to mass production a twelve-inch plant in Taiwan.

5. Amber Chung, "FSC Fines UMC's Tsao NT$3m," *Taipei Times,* April 21, 2005.

6. Mike Clendenin, "China's Drive for IC Foundry Market Unnerves Taiwan," *EE Times,* October 4, 2001.

7. The most recent U.S. weapons package, worth a costly $18.2 billion, was bitterly protested. Its government backers insisted that it would help Taiwan maintain a balance of power with the mainland for the next thirty years. Alice Hung, "Thousands of Taiwan People Protest U.S. Arms Deal," Reuters, September 25, 2004.

8. See Anita Chan's account in *China's Workers Under Assault* (Armonk, N.Y.: M. E. Sharpe, 2001); and chapter 3 of You-tien Hsing, *Making Capitalism in China: The Taiwan Connection* (New York: Oxford University Press, 1998).

9. Chin Chung, "Division of Labor Across the Taiwan Strait," in Barry Naughton, ed., *The China Circle: Economics and Electronics in the PRC, Taiwan, and Hong Kong* (Washington, D.C.: Brookings Institution Press, 1997), 173.

10. "Chinese Mainland to Greet Another High Tide of Taiwan Investment," *People's Daily,* February 2, 2005.

11. This two-handed game was called by Beijing after the 2004 election, when the Taiwan Affairs Office declared that it would not welcome Taiwanese investors who openly espoused the DPP's sovereignty moves. Hsu Wen-Lung, high-profile founder of the Chi Mei Group—massively invested in petrochemicals and electronics in the PRC—was criticized in a *People's Daily* editorial for his bankrolling of DPP's causes. " 'Green' Taiwan Businessmen Not Welcomed: Official," *People's Daily,* June 15, 2004; Jessie Ho, "Chi Mei Boss Holds Good China Cards," *Taipei Times,* June 8, 2004.

12. *Taipei Times Taiwan Yearbook, 2004* (http://ecommerce.taipeitimes.com/year book2004/P135.htm).

13. Jason Dedrick and Kenneth Kraemer, *Asia's Computer Challenge: Threat or Opportunity for the United States and the World?* (New York: Oxford University Press, 1998), 151–52.

14. MacWilliam Bishop, "Taiwan High Tech Jobs to China: Fact vs. Fiction," *Asia Times,* August 10, 2004.

15. Chin Chung, "Division of Labor," 190.

16. Qiwen Lu, *China's Leap into the Information Age: Innovation and Organization in the Computer Industry* (New York: Oxford University Press, 2000), 6–9.

17. Denis Fred Simon and Detlef Rehn, *Technological Innovation in China: The Case of the Shanghai Semiconductor Industry* (Cambridge, Mass.: Ballinger, 1988), 1–19.

18. Jonathan Spence, *To Change China: Western Advisers in China, 1620–1960* (New York: Penguin, 1980).

19. Kenneth Flamm, *Mismanaged Trade? Strategic Policy and the Semiconductor Industry* (Washington, D.C.: Brookings Institution Press, 1996), 36–37.

20. Lu recounts the history of these companies in *China's Leap into the Information Age.*

21. Jean-François Huchet, "The China Circle and Technological Development in the Chinese Electronics Industry," in Naughton, ed., *The China Circle,* 277.

22. Helen Sun, "Yangtze Delta Boom Queried," *Shanghai Daily,* November 8, 2004.

23. Simon and Rehn, *Technological Innovation in China,* 136–39.

24. In Jiang Zemin's words, "The state has invested a lot of funds in these SOEs, but the achievement is not as much as we expected. So we will no longer make direct investment in this industry. We will instead make efforts to provide a better environment for domestic and overseas investment with better policies, laws and infrastructure." Clendenin, "China's Drive for IC Foundry Market Unnerves Taiwan." For a typical official commentary advocating the crucial national need for a microchip industry, see "China Must Accelerate Construction of the Important Chip Industry," *People's Daily,* June 25, 2004.

25. Flamm, *Mismanaged Trade?,* 17.

26. Keynote Address of Kenneth Juster, Undersecretary of Commerce for Industry and Security, at the U.S.-Taiwan Business Council and the Fabless Semiconductor Association Conference on "Taiwan and China Semiconductor Industry Outlook, 2003," San Jose, California, September 15, 2003.

27. The lobbying was part of a vigorous debate on the reauthorization of the Export Administration Act (1979), the legislation that regulates the dual-use approval process. The lobbying effort was backed up by the neoconservative powerhouse Project for a New American Century (http://www.newamericancentury.org).

28. John J. Tkacik Jr., "The U.S. Must Face Up to China's Trade Challenges," Backgrounder no. 1698, Heritage Foundation, October 23, 2003 (http://www.heritage.org). See also Seth Cropsey, *Safeguarding Defense Technology, Enabling Commerce: A New Balance in the New Economy* (Washington, D.C.: American Enterprise Institute Press, 2002).

29. Iris Chang describes these espionage cases in the 1990s in *The Chinese in America: A Narrative History* (New York: Viking, 2003). Also see Wen Ho Lee with Helen Zia, *My Country Versus Me: The First-Hand Account by the Los Alamos Scientist Who Was Falsely Accused of Being a Spy* (New York: Hyperion, 2001); and Dan Stober and Ian Hoffman, *A Convenient Spy: Wen Ho Lee and the Politics of Nuclear Espionage* (New York: Simon & Schuster, 2004).

30. "US Sees a Spy in China's Lenovo," *Asia Times,* January 25, 2005.

31. For a semi-official Chinese response both to this deep-seated American paranoia and to Washington's uses of export controls, see Cai Yumin, "US, Don't Be Doubtful of Everything: A Commentary," *People's Daily,* October 12, 2003.

32. Li Heng, "Intel to Assemble and Test Pentium 4 Microprocessor in China," *People's Daily,* May 10, 2002.

33. By far, the majority of these IC houses would burn through their initial capital. Mark LaPedus, "China's IC Design Houses Struggling for Survival," *EE Times* May 25, 2004 (www.eetimes.com).

34. Kathy Chen and Evan Ramsted, "China Sees a New Way to Steer Tech Market," *Asian Wall Street Journal,* April 23, 2004.

35. Elizabeth Becker, "U.S. Files a Complaint Against China at the WTO," *New York Times,* March 19, 2004.

36. Edward Alden, "China and US Resolve Dispute over Chip Taxes," *Financial Times,* July 8, 2004; "China Changes Tack on Incentives for Chipmakers," *Financial Times,* July 9, 2004. The State Administration of Taxation also increased its tax rebate on exports of electronics from 13 percent to 17 percent in November 2004.

37. George Leopold, "U.S., China Agree on Technology Export Inspections," *EE Times,* April 28, 2004.

38. To this day, the company's response has been evasive, and the class-action lawsuit on the part of former employees has proceeded painfully slow. Taiwan Association for Victims of Occupational Injuries, "RCA in Taiwan" (http://tean.formosa .org/campaign/hightech/rca/qafacts.html).

39. The Silicon Valley Toxics Coalition (www.svtc.org) has amassed the most extensive documentation of the industry's deadly ecological footprint. A Taiwan case study is included in the Nautilus Institute's California Global Corporate Accountability Project, *Dodging Dilemmas?: Environmental and Social Accountability in the Global Operations of California-Based High-Tech Companies* (May 2002). Among the books that describe the toxic underbelly of microchip manufacture are Dennis Hayes, *Behind the Silicon Curtain: The Seductions of Work in a Lonely Era* (Boston: South End Press, 1989); Chris Carlsson and Mark Leger, eds., *Bad Attitude: The Processed World Anthology* (New York: Verso, 1990); Robert Howard, *Brave New Workplaces* (New York: Viking, 1985); Elizabeth Grossman, *High Tech Trash: Digital Devices, Hidden Toxins, and Human Health* (Washington, D.C.: Island Press, 2005); Lenny Siegel and John Markoff, *The High Cost of High Tech: The Dark Side of the Chip* (New York: Harper & Row, 1985). Also see Sandra Steingraber, *Living Downstream: An Ecologist Looks at Cancer and the Environment* (Reading, Mass.: Addison-Wesley, 1997).

40. Leslie Byster and Ted Smith, "From Silicon Valley to Green Silicon Island: Taiwan's Pollution and Promise in the Era of High-Tech Globalization," Report by Silicon Valley Toxics Coalition, International Campaign for Responsible Technology, and Taiwanese Environmental Action Network, 2001 (http://www.svtc.org/icrt/asia/ taiwan3_01.htm).

41. To cite only a few milestones, Syntec, Taiwan's first IC design firm, was commercialized in 1982, TSMC was spun off in 1987 from a technology agreement with Philips, and Taiwan Mask Corporation followed one year later, completing the IC value chain.

42. Alice H. Amsden and Wan-wen Chu, *Beyond Late Development: Taiwan's Upgrading Policies* (Cambridge, Mass.: MIT Press, 2003).

43. World Bank Group, *The East Asian Miracle: Economic Growth and Public Policy,* World Bank Policy Research Report (New York: Oxford University Press, 1993).

44. Jeffrey Henderson, *The Globalisation of High Technology Production: Society, Space and Semiconductors in the Restructuring of the Modern World* (London: Routledge, 1989).

45. AnnaLee Saxenian, "The Silicon Valley–Hsinchu Connection: Technical Communities and Industrial Upgrading," *Industrial and Corporate Change* 10, no. 4 (2001). According to Saxenian, a similar pattern is now developing in the relationship between Chinese engineers in Silicon Valley and the IC industry on the mainland. *Local and Global Networks of Immigrant Professionals in Silicon Valley* (San Francisco: Public Policy Institute of California, April 2002). See also Jinn-yuh Hsu and Alan Smart, "The Chinese Diaspora, Foreign Investment, and Economic Development in China," *Review of International Affairs* 3, no. 4 (Summer 2004): 544–66.

46. "Shanghai Sets Up State Technology Transfer Center," *People's Daily,* May 27, 2003.

47. Xue Wen, "SMIC to Work with Chip Design Company," *Shanghai Daily,* December 10, 2004.

48. In March 2004, a group of industry veterans, mostly from Taiwan, announced plans to back Nano Semiconductor Manufacturing Corp. to the tune of $600 million in a chipmaking venture that would begin production in Ningbo by September 2005. "Taiwan-Backed Co. to Invest $600m in China Chip Plant," Reuters, March 19, 2004. In February 2003, Nanjing also saw the groundbreaking of a major semiconductor project for six- and eight-inch fabs, funded by an international consortium of backers. "Semiconductor Production to Expand," *China Daily,* February 25, 2003.

49. Richard Read, "China Makes Room for Religion," *Salt Lake Tribune,* February 15, 2003.

50. "China's First Chip Foundry Chock Full of Orders," December 6, 2001 (www.chinaproducts.com/eng2/content/conts1995.php).

51. David Noble offers a generous survey of the links in his wide-ranging history, *The Religion of Technology: The Divinity of Man and the Spirit of Invention* (New York: Knopf, 1997).

52. Horng-luen Wang, "What's It Like to Be Shanghaied?" (unpublished manuscript).

53. You-tien Hsing, *Making Capitalism in China,* 132.

Index

Page numbers in *italics* refer to illustrations.

Index

communism:
   Chinese, 5, 8, 25–26, 39, 41–42, 46,
     53–58, 67, 68, 73–74, 91–92, 96–97,
     106–7, 108, 112–14, 133, 134, 139, 140,
     153–55, 176, 183–84, 189–91, 197, 198,
     202–6, 210, 232–33, 239–40, 250, 262,
     263
   political nature of, 5, 25–26, 41–42,
     73–74, 134, 153–55, 189–91, 197, 250,
     262, 265–66
   U.S. opposition to, 67, 68, 176, 202–3,
     239–40
computer industry, 34–35, 80–81, 91–130,
   134, 232, 233, 241, 246
Confucianism, 103, 264
Coordinating Committee for Multilateral
   Export Controls (COCOM), 239–40
corporations, multinational:
   accounting methods of, 63–64, 142
   culture of, 44, 144, 182–83, 195–96, 222,
     253
   government cooperation with, 5, 19, 55,
     88, 89–90, 118, 168–69, 189–91, 204,
     207–24, 250, 265, 266
   joint ventures of, 30, 46–47, 51, 127, 128,
     140, 169–71, 187–88, 206, 208,
     218–19, 233, 234, 240–41
   management of, 13–19, 25, 34–38, 47,
     48–49, 57, 59, 64, 69–72, 77, 78,
     95–96, 100–106, 109–11, 118, 124–30,
     132, 150, 155–62, 176, 177–83, 186–96,
     199–200, 203, 211, 222–23, 229, 236,
     253, 254, 258, 260, 263
   profits of, 12, 25, 28, 36–37, 48–49,
     51–52, 62–64, 72–75, 82, 83–87, 98,
     101, 104, 118–19, 120, 138–39, 140, 150,
     168, 186–89, 192, 195, 199, 202, 203,
     218–20, 223–24, 246, 262, 266–67,
     278*n*–79*n*
   stock prices of, 37, 83, 149, 250–51
   taxation of, 8, 17, 19, 26, 32, 48, 63–64,
     81–82, 84, 88, 98, 118, 139, 191, 193,
     207, 208, 213, 218, 220, 230, 266–67
CSMC, 234–36, 253
Cultural Revolution, 41, 54, 106–7, 130,
   208

Dalian, 105, 123, 156, 215, 216
Democratic Party, 27

Deng Xiaoping, 41, 42, 56, 113, 199, 235
developing countries, 4, 6–7, 32, 120,
   132–33, 155–56, 168–69
DiBattista, Mark, 82
Dobbs, Lou, 11–12
dollar, value of, 62, 83, 85, 89, 219, 267
Dong Yuehua, 215–16

East Asia, 20–21, 37, 48–49, 61, 68–72,
   106, 226, 231, 241
East India Company, 137
English-language skills, 94, 107, 109, 115,
   118, 124–25, 127, 142–45, 149, 150, 162,
   181, 188, 215, 222
Enron Corp., 214
entrepreneurship, 69, 81, 110–11, 132, 140,
   183, 184, 235, 245, 263
environmental issues, 3, 4, 9, 21, 25–26, 33,
   68, 153, 165–66, 204, 205, 207, 212,
   243–44, 253, 265, 266
European Union (EU), 6, 21, 91
Evans, Don, 87, 202
Export-Import Bank, U.S., 28, 79–80
Exporting America (Dobbs), 11

"face," 102, 128, 159, 170–71, 195–96, 222
Fair Currency Alliance, 86, 278*n*
foreign direct investment (FDI), 40–41,
   42, 46, 51–52, 155, 164, 172, 207, 208,
   266, 275*n*–76*n*
foreign exchange, 9–10, 32, 62, 83, 85–89,
   192
Fortune 500 companies, 40–41, 55, 84, 165,
   214
Four Hundred Million Customers (Crow),
   51
Four Modernizations, 113
Friedman, Milton, 41
Friedman, Thomas, 6–7, 77–78, 79,
   281*n*
Fujian province, 17, 49, 229

Gartner Group, 29, 132, 151, 156
Gates, Bill, 108
General Electric (GE), 4, 30, 156, 194,
   219
General Motors (GM), 4, 30, 52, 61, 129
George III, King of Great Britain, 50
Gini coefficient, 56

299

Index

Index

Index